Of Love and Sanity

Ian Nimmo White

Petrel Publications

of Love and Sanity is a novel dedicated to the memory of
James Glanville Lewis (1923-2015), a former Chindit who
fought against the Imperial Japanese Army in Burma in 1943.
Although captured and tortured by the enemy, and suffering
a total breakdown when he returned to England, he dedicated the rest of his life to the service of young people. The
more disadvantaged the youngsters were, the more of his
time he gave them. They came to regard him as a shaman,
and when he died, in his nineties, he had become a renowned
humanitarian.

Acknowledgement

THE AUTHOR WISHES to thank the adopted family and many friends of Jim Lewis who have supported this book, in particular Duncan Simpson and Michael Innes.

The Author

IAN NIMMO WHITE was born in Paisley in 1948 and educated at the John Neilson Institution, Jordanhill College Glasgow and Dundee University. From 1972 until his retirement in 2007, he worked in Fife's Youth and Community Service.

In 2010 he took on the role of Organising Secretary of the Tay Rail Bridge Disaster Memorial Trust, playing a major part in the eventual erection, on Tayside in 2013, of memorial stones to the victims of the tragedy. He continues to work in heritage and genealogy.

For twenty years he has been a regularly published poet in both English and Scots, and is currently listed on the *Live Literature Scotland* Scheme, which enables him to be booked by primary schools so that he can bring poetry alive for the children. *Of Love and Sanity* is his first novel.

He lives with his wife Janice, a retired librarian, and their golden retriever, Brora, in Leslie, Fife. They have three sons, two daughters-in-law and one grand-daughter.

Crack Willow 1980

WILLIAMS ENTERED HIS office in West Street that Monday morning as punctual as ever. His army training had never deserted him. His secretary, Mrs Crossley, had watched his approach from some distance, decided he was in the darker of the two moods he normally betrayed and, only half-raising her head, said:

'Good morning, Mr Williams.'

'Good morning to you, Ma'am.' The boss was brusque.

And this confirmed he was indeed in the dark side of his persona. Had he been otherwise, he would have addressed his loyal servant as 'Mrs C'. To those who didn't know them this sounded condescending but it soon became clear that the two of them trusted each other implicitly and the latter term was in fact one of endearment.

Having sussed him out, Mrs Crossley decided she would not approach him with the morning mail until 9.30.

A confirmed bachelor and set in his ways, Tom Williams was 57 years old and beginning to tire. The world, and more importantly the service he had dedicated himself to thirty years before, was changing too fast and he couldn't understand why younger colleagues never made it to work in time. But if it became intolerable, at least he knew he only had eight years to retirement.

He made his way into the back office which was much larger than the reception where Mrs Crossley toiled, but it had to accommodate Williams and his three professional subordinates. Under ideal circumstances he would have had his own room but this was the youth and community service, a non-essential arm of local government. As needs must, the devil and Williams would drive. And anyway, he enjoyed company and reflected he'd done well to get this former chip shop in the burgeoning new town of Crack Willow. Opportunities for professional confidentialities were rare but Williams was an original and passionate practitioner. It was more important to him that he present an open door to the public.

And in Crack Willow he was a stand-out, old-fashioned of appearance in his bow tie, tweed and twill, all topped with a deer-stalker hat, and most impressive of all, speaking in his plum and proper English accent. Conscious of being employed by a labour dominated council, he would occasionally declare his pride in having been born to a mining family in the Rhondda Valley of Wales. It didn't cut much ice. To most of them he was just plain posh. Williams cared not a jot. Whether loved or hated, his only concern was that people did not ignore him.

To make the cramped room even more so, an additional desk had hurriedly been put in place the Friday before around closing time. A new colleague was on the way, on the rebound from some controversy on the other side of the region. Williams guessed it was only a temporary measure for six weeks. He would put up with it, be at all times courteous to the man, make sure the others followed suit, then send him on his way with all best wishes for the future. The chap was due at 10am

Between 9.15 and 9.30 his three colleagues arrived one by one, all to a greeting of:

'Good afternoon.'

'Good morning to you too Tom,' replied the first, Mike Wellsley.

Mike was just seven years younger than Tom, had recently married for the second time, and had four grown-up children by his first marriage, all of whom had long since flown the nest. He was an all-rounder who at different times had been an electrician and a policeman before undertaking training in youth and community service. He was thoroughly experienced and best knew how to handle the old man.

There was a rattle then thump of the front door announcing the arrival of the second, Peter Stanley, a single young man in his late twenties. Peter was awkward, both physically being five stones overweight and also in his dealings with people. It didn't help that he came from a privileged background, and whilst well-intentioned he struggled with the client group. Colleagues often saw him as a square peg in a round hole, better suited to a different line of work.

'Cheers Tom,' he just about replied, then sat down at his desk to read his paper.

Enter the star of the team, deliberately last but not least, Roger Jenkins. At 22 years of age he had joined the service only six months previously. He had done the very latest training which was changing the service from youth and community to community education, and as far as he was concerned, nobody before him had done it right. He was good, knew it, and would make sure everyone else would soon know it as well. He wasn't married but was in a steady partnership, quite novel for those times.

'Good morning Tom,' he said, bright as a button.

Williams liked Jenkins, in spite of the brashness and bravura. He had the potential to be the best community worker he had ever known. But just occasionally he would give him a rap on the knuckles just to remind him of who was in charge.

'Roger, I saw that you left work again at one o'clock last Friday. You and I must have a talk sometime about those two and a half day weekends of yours.'

Tom, I worked morning, noon and nights from Monday through to Thursday last week.'

'Not the point, dear boy. It's how the public perceive us that matters.'

The Monday morning salutations were interrupted by Mrs Crossley who had finally got all the mail and other admin together:

'Your mail, Mr Williams,' she said, depositing the opened letters on his desk.

'Thank you Mrs C, I'll call you when I'm ready.'

Williams was by now defrosted and in an altogether lighter mood. He filtered through his letters, quickly sorting them into three piles, one he would respond to that day, the second the next day, the third whenever. The last pile was invariably the largest and growing by the day.

'Has that chap from the architects' department replied to you yet, Tom?' queried Mike Wellsley.

'He certainly has.' Tom passed him the letter.

'Ya boy! Send him a rocket, Tom.'

'No, I shall sit on this for twenty-four hours until I've cooled down and had time to think. Then I'll send him a rocket.'

This was all about a community hall in the nearby village of Carriston, the responsibility for which was shared between the local community and the West Street office. It had been built only recently in the style of a medway hut with the floor propped up by a uniform series of jacks, but only a few days ago the senior citizens' dancing group had backed off as a small hole appeared in the floor. Now the local management committee wanted to know, through Tom, what the Council were going to do about it. Tom had passed on the question to architects' department with the added enquiry, if there was to be a delay, whether or not the hall was safe enough for the programme to continue and if the architect would kindly give him a formal reply one way or the other. This morning's reply had been terse:

I'm sorry, we don't normally do that sort of thing.

Changing the subject, Williams shouted out:

'Mrs C, will you take some letters please?'

Mrs Crossley came through at speed, notepad in her left hand, a pencil in her right. It took her only ten minutes to handle his dictation and return to her typewriter. Williams sighed:

'Dreadful business this, seen it all before. It's called the *I'm in charge* syndrome. Promote them suddenly to high authority and it goes straight to their heads. Well, we shall see.'

The two younger colleagues, Stanley and Jenkins, exchanged a wry smile. They just knew the wily old fox was going to make the architect dance.

Enter Mrs Crossley once more:

'That's Mr Gray for you now, Mr. Williams.'

'Right chaps, could you possibly huddle in the front office, it should only take a few minutes? Thank you Mrs C, show Mr. Gray in.'

John Gray, a man in his mid-thirties now and married with three children, came in, exchanged greetings with Williams and after the shortest of briefings on the work done by the team, was shown his desk by Williams and given some files to study for a few days. The boss saw no point in raising the issues which had brought Gray to Crack Willow, and Gray was not of a mood to volunteer any of it. Williams made note of how worn Gray looked. This was not the young man who had joined the service ten years before, the young man Williams had made a point of going to watch one evening in action, the young man who had impressed him with his ability to handle fifty volatile working class teenagers in one of the region's most rundown youth centres. Clearly, Gray had undergone a traumatic experience. But

Williams wasn't overly concerned, he knew all about pain. So he kept a professional stance:

'Just one more thing, John. We wear collar and tie in this office, whatever the circumstances, collar and tie.'

For fifteen years Gray had worn an open-neck shirt and pullover, from his days as a volunteer in a mission society in Glasgow, through his professional training, and throughout his service to date in old and ramshackle youth centres. He didn't exactly like the way this rule had been explained, but he was well aware of Williams' formidable reputation and thought to himself *When in Rome*.................He would get a tie.

The following morning early on, Williams barked at Mrs Crossley:

'Mrs C, would you get me that architect fellow at regional headquarters please?'

A long silence later, Mrs Crossley buzzed her boss:

'Mr Stirling is on line for you now, Mr Williams.'

Everyone pretended to be busy but cocked one ear intently.

'Ah yes Mr Stirling..........Yes..........Yes.........Yes.........
You can't say whether the hall floor is safe or not. Well, in that case I'll write first class to the chairman of the village committee informing him it's unsafe..........What do you mean I can't do that? I can and I must, the safety of the users comes first.........Of course, I can't be responsible for the newspaper reaction............
Now Mr Stirling, no need to raise your voice like that, if volunteers get upset about not being able to continue with their programmes, often as not they go public............Yes, I agree, it's a tricky

situation..........Of course you can have a few hours to discuss it with your director......Yes, yes, good morning to you too, Sir.'

On Thursday next Mike Wellsley entered the office grinning from ear to ear:

'Tom, guess what? There are workmen crawling all over the foundations at Carriston Community Hall.'

'Well well, what a nice surprise. Jolly good !'

The workload

The West Street office had an overview of youth and community work in roughly twenty communities, half of them precincts within the new town of Crack Willow and the other half old outreach villages encircling the town.

The priority service was youth work and the public halls in those communities ran evening youth clubs led by part-time youth leaders who had been appointed and trained by the professional staff at West Street. The duties of the professionals included visiting the youth clubs, supporting the youth leaders and advising the halls' management committees on youth club programmes. Additional services which involved the daytime use of the same community halls were, among others, helping young mothers to start up and run playgroups for their children and support to senior citizens' groups.

Beyond the work with community halls, the professionals could find themselves as link officers between the fast growing movement of residents' associations negotiating with their local authority landlords. And there were special projects like the *Big Summer Show,* a play scheme for the town's children throughout the school summer holidays which involved the whole community by way of young volunteers in the late teen, early twenties' age group and programmed events for adults in the evenings.

The *Big Summer Show* was a source of great pride to Williams. Although his brainchild, its main practitioner had been a pupil of his in youth work, David Samson, only 15 years old when they first met each other. David had done well and been recently promoted to the same level as Tom in another area of the Colliershire region. To Williams, never having been a family man, David was one of only two young men who had ever come close to being his son.

Williams missed David but it was time to move on, and he had a new initiative simmering away on his back burner. This was the heyday of the one and only Margaret Thatcher, and there were a growing number of young people joining the dole queue. At the next staff meeting, he would reveal his plans for making a small contribution to the reversing of this unhealthy trend, something which would dovetail proudly into their skills.

The Kwid Kids

Weeks later a professional staff meeting had been scheduled for 10am of a Tuesday morning. Waiting on the word of command, while Williams and Mrs. Crossley dealt with necessary admin, Wellsley read his morning paper while teasing dirt from underneath his nails with a small screwdriver. Amazingly, he carried a wallet of tradesman's tools in the inside pocket of his office suit jacket. They came in handy for small jobs at the office or the community centres he visited. Rather than wait months for the council's works department, he could do a DIY job on the spot and no-one need ever know. Stanley settled his nerves by amusing himself with the constant twisting of his Rubix cube while Jenkins hammered on with his report writing appearing to be annoyed that he was going to be interrupted by yet another staff meeting organised without any agenda on the subject matter.

'Thank you Mrs C, I'll sign these letters when you're ready.'

The crisp tones of Tom Williams had shattered the murmuring half-silence of his colleagues.

'Right lads, let's get to it.'

This was without doubt a male preserve, Williams' male preserve. And in the early days of 1980 there was a while yet to go before female equality, even longer to young women with attitude. Women never seemed to be a serious part of Tom Williams' history, and even if they had been, he never talked about them. And yet he was not without feeling for them. He had worked with them in voluntary organisations in his past, had grown to admire them, and they had grown to admire him. He just didn't want them too close.

The four colleagues gathered around the table. Gray was absent on sick leave. This had not surprised Williams. For weeks Gray had sat in his corner in almost total silence. Youth and community workers didn't do that sort of thing. Clearly, he was not a well man. Williams spoke first:

'The thing is, we've got to do something about all those young people hanging about the town centre. They're on the dole and the likelihood of them getting jobs must be very slim. I feel for them, I really do.'

'What do you suggest, Tom?' Wellsley begged, anticipating something big was coming. He knew the old man only too well.

'I thought we could take turns on a rota basis and go down the town centre for a couple of hours at a time, make contact with them, get to know them.'

Wellsley and Stanley did not respond, but their faces betrayed them. Wellsley wasn't keen and Stanley had gone a shade of white. The very concept had him in a panic. But Jenkins had considered it professionally:

'I think that's an excellent idea, Tom, but we're a bit low in number right now.'

'I've thought about that, but it's not as if we're snowed under in the mornings. The nature of our work is such that most of it is done later in the day. We could split into two pairs and each pair could do two sessions of two hours each week.'

'Even so Tom, if we do manage to make contact with them and establish relationships, what are we going to offer them?'

'Good question. There is of course all the organisations with whom we have contact. We could offer them some voluntary work there. But I was thinking of something else, something different which would counter the unemployed position they're in, and something which would raise their self-esteem – a new community service project they would run by themselves.'

Wellsley was still a bit dicky about the idea of wandering around the town centre approaching lads in their late teens who more than likely would be less than impressed by a strange middle-aged man wanting to talk to them, not to mention an even older man in a deer-stalker hat. However, he could see it was basically a sound idea.

Once Williams had a bee in his bonnet there was no stopping him, so minutes later they were consulting their diaries and plotting a duty rota for the new project. Each of the two pairings would have an older man partnering a younger man. They would start the following Monday morning.

Sensing they were more or less finished, Mrs Crossley cut in:

'Mr Williams, there's a young lady here to see you.'

'Good morning friend, do come in.'

The young woman was from the YM/YWCA delivering papers to him for signing. Williams was chairman of their board. The task took seconds.

'Thank you friend, have a nice day.'

On the way out, she stopped in the front office to make an aside to Peter Stanley:

'I didn't like that *friend* bit. It's so patronising.'

She couldn't have been expected to understand. Tom Williams was a Quaker and had been for many years. And Quakers often called people friends on first meeting. They were an unconventional Christian body suiting Williams down to the ground. They didn't ram their beliefs down people's throats, preferring to express them by deed in the day to day course of their lives. Neither did they believe in the hierarchical structures put in place by other Christian organisations, preferring to allow each man and woman to make their own peace on a direct line to their God.

I have feet of clay, the old man would often say to his colleagues.

By the second week of the town centre project, John Gray had been hospitalised. It was diagnosed a sister disease of tuberculosis, but nobody could figure out where he'd caught it. On top of his low mental condition, things did not look good to his colleagues. But Williams remained philosophical and hopeful, for he had known worse, much worse.

At least Gray was now pleased to know what had been wrong with him and be told he would fully recover within six months. As he lay in his hospital bed, he reflected on what had happened to him in the previous six months. He'd completed a successful eight years at Roundhill in the central area and felt it was time to move on. So Colliershire's regional director had phoned him and flagged up what he described as a great opportunity – Manager of Bakersfield Centre in the western area. The job offered an increase in salary. What the director omitted to tell him was that the previous incumbent had taken off with his girlfriend to Germany having misappropriated £5000 of the centre's funds. Gray accepted the job and would go on to learn about the felony and its consequences in his first few weeks of duty. He then demanded of his bosses, four of them in all up to the executive head of the service, that they show some remorse on behalf of the Council by reimbursing the full £5000 to the centre's management committee. Between them they couldn't muster the strength of character to do that, so Gray, utterly disillusioned, wrote the director a letter of resignation. Realising that Gray was not as naïve as they'd thought, they bounced him back eastwards again on a transfer, this time to Crack Willow, and looked for another fall guy.

In the third week of the town centre project Williams dropped a bombshell:

'I won't be going down with you in future..........Yes, yes, I know, but just think for a minute. Imagine you're an unemployed 16 year old hanging about with your mates in the bowling alley and having good crack. Suddenly an old codger dressed like me, talking like me, starts chatting you up. What's he supposed to think? No, no way, it's not working.'

Mike Wellsley was annoyed. He'd given in to Tom on the project's concept and now this.

'I'm sorry Mike, sorry to Roger and Peter as well, but there's a student coming on placement next week. A young lady if you please. In a sense she'll be getting thrown in at the deep end, but so what, it'll be good for her.'

Accordingly the project was adjusted, Wellsley and Stanley together as usual, Jenkins with Marie, the new student. Stanley had been in the nerves throughout those first sessions and projected as such, but he was in good company. Wellsley had an easy manner, born of his days in the trades, and was able to talk comfortably with unemployed young people.

Marie was a welcome addition, not just for making up the staff complement, but for her essential contact with girls, initial contact by her male counterparts alone being too risky. She also had the company of Jenkins who was not long graduated from the same college. They would discuss theory with great passion as they went along.

Two youngsters, Mathew and Bobby, sat in the bowling alley, not enough cash to play a game, but enough to patronise the soft drinks bar and be allowed to hang around. Wellsley spoke to Bobby first and told him the reason for the visit. Bobby responded:

'Yeah, we know about it. Got told Friday by that weird old sod, the one wi' the funny hat. He's not a poof is he?'

Mike laughed:

'No, it's just his way, he wouldn't mean you harm. How do you pass your time?'

'Mostly hangin around, ye know? Go down the park, play footie, job centre once a week.'

'Any luck?'

'No chance, nothin', always the same.'

Mike told them about the office in West Street and gave them an open anytime invitation. This came as a surprise for they had always regarded themselves as outsiders spurned by the system. They seemed genuinely flattered, so accepted.

Jenkins and Marie had some success as well, making contact with a lad called Phil and his girlfriend Susie. In the office Jenkins was full of the patois of social group work, but he'd been raised by a working class family, so was ably streetwise for such a situation. The team returned to base at 4 o'clock satisfied they were at last getting somewhere.

Momentum gained, it wasn't long, two weeks or so, before some nine teenagers were gathered in the back room of the West Street office and seated alongside the professional staff. Their names were Bobby, Susie, Phil, Donald, Derek, Steve,

Bruno, Dod and Jim. They had accepted the original invitation in twos and threes at first and this meeting had been set up on the strength of it. Up to fifteen had been expected, so the staff thought this a reasonable turnout given the age group.

Williams kicked off:

'Good morning, ladies and gentlemen.'

Quite deliberate, for he had a good idea they'd never been addressed as such before. Whether they liked it or not, he had their attention.

The conversation went on to explore the possibility of setting up a community service project where members would go out to very elderly or disabled people, to dig their gardens or bring in much-needed provisions, all in return for a few pounds which would go back into the kitty for ongoing running costs. For the gardening, if the tenants didn't have their own, second hand tools would be provided. Mike Wellsley was just the man for that. But at one point, Phil blurted out:

'Hold on a mo! Why should we do all that for folk with nothin' in it for us?'

As always, Williams had the answers, and one by one he bent back the fingers of one hand as he announced them:

'Firstly you get the chance to meet and make friends with old people and people less fortunate than yourselves, secondly it's something worthwhile to do with your time. You're also changing what some of the community are thinking about you. Although we know it's not true, some people view lads on the dole as scroungers. Last but not least, it's something you can put on an application form when you're applying for future jobs. And if all goes well, there are people here who'd be glad to referee for you. There are loads of reasons, Phil.'

Wellsley, Stanley, Jenkins and Marie gave off similar positive vibes and one by one the young people were convinced. By the end, they had projected a tentative starting date. Meanwhile, Jenkins would see to the necessary publicity, Stanley would draw up a list of people phoning in for assistance. The members would divide up the town and knock on doors. A bank account to govern the project was to be set up, and all that remained was a name for the project. Bruno had a suggestion:

'What about the Quid Kids? After all, we'll be asking folks for a few pounds for the jobs we do for them.'

'Let's spell it differently, make it sound catchy,' said the old man. 'Kwid Kids.'

He wrote it out in large capitals on an A4 and turned it round for them to see.

'Yeah, yeah,' they agreed in unison.

After the meeting it was time to close the office. Last to leave were Jenkins and Williams. The younger man had been impressed:

'That was good, Tom. How did you get them hooked so quickly?'

This came as a surprise, for Roger wasn't known for giving compliments to colleagues. But Williams still had a sharp response:

'Well of course, dear boy, group work is an art form, not a science.'

Fast forward ten days and everything was in place. Williams was excited again, it made him feel younger. But first off today he had a delicate duty on his plate. John Gray, although far from fully fit, was returning to work. Williams made a point of going in a few minutes earlier:

'Welcome back, dear boy.'

This was genuine, but Gray wished he wouldn't call him boy. He was a married man with three children.

John Gray was a shy and self-conscious man who always had difficulty joining clubs or associations. At school he was never really one of the boys, even less likely to chase girls, but the one thing he did possess was a good intellect. He had a first class memory, was good in number and language, admittedly of the written not spoken variety, and could solve problems. When training as a youth and community worker he was quite unnerved at times by the fact his fellow students came from all over the world, some of them more experienced than he in the ways of that world. He wasn't even sure of why he had joined the service in the first place. He was 20 at the time and all he knew was that he hated his job and while working voluntarily in the evenings at a mission in Glasgow's East End, he felt a peace he'd never known. Although surrounded by sixty volatile and underprivileged teenagers, he was, for some strange reason, comfortable. The fact that he was a talented sportsman certainly helped, the kids looked up to someone like that. So as soon as he found out he could do this for a living, he was out of the traps like a greyhound. When he qualified he took on the management of an old miners' institute in Roundhill and turned it into a successful youth centre. It suited his persona just fine, he did it pretty much on his own and on his own terms.

And now he had a mountain to climb. He had to start again, and this time he would have to operate as one of a team. He wasn't quite sure of what to make of Wellsley, Stanley or Jenkins. And as for his boss – waow !

When Gray entered, Williams came straight to the point:

'John, you're not fit enough to be full time as yet. I think you should work half time for the next six weeks. Whadayathink? We'll keep you on full pay.'

Gray was surprised but grateful. He himself was aware he wasn't yet at full strength.

'I've asked Mike to take on some of your outreach work in the meantime and would like you to spend your time in the office having a look at the state of play with the *Big Summer Show*. It's a bit rundown I'm afraid.'

Gray had mixed feelings about this. The *Big Summer Show* was a daunting assignment but it would give him a chance to concentrate his mind and something in which to sink his teeth.

After reading the papers for a while he sighed to himself. Yet again he had a resurrection job to do. The treasurer, a housing officer by day, had left his wife, children, job, *Big Summer Show* and all, for a blond secretary half his age. They had taken off for sunnier climes. The *Show* was in debt to a fair old tune, so the first thing for Gray to do was post off applications for money. In truth, it didn't bother him, he was glad to have work again. He was also glad to have been born with something in the genes of all Glaswegians – a sense of black humour.

The next months went by in an atmosphere of great industry. The *Kwid Kids* came and went with stories of the jobs they had just done and the people for whom they had worked. Many of those souls had interesting pasts and told the *Kids* fascinating tales in the intervals between work when tea and biscuits ruled. Also, there were stories of the on-the-QT backhanders the *Kids* had been given when saying good-bye. Meanwhile, John Gray worked away happily in his own company and eventually got the *Big Summer Show* out of financial trouble. It would be a very thin programme that year but Gray was confident he could get it back to normal by the next year, even if it would never be quite the enormous show it had been in its heyday.

Williams enjoyed the banter. It reminded him of the special relationships he had with his buddies in his old army days. Late in a busy day the *Kids* would surround his desk and hang on his every word. This made his colleagues jealous at times, for what could they possibly see in this enigmatic, posh old codger? In fact they saw a man they could trust, a man who would tell them the truth about themselves and about life itself. Williams had always been clear about his job. He wasn't there to turn young people into successes overnight, but help them to cope with what they had, then help them on to the first rung of the ladder, then finally, stand back and watch them climb the rest of the ladder for themselves.

Not that things always went smoothly for the *Kids*. On one occasion Mrs Crossley flew into the back office in a flutter:

'That's Mrs Ritchie on the phone, Mr Williams. She's in a terrible rage. Derek's done her front garden and it's in a worse state than when he started. She's coming in to see you at two o'clock.'

'Very well, Mrs C,' her boss said, obviously unperturbed. He knew Mrs Ritchie to be a widow and lonely. She was a gifted artist and dressed well covering herself in jewellery. She was also a valuable volunteer, for she kept a weather eye on an old children's home next door to her which was now used as a meeting place for voluntary organisations. He also knew that Derek wasn't the brightest star in the universe, and by a sheer co-incidence had lived in that old children's home from when he was orphaned at age 12.

2 o'clock arrived. One of the good things about the office was the huge front window. You could see someone coming from way off. Standing in readiness in the front room, Williams picked up Mrs Ritchie advancing at speed, a woman on a mission. She was well prepared for what she was going to say but didn't get the chance:

'Oh I say, Ma'am! Where on earth did you get that beautiful brooch on your dress?'

Disarmed and forgetting her speech altogether, she purred with delight:

'Oh, do you think so Mr Williams? In fact it was my mother's and her mother's before that. There was rumour in my family that it once belonged to a Duchess.'

'Oh I say, Ma'am!'

Mrs Ritchie then remembered the reason for her journey:

'Now Derek…'

'Yes, that was silly of Derek, but I'm sure we could send Iain Mackay up with him to help him sort it out. Iain was a gardener before he had that stroke. But you're right to be annoyed, very careless of Derek. And to think he's done a good job of the garden next door to you at the community house. He lived there as a child you know.'

'Oh no, he wasn't, was he?'

'Yes, I'm afraid so, an orphan.'

'Oh the poor boy.'

After the customary cup of tea and a long chat about famous painters and classical music, Mrs Ritchie took her leave, not only satisfied but utterly enchanted, and just a tad remorseful.

Seated at his desk again, Williams looked across the divide to where Gray sat and busied himself with applications from young people who wanted to come to Crack Willow for the school holidays and work as volunteers on the *Big Summer Show*. Williams thought to himself:

This man's really good, but I wonder if he'll ever be able to work as one of the team.

By the beginning of the next year, the office and the *Big Summer Show* planning had a more settled look about it. The *Kwid Kids* however were struggling. Quite naturally, some youngsters had tired of it and others had managed to get jobs. The diehards who were left needed a fresh challenge.

Williams peered through the front office window into the middle distance. Wellsley had seen that look before and prepared himself for a revelation which would inevitably land more work on his plate.

'Just thinking Mike, why don't we do something daft? The *Kids* could build a raft and sail it down the River Latham to the sea, having been sponsored beforehand in aid of a charity of their choice.'

For a moment Wellsley thought, hoped, the boss was pulling his leg. He waited for a smile to spread across Tom's face. No such luck, he was deadly serious. The logistic implications and the health and safety hazards were very shortly searing through Wellsley's brain.

'Tom, for goodness sake don't go there. Somebody's going to get hurt.'

'Oh come on Mike, we can do it. Just think of how much the publicity will do for the lads and the whole experience for their self-esteem. And anyway, they do need a new direction.'

Jenkins had overheard and let out a yell:

'Yes, yes, yes. Brilliant !'

Stanley grabbed a file, thrust it into his case, informed Mrs Crossley he was off to one of his community centres, and almost went through the front door without opening it.

'I think we can take it that Peter ain't keen,' said Williams laconically.

The Kon-Tiki Kids
Like many men of his generation Tom Williams had been inspired by Thor Heyerdahl's *Kon-Tiki* expedition of 1947. It was

a voyage by raft across the Pacific Ocean from South America to the Polynesian Islands, led by Norwegian explorer Thor Heyerdahl. The raft was named *Kon-Tiki* after the sun god Viracocha, for whom *Kon-Tiki* was said to be an earthly name. Heyerdahl eventually wrote a book of the same name, a chronicle of his adventures, on the back of which an award-winning documentary film was made.

'What's the problem now Tom,' said Bobby when he entered the office. He was with his older brother Mathew who hadn't taken up with the *Kwid Kids* but was now curious about Bobby's fascination with this office. Bobby continued:

'Is it that chancer again, the one who's on the gargle and never knows what day it is? We've told him three times he's well fit to dig his garden for himself.'

'No Bobby, it's not a job request. Mike and I have a new idea.'

'Whoops! Exit stage left.'

Jokingly he turned round and feigned a move towards the door.

Wellsley looked quizzically at Williams. The idea was nothing to do with him.

Bobby continued:

'You just don't get it do you, Tom? I've been on this gig for a whole year and I still ain't pulled a job.'

'Yes I know, and you deserve better. I just thought you might like to go on an adventure.'

'Oh yeah, like a holiday you mean?' Bobby sat down.

'Well not exactly. It's something more exciting than that.'

Williams recounted the story of Heyerdahl's *Kon-Tiki* expedition and then revealed his plan to the two lads.

Mathew and Bobby had endured a hard childhood which included the loss of their father at only 40 years of age, a tragic suicide. Their mother, struggling to cope in the aftermath with six children, took her daughters with her to a new home in Crack Willow and placed the two boys in care. Mathew was 15 and Bobby 13. Mathew looked out for his younger brother but he couldn't always be at his side. Bobby was tortured by emotions he couldn't understand himself and on one occasion attacked a member of staff.

When they were old enough to go out into the community themselves they were helped by a local minister who knew Tom Williams well and thought his office could find things for them to do while they tried to get a job.

'You beauty!' exclaimed Mathew jumping out of his seat. He was ecstatic. Bobby followed suit:

'When do we go?'

'Woa woah!' cautioned Wellsley 'We've got a whole load of things to work through before that.'

There was a garage in a car park to the rear of the West Street office. Years before Williams had managed to get the use of it from the authorities for a peppercorn rent. It had become a glory hole for the *Big Summer Show* but now it would be used as a workshop for the aptly named *Kon-Tiki Kids*. Wellsley came into his own, advising the lads on how to construct a raft. There was Donald, Bobby and Mathew, and a new face, Gerry. Only four were needed to man the craft.

On the first day of work, only one hour in, Bobby let slip something he'd been holding on to for dear life:

'Mathew, have you told Tom and Mike that you can't swim?'

Mathew gave his young brother a look fit to kill:

'What does it matter? It's only a river a few yards wide and when you stand in it, you're only up to the waist.'

Mike had to put the foot down:

'I'm afraid it does matter, Mathew. In some places there are fast currents and there are dark pools with hidden depths. I'm sorry Mathew, you can't go.'

The disappointment on Mathew's face was palpable. He continued to work on for twenty minutes then sloped off in a huff.

Mike had gathered the simplest of materials for the job in hand – large blocks of polystyrene for the main body of the raft, and dowelling to be run through holes screwed through the blocks for holding them together. The dowelling was just a collection of large broom handles, which would be secured by ropes. Finally, working from his garage at home, he had crafted wooden blades to be attached to dowelling so that paddles could be made, one for each crewman. With Williams they had all agreed that the raft be built at no cost whatsoever. The task was completed within a week.

Meanwhile, the old fox Williams handled the seemingly impossible, the cheering up of the truculent Mathew:

'Tell you what old friend, why don't you give the old man a hand? There's admin to do for the project, like liaison with the newspapers, sponsor forms to be made up with the names of the charities who will benefit, and permissions to get from the paper mills along the river, not to mention the Crown Estates people. Then there's advice on health and safety, the list goes on and on.'

Mathew chewed on it for a day or so and returned to the office uplifted. He liked the idea of doing admin, it made him feel important, and having been born into the industrial heartland of the big city, he had a good gift for the gab. Working with newspaper journalists was the dog's bollocks.

The three lads were made up to the complement of four with the arrival of Tim, Donald's younger brother. A date was set for a Sunday in late September. The activities surrounding the *Big Summer Show* would be over by then so wouldn't get in the way. And the team decided they would take a recce the week before the voyage by walking the bank of the river so they could take notes on any possible hazards.

It took a while for Mathew and Williams to get the necessary permissions but if it hadn't been for the old man's ability to worm his way around bureaucracy, it would have taken a sight longer. The newspapers were a knockout, massively interested, and the team wasted little time going round houses, knocking on doors and getting Mathew's sponsor sheets filled in. There were very few refusals.

The weather was fine on the recce, and along with Mike Wellsley the lads recorded the stretches made impassable by huge rocks and one particularly large fallen tree – an oak. A plan was made so that the raft could be lifted out of the water at those points, carried along the bank and relaunched.

Where there were low bridges the strategy would be to lie down flat until they were through. Special cognisance was taken of a long weir, but they felt they would be able to ride it.

On the morning of the big day the team, including Mathew, assembled at the car park behind the office. The weather was overcast with a mixture of rain and sunshine forecast. Wellsley had pre-booked a minibus and trailer from a local school who were only too pleased to be mentioned in the publicity. The raft was secured to the trailer and the team sat inside the bus with all they needed, including lifejackets, paddles and helmets. Wellsley then drove to a bridge over the Latham River at Crack Willow's town park, the jump-off point. The lads were dressed in their normal clothes except for thick socks and kagoules – trainers, jeans and polo-neck pullovers. An extra man had been enlisted by Mike, Iain MacKay, the chap who had helped Derek redo Mrs Ritchie's garden. Iain had been an officer in the Boys' Brigade for many years and was experienced in outward bound activities. He had agreed with Mike, who would be too busy driving the bus and trailer point to point on the route, that he alone would walk the riverbank alongside the raft, carrying ropes to be used if it ever got out of control. Mathew was to assist Mike.

Before the signal for go, MacKay gave them a word of caution:

'Watch out boys, there's been a lot of rain in the last week and the level of the river's gone up.'

Helmets and life-jackets on, there was a couple of minutes for final checks. Then all were on board. The skipper of the raft was Donald, an exceptionally tall and strong lad:

'Cast off me lads, for port o Latham or bust !'

The crew let out a yell and they were off. The test had begun. They paddled well and reached the first low bridge, a little less than a mile downstream. As planned they lay down flat but the high river level meant that there was less clearance for the raft. It bounced off the undersides of the bridge one to the other, lost its stability and within seconds the crew were all in the drink.

The initial shock of hitting the water impaired their thinking for a few moments and the water level ensured they had to swim. Bobby was able to grab the branch of a tree, then pulling himself to the bank, the tree itself. Iain Mackay took to the water and along with one of his ropes and the immensely strong Donald was able to secure the raft which had threatened to continue downstream and leave them. Gerry and Tom somehow managed to reach the bank a little further down. But one paddle was lost.

Like seaside bathers the shock gave way to a feeling of exhilaration. It never entered their heads to quit. Au contraire, the experience only served to heighten their resolve. Off they moved again to be cheered up by a long passage of relative calm and good sailing. It lasted for three miles.

A second low bridge, an ancient one, was approaching but this time there was enough clearance. What they hadn't noted on the recce though were the overhanging bramble bushes. No reason to of course because of the then low water. Now for real, even lying down, their kagoules and jeans, and painfully the backs of their hands, were badly scratched. All four cursed like troopers.

Allowing for three further stops to avoid their pre-recorded no-go areas, they were now well past the half way mark, the river had widened, the going was good. And then the long weir appeared.

'Down me lads, down!' commanded Donald.

They obeyed but again they had miscalculated. When the raft hit the weir its speed increased two-fold. The crew could feel the adrenalin rush and their stomachs turn. At the end of the weir, the raft came to a sudden halt. It had hit dozens of small rocks half-hidden by the water, and raising itself at the rear end, spilled its human cargo once more into the drink, only this time into a shallow drink. They were sore, very sore, and now they had nothing to blame but themselves. When the water was low the week before, they should have made a note of the rocks.

It took some time to recover from this one. The raft was secured to the bank. The sun was out so began to warm their soaking clothes. They were joined by MacKay, Wellsley who had parked there to await them, and Mathew who had endless fun ribbing them for what he'd just witnessed. They all sat down to eat the packed lunches and drink from plastic cups filled with hot tea poured from thermos flasks, all provided by Wellsley.

Refreshed and re-invigorated they checked the raft for damage. Thankfully, as it turned out, it was only superficial, so they started the last lap of their voyage. A mile was completed before they heard voices ahead. The townsfolk of Latham, who had followed the publicity keenly, were gathered on both banks of the river to clap them and cheer them as they passed.

These four lads had not enjoyed a normal childhood, so they were not prepared for the reception. They found it a bit overwhelming and it would be years before they were able to look back on it with true fondness. For the moment, the only emotions were those derived from suddenly becoming famous.

On the Latham estuary they heaved to just before the gigantic power station and hardly made the bank when they were besieged by a multitude of journalists and cameramen. Wellsley and MacKay intervened to restore some balance of order, and at one point had to draw the line and suggest to some of the press they make their way to the community centre where the lads were headed for a warm shower, a change of clothes and refreshments.

Donald quipped to the other three that one young female reporter, whom he described as a bit of all right, had asked him what their next challenge would be. He'd told her the English Channel and claimed she'd believed him.

'Maybe that'll be in the papers,' joked his young brother Tim.

Welcoming them at the community centre was an overjoyed Williams. His lads had done it. He reflected on the teamwork this would have taken and his mind drifted off to a far-flung time and place where a mighty river was crossed by himself and a group of buddies who totally relied on each other for survival.

In the days that followed the Latham adventure, Williams and Mathew got their hands on every appropriate newspaper, and together with the raft crew, Wellsley, Jenkins and Stanley, they scoured them for all the photographs and full page features.

Within a few weeks, their fame having gone before them, all four lads had secured jobs. And in the years ahead, Donald and Tim would go into the building trade. Bobby, having served an apprenticeship in painting and decorating with the local district council, went on to run his own successful business.

Gerry Irwin was the one for whom Williams felt the most, for his childhood was by far the worst. He had been orphaned when his mother and father both died of cancer. It was difficult to raise any sort of conversation with him and he often stood on the fringe of things in a deep silence with dark clouds over his brow. But he broke his silence six months later:

'I need to tell you something, Tom.'

Realising this was unusual and therefore important, Williams cleared the back office:

'Go ahead, boy, go right ahead.'

'You know when we collected the sponsor money?'

'Yes?'

'Well, the names and everything were written in pencil. I rubbed out the last ten and spent the money on myself.'

Williams had been too long in the game to react with anger or disapproval. He saw the owning-up as a measure of the regard in which Gerry held him and an indication there was hope for the boy. He responded:

'Well boy, when you can manage it, that money will have to be returned. It belongs to charity. But I'm glad you told me, it was the right thing to do.'

'Thanks Tom, I'll do that.'

When Williams closed his office that evening, he thought to himself:

That's why we do it.

A strong relationship would grow between Gerry and Tom. A year later Gerry handed him a £50 cheque made out to 'Tom Williams' and asked him to divide it between the three charities who had benefited from the raft adventure. A few years later, Gerry Irwin became Tom Williams' adopted son.

Chapter 1

Burma 1943 – the buddies

'STORK!' ROARED SERGEANT McKinlay, forgetting in his moment of outrage that the first rule of jungle battle was to be as silent as possible. He reverted to a loud whisper:

'Can ye no keep yir bloody fire under control? Ye micht as weel send the bastards smoke signals while ye're at it.'

'Bastards' was the term applied at all times to the enemy by McKinlay. Born in Aberdeen he was a soldier to his fingernails and toenails like his grandfather and father before him. They had served in the First Boer War and World War One respectively, the father having gone over the top in the charge of 1st July 1916 at the Somme, arguably the most notorious day in the history of the British Army. McKinlay Senior had lived to tell the tale, but was badly wounded and never the same man again.

Sergeant McKinlay of Burma was a man renowned throughout the brigade. Rumour had it, depending on the tale teller, he had killed any amount of Japanese soldiers up to twenty, most with a bullet, he was a crack shot, and a few by broken neck or back. When he was around, his men addressed him as 'Sarge', when not he was 'Mad Mac'. He was fearsome, no less so on account of his almost incomprehensible Doric dialect which was laced with the foulest language a trooper could muster:

'For fuck sake, Stork, pit the bugger oot and stert again.'

'Okay Sarge, gotcha.'

Mad Mac and Stork were muckers. That meant a pair like all the other pairs who cooked, ate and rested together. Stork was also one of Mad Mac's corporals in the platoon, one of three rifle platoons in the column.

Stork was a gangly awkward man. His original name in the army had been Tiny Taylor due to his height of 6 foot 3. But the weeks of continuous marching in this column of the brigade with a pack of seventy pounds on his back, the reliance on the inadequate K-rations which placed the men on a downward spiral to starvation, not to mention the strength sapping climate and being laid low by a bout of dengue fever the year before, had reduced his weight from 13 stones to 9, making him look a dead-ringer for a stork. And now he was presenting symptoms of beriberi as his feet were beginning to swell up and be painful. He longed for the next stream they might tumble on, just to dangle his legs in the cool and healing water.

'Wid ye jist luik at they twa ower there?' McKinlay was pointing at Smudger and Kiddo.

'Yes Sarge, they're always at it, every time we bivouac.'

Smudger Smith carried a pocket-sized chess set in his pack. Now he was sat down with Kiddo to continue the game they'd started the day before. A bit of a DIY craftsman, he had altered the set by gluing pegs to the bases of the figures which could be fitted into holes he had made in the black and white squares of the board. This was ideal for keeping a postponed game alive when breaking camp, for rests like this were never more than an hour or two and were used for several other functions.

'Your move,' Smudger said to Kiddo. His own move had taken seconds and he was closing in on a checkmate.

The pair of them were so engrossed they wouldn't have noticed if the alarm was raised and Stork commented on it.

'Theh'll bloody weel notice me,' said McKinlay.

Kiddo and Smudger were kindred spirits. Neither had wanted this war. When conscripted, Kiddo, real name Bernard Markham, had been destined for a career in piano teaching, music was his greatest passion followed by poetry. He had been raised in Hampstead, London, and for all the world had the proper English accent to confirm it. The men called him 'Kiddo', for he was the youngest by years.

Smudger Smith loved history and literature, and came from Devon, not far from Kiddo's roots. He cut an odd figure, very small, and for close working had to wear little circular glasses with strong lenses. The men wondered how he had ever been able to handle far less shoot a rifle. But he was longsighted and had passed training school with flying colours.

The only difference between the two was that Smudger had been assigned to the campaign. Although it was quite common among servicemen, Kiddo had volunteered for the worst possible reason. On his first home leave from army service, he discovered his girlfriend had married one of his friends, and the Burma ticket became a suicide mission. Now he was having second thoughts. What had he let himself in for?

Nearby were Thomo, alias Bill Thomson, and Stinka. Thomo had complained to Mad Mac on several occasions about what it was like to muck with Stinka, that if you were downwind of him the smell was atrocious, and begged his sergeant for another mate. The answer was always the same:

'Nae bloody chance, get on wae it laddie.'

However, on this occasion McKinlay had some sympathy:

'Jesus Christ Stinka, pit a stone on they socks o' yours or theh'll waak awa thirsels.'

'I'll wash them when next we reach water, Sarge.'

'That'll no be for a couple o' days yet. Ye've got fower extra pairs o' socks in yon pack o' yours. Cheynge them noo or nane o' us wull be able tae breathe the next time we get some sleep.'

'Okay Sarge.'

Apart from the obvious reason for his nickname, Stinker Manley was not a pretty sight. The only time he went to the dentist was when he was in terrible pain. The result over the years was two rows of teeth with at least one gap, often more, between each tooth. Back in civilisation he had been a night-mare to behold for any drill sergeant at morning parade. And if berated by his mates for never washing or shaving, he had the perfect reply:

'Them folks who have to wash every day must be very dirty, yeah?'

Thomo had been born and raised in Australia, but his family moved to Newcastle when he was 12. When he spoke it came out in a curious mixture of Geordie and Oz. Both he and Stinka, for all the latter's faults, were damn good soldiers and bull's eye shots.

The buddies settled down in their pairs for tucker and rest. As was the custom, one prepared a meal, the other some char. Stork and McKinlay began to blether:

'That was some march we did during the night, Sarge. How many miles do you think?'

'Fifteen Ah'd say, give or take. It wis a guid track, nae slashin needed up front.'

The brigade of 3000 men had been divided up into eight separate columns, and each column was led by a group of slashers who cleared the way ahead if it was heavy with undergrowth. A track of five feet in width was necessary to allow the mules and their heavy side packs to manage comfortably.

'But during the night, Sarge? I know it's done because it's too dangerous to take a long track in daylight, but it was murder.'

'Ach Stork, ye're only sayin this cause yir feet are sae sair. Dinna worry, son, Ah'll find ye watter soon.'

'Cheers Sarge. Although, I was wondering what Wingate's got in store for us now. Those rations are getting low, we'll need another air-drop soon.'

'Oh yes, the good old RAF.'

McKinlay had switched to English, always did when he fancied a bit of sarcasm:

'The pin-up boys of the services, clean as a whistle when they land, clean as a whistle when they take off, and of course clean as a whistle when they don't have to land at all. Three cheers for the fly-boys.'

He made a dummy salute and with his free hand, placed a forefinger above his upper lip to mimic a moustache. Stork laughed. Despite all the pain and suffering, the hard going, the constant pangs of hunger and the dehydration from never having enough water to drink, he felt safe in the hands of his sergeant. His buddies felt safe too and once they'd got used to Mad Mac's rebukes and foul language, they welcomed his leadership. They'd lost their commanding officer some way back. Badly wounded in a skirmish which took the lives of five of the platoon, he ordered the men to leave him behind. They gave him a canteen of water, three grenades, and enough morphia for him to take a lethal dose. They never saw nor heard of him again. Major Bissett, commander of the column, had no other officer to spare but knew McKinlay well and viewed him a safe pair of hands.

Suddenly there was a huge explosion about a mile or more ahead which rocked them all to the core.

'Ay ay! The commandos. Theh'll hae blown yon viaduct.'

The blast was followed by a ratatat of gunfire.

'That'll be the Japs engaging,' said Stork.

Yup, the bastards are nivir faur awa.'

The morning had taken on a new aspect. The sky was a rare blue and an orange sun was slowly climbing out of the distant dark mountains. The buddies sighed. There were some occasions when this godforsaken country could look stunningly beautiful.

Mac shook Stork out of his awe:

'Whit dae ye mak o' the young'un, Kiddo, or if you prefer, Bernard? Is he no a fairy or what?'

'I don't think so, Sarge. Okay, so he talks posh and likes classical music and poetry, was brought up in Hampstead, but.........

Mac cut him off:

'Hampstead indeed. Well I do beg your pardon. Ther are mair millionaires per squerr mile in thon place than in onie ithir place in the hale o Britain. Ah've cheynged ma mind, Ah'm keepin in wae him. But Ah still think he's a fairy.'

Stork got on with the meal but looked forlornly at the K-rations. The K was short for Kelloggs, the rations being made up in their main base in America. It wasn't a delightful menu – tins of spam, hard biscuits which were difficult to eat but could be dunked in tea to make a satisfying porridge, a little rice never enough, processed cheese, nuts, raisins, dates, cigarettes, matches, tea, milk, sugar and salt, and sometimes chocolate if the men were lucky. A boost in protein was available now and again from mule steak, if a pack animal had collapsed and died the day before of exhaustion. If they stumbled on a Burmese village, the locals were usually generous and fed the men adequate and properly cooked rice with onions and other vegetables.

'What do you think of our brigade commander, Sarge?'

'Orde Wingate? If ye ask me, he's a bloody madman, a total fruitcake. But ther's nae doot, he's jist the man for the job. The bastards are aff thir heids as weel, but nae match for oor boy. That's why he merches us aa in columns. Ye cannae attack a column and win. It disnae present a solid front, and if wan part gets fucked, the ithers can redeploy and pick the bastards aff. He'll dae for ma boss.'

Stork laughed and nodded in agreement. The Brigadier, Orde Wingate, had gained an earlier reputation as an expert in guerrilla warfare operating special forces in Palestine and Abyssinia. A confirmed Zionist, he had played an initial role in the encouragement of the Jewish people towards what would eventually become their own state of Israel in 1948. He came to the notice of Churchill in late 1938 who thought him one of the most extraordinary and eccentric soldiers, and indeed men, he had ever met. Incredibly single-minded and determined, he brooked no opposition from colleagues whatever their rank, and was totally committed and loyal to his men. They were inspired by him. The Japanese were unstoppable by early 1942 when they conquered Burma. So the following year Wingate parachuted his men into the country behind Japanese lines, divided up his brigade into two forces, one diversionary, the other major, and both forces were to blow up bridges, cut railway lines and ambush Japanese patrols. The two forces would then meet up east of the Irrawaddy river and attack the main railway line from Lashio in the East to Mandalay in the West. The plan seemed crazy but up till now was working. Wingate was at least a match for the Japanese, his strategy called Long Range Penetration with the campaign coded *Longcloth*. The total brigade was only 3,000 men drawn from eight regiments, four British, four Gurkha, and he put them into a mix in each of eight equal and separate columns, comprised of three infantry platoons, a support platoon with mortars and Vickers machine guns, and a commando platoon for blowing bridges. His men would go down in history as the Chindits which was less of a mouthful than Long Range Penetration Force. Wingate coined the name from the Burmese Chinthe, a mythical half lion half eagle, statues of which guarded the pagodas of Burma. He saw the name as a metaphor for the partnership between his ground troops and supporting air forces.

The Gurkhas were represented in Mad Mac's platoon, one pairing of muckers being Shankar and Ganesh. And if ever his men needed reminding of the value of these fine soldiers, he would quote from a famous British general:

If a man tells you he's not afraid of dying, he's a liar, unless he's a Gurkha.

Shankar and Ganesh enjoyed their bivouac meal better than their British mates, simply because they knew how to cook rice and mix it with the right concoction of vegetables and fruit. They were last to eat. Despite the hunger they waited until it was cooked through and through.

After the meal the men cleared up and put their fires out. Only groundsheets were left out so that the men could rest awhile before moving on, and the Lee Enfield rifles lay beside them if a sudden alarm was raised.

'Stinka! What the fuck are you playin at?' roared McKinlay, once again forgetting the rule of silence. Stinker had gone just ten yards and was dropping his shorts.

'Ye ken the rules, man. Go a hunner yards at least and tak a spade or somethin'. Goad almighty, the man's an erse.'

In the interests of sanitation a soldier had to distance himself from his group to take a dump and had to take a digging implement with him, to lessen the chance of disease entering his platoon's supplies of water.

'And Thomo, fuck sake, gie yirsel a shake and luik sherp. Tak yir rifle, go wae him and watch his back.'

'Yes Sarge,' replied the two men in turn.

McKinlay and Stork now realised there wasn't going to be much rest now and worried about the fact the men hadn't slept much in the past three days:

'Seriously Sarge, what are our chances of survival?'

'Nae better than fifty fifty, auld freend. But Ah'll tell ye wan thing. They bastards wull nivir tak McKinlay alive.'

A further ten minutes passed and the whistle for departure sounded. Mad Mac hated it, for he thought his father would have heard the same whistle calling him over the top into no man's land. It was a haunting sound.

The going was harder now and progress was slow. Up ahead the slashers were at it non-stop. It was estimated by the column commander if it continued for the whole day they would be lucky if they managed three miles. The packs weighed the equivalent of half that of a man who had been reduced to 10 stones and the straps cut into his shoulders on an arduous trek. Nicknamed 'Everests' because of the prolonged effort, they typically contained three grenades, a groundsheet, spare shirt and trousers, four spare pairs of socks, jack knife, rubber shoes, toggle-rope, canvas life-jacket, mess tin, ration bags, water bottle, water carrier, and other odds and sods. The men also carried their rifles, side-arms and bayonets.

McKinlay's platoon was the third in the column and it served to protect the rear, although it also served to put them most at risk. About midday, he ordered his men to stop. His instincts born of hard battles were on high alert. The sudden clearing to their right had high rocks at the end and the jungle birds had fallen silent, all the ingredients for a Japanese presence. In a loud whisper Mac gave out his instructions:

'Move very slowly backarts intae cover, my lads, and present arms, point them at they rocks.' The Japanese were courageous do or die soldiers, but they were badly organised. And when they fought it was for their Emperor, not for their officers.

Suddenly, a bloodcurdling yell tore through the air and a forty strong force of the enemy jumped from cover like rabbits out of their burrows. And they kept yelling as they charged across the clearing shooting randomly as they went. It was a big mistake, for rifle platoon 3 was ready for them.

'Wait my lads, steady, steady…….Now, pick your man, and fire at will !'

It took less than a minute. A crescendo of volley fire zipped into the bodies of the Japanese soldiers until 90 percent of them had collapsed like playing cards and either lay dead or fatally wounded. Realising they were defeated, the four still standing dropped their rifles. Kiddo and some of the younger men raised their weapons to finish them off but their sergeant stopped them with the voice of experience:

'Easy my lads, cease firing, not needed now.'

The enemy soldiers looked straight at them and bowed, then took out their side arms. Kiddo raised his Enfield again.

'I told you to cease firing, boy!' roared McKinlay.

Kiddo complied, then gasped as the Japanese foursome raised their pistols to their temples and almost simultaneously pulled the triggers. As Shankar and Ganesh moved around the few of the Jap platoon who were still alive to despatch them with mercy, Smudger and Kiddo held on to teak trees and were physically sick.

It was not a total victory. Mad Mac was duly informed that it had come at the cost of three of his men's lives. They were buried in shallow graves marked with bamboo crosses. The bush hats they had worn were hung on top.

When they took up marching again and for a long time into the afternoon no-one spoke. Their thoughts were their own. Smudger, the amateur historian, remembered the immortal words of the Duke of Wellington:

Next to a battle lost, the greatest misery is a battle gained

The memory of the four Japanese suicides would stay vividly with them for days. And like the rest of the column they were becoming exhausted, beyond tired. Major Bissett who had heard about the attack and was becoming concerned about sniping further up the column decided to call a halt one hour before dusk, which at this time of year would fall quickly and soon. When they finally bivouacked, it became clear to McKinlay his men were down both physically and emotionally. He scratched his mind for something funny to say that would lift them, and he got his chance when Smudger went off for a dump with Kiddo in tow as look-out.

'Ther goes oor expert on Oscar Wilde and the ither yin, ye ken, the wan wha wrote aboot the mail train.'

'W.H. Auden,' prompted Stork.

'Ay, and a richt perr o' poofs theh were and aa.'

'Oh Sarge, give the boy a break,' said Thomo.

'Ferr enough, but when Smudger comes back, tell him tae sleep wae his erse against a sturdy tree the nicht.' The company were beside themselves with laughter. The tonic had worked. On his return Kiddo said:

'Did I miss something, what was so funny?'

Fires were put out an hour after bedding down and few men had difficulty sleeping. One such was Kiddo. He cursed himself for having volunteered, and now he was terrified. He tossed and turned until 2am when he finally dropped off.

The next morning dawned with more of the same, heavy undergrowth to be hacked through and slow progress. But around midday they got word from up ahead that a small river had been found. It was quite fast flowing which was ideal for their needs, for the banks of slow or static water could harbour all sorts of dangerous diseases, together with some interesting friends – ants, centipedes and leeches for just three.

In groups they took turns at the water so that the momentum of the column was maintained. Water containers were filled, men slaked their thirst, washed and bathed their sores. And look-outs were posted. The Japanese were never far away from water in anticipation of a band of thirsty British soldiers.

'Oh that's so much better,' sighed Stork, 'I can literally see the swelling in my feet going down.'

'Guid man, Stork, ye can tak as lang as ye like, we cannae afford tae lose men like you.'

Smudger and Kiddo played in the water like children, but had to be told to keep their voices down. Stinker at last had a chance to wash but had to be led to the trough by the scruff of the neck and thrown in by his mates. When finished, Thomo told him to change his socks or he'd be tied to a tree and left behind. He complained bitterly throughout his ordeal.

Shankar and Ganesh went through their own routine inscrutable as ever. Whatever the situation, they never seemed to betray any emotion. And at all times they were inseparable from their khukuris, or kukris, a sizeable, inwardly turned broad knife which doubled as a useful utensil and a devastating weapon.

At last refreshed, the column continued on its way and was lifted once more by the sound then sight of allied planes. The wireless operator had done his job early in the morning at breakfast and had negotiated the next drop zone. The zones were found not only by map and compass, but were also chosen for features close by which could be made out from a long way off. The same tactic was used when columns wanted to rendezvous with each other.

'Thank the Lord, more rations at last,' said Stork as he sank to his knees.

Day followed laborious day, night marching alternating with day marching until the men lost track of time. But eventually, word was passed down the line that Wingate intended to go ahead with his plan of crossing the Irrawaddy. Many received this news with dismay, for they were already weakened and wanted to turn for home base in India. But Wingate was not a man to cash in his chips too soon.

Another column was already approaching the river, and had paused to change plan and cross at a different point, for a massive Japanese force were closing in from the South. The column commander had rubber boats but didn't feel they were adequate, so he took a risk and delayed while some of his men took a recce into a nearby ferry town where better dinghies were in plentiful supply and the villagers, whether friendly or pro-Japanese, had no choice in the matter. The boats were commandeered. Bissett's following column would reap the benefit of this commander's resourceful thinking:

Bend by bend, the men could detect the increasing sound of a large body of moving water. Even Mad Mac and his lads, bringing up the rear, could hear it clearly.

'Looks like we're crossin efter aa. Ah jist hope that bloody madman kens whit he's daein.'

It took fifteen minutes for a column like this to pass a given point, so there was inevitable frustration for the platoon as a queue began to develop and men in front of them bunched up. It seemed an eternity before the lads were at last able to stand back and take in the view of Burma's greatest river, the Irrawaddy. It was anything from half a mile to a mile wide depending on a favoured crossing point, but the monsoon season wasn't due for six weeks yet, and there were two great sandbanks protruding from the river, as if arranged to function as stepping stones. The previous column had used them well to ferry its men in relays. And this had also served to leave Bissett's column more than enough boats to spare. At the very end of the exercise, the riflemen took to the boats, only to hear that familiar bloodcurdling cry. The Japanese had arrived, a little too late to make an impression that mattered and only to discover that the surplus dinghies had been holed.

Nonetheless, they were able to fire at the embarking riflemen. And with Ganesh late into the water, Mad Mac had to howl at him:

'For fuck sake Ganesh, get on board!'

Ganesh remained in the water, using all his strength to push the last boat as far out as possible. Then he stood upright and looked at McKinlay:

'Good-bye, my Sergeant. Good luck.'

He turned towards the Japanese soldiers. Before he fell he had stopped four bullets and despatched one of the enemy with his kukri. And he lay at the water's edge, a stone's throw from the body of a British soldier.

Chapter 2

A strange relationship

BY 1985 THE West Street office in Crack Willow was much changed.

In late 1983 Peter Stanley saw sense, and realising his future lay elsewhere, left the youth and community service for a career in the licensed trade. On the day of his departure Tom Williams assembled the staff in the back office. Peter had been sent on a dummy errand:

'Now listen up. Not one of you has given any thought to this man's leaving. I've bought him a bumper sized book on classic cars, you know how much he loves his cars, and a card to go with it which I expect you all to sign.'

The company looked suitably guilty then searched for their pens. Mike Wellsley and John Gray took out their wallets as well and offered Williams a fiver each to offset his costs. Their boss waved his hand in a gesture of polite refusal. When Peter returned, the presentation took place, and after a humble and hastily prepared buffet was consumed, he took his leave and went off to pastures new.

A year later, Williams sustained an unexpected blow. His loyal servant, the super-efficient Mrs Crossley had to tell him her husband was being moved by his firm to the Scottish Borders. Within a month she was off with her family and Williams contemplated life without the irreplaceable Mrs C. However, he went through the motions of advertisement, selecting applications, interviewing candidates and finally appointing the ably qualified Mrs Hunter.

Throughout 1984 Mike Wellsley and Roger Jenkins had itchy feet. The constant to and fro of unemployed youngsters was proving too much. Sometimes the ex-policeman in Wellsley would come to the fore. He had given his all to the *Kon-Tiki Kids* but they had been exceptional. Other lads were not so biddable and Mike would often refer to them as 'plasters'.

Roger Jenkins went hard at both his written work and his social group work in the community, and was fast coming to the notice of those in high office and those in political power. Sometimes he thought that the aimless lads who gathered around Tom Williams' desk were an unwelcome distraction. In the cramped working conditions of the office this was to some extent understandable, and by late in the year Wellsley and Jenkins had secured permission for a new office, ostensibly a classroom in the local primary which had fallen idle in the wake of a drop in the school roll.

Meanwhile, John Gray was quite content. He had recovered from a serious illness and the debacle surrounding his previous job. Whatever else fell on his plate, for six months in the year he was thoroughly occupied with the *Big Summer Show*, and since the late sixties when he worked in the east end of Glasgow, he had never felt ill at ease in the company of needy young people.

At the start of New Year 1985 a lorry pulling a long low-loader drew up in front of the office. Wellsley and Jenkins along with the driver, and with the help of a robust trolley, busied themselves moving what they would need out to the vehicle – desks, chairs, filing cabinets, other odds and ends. Williams remained at his desk, inscrutable and silent.

When finished, his two colleagues approached his desk to exchange parting gestures. What they got came totally out of the blue:

'Well, good luck. Now make sure you've got everything, because you're not coming back.'

Clearly, Williams had viewed the parting as an act of betrayal. And just like Jenkins and Wellsley, Gray too was shocked by Williams' frosty au revoir. As they turned for the door, they offered Gray the chance to go with them. He thought that a strange thing to ask so late in the day, and then thought to himself:

There's a lot going on here, so I'm staying put.

Gray well knew that the professional team would continue to come together regularly for meetings under the leadership of Tom Williams, but could see the relationships between the four men could never be the same. Williams' comment had shown him a side of his boss he hadn't seen before, but something he couldn't put a finger on, something instinctive, was keeping him next to the old man.

In the West Street office the weeks that followed the break-up were quiet, weirdly so. Mrs Hunter was a very reserved person and tended to arrive, do her work very ably, then go home. Williams had gone into a shell and hardly spoke. The Government had started a Youth Opportunities Programme and two teenagers had been assigned for a period to the office. Oddly, Williams took little or nothing to do with it, leaving them both in Gray's hands. It seemed as if the great youth worker had run out of steam and had one eye on the clock and the countdown to retirement in 3 years' time.

Gray busied himself as best he could, popping in and out in a combination of routine work and preparations for the 1985 *Big Summer Show*. But occasionally, when confined to his desk, he would glance across the now much widened divide at his boss and try to second guess his thoughts, but to no avail. Gray was puzzled by him:

What a complex man Tom is. To be born in Wales in The Rhondda Valley, a mining stronghold, and yet speak such proper English, wear clothes traditionally associated with toffs, never to have had another relationship after losing his fiancé, and seemingly by design, to have seen active service in the British Army but never to talk about it, in fact never to talk about any of his life prior to 1963, the year of his arrival here in Colliershire. And yet he wants to know everything about others, particularly disadvantaged or troublesome young people for whom he will give his all, no matter what their past. How am I going to get on with this strange old codger on my own?

Clearly the two men were vastly different, but they both knew they had at least two things in common. One was a keen sense of humour, albeit arrived at through real, day to day experiences and roundabout ways.

Williams was renowned as a dreadful driver and those who knew all about it made every effort to avoid ending up in the front passenger seat of his car. In his Glaswegian humour Gray told one poor soul to take a paper bag with him to put over his head if the experience proved too much.

One December when consecutive falls of snow had created extremely icy conditions, Williams had been returning from an evening committee meeting when he managed to bounce his car three times off a bridge over the River Latham.

And Williams had double standards about driving:

Just months into their new partnership, Gray reversed out of his carpark bay, across West Street and straight into another car. He knew whose car it was, the man stopped there occasionally to get golfing tickets from the parks department next door. He waited for the man to return, then swapped insurance details with him. Later in the office he recounted the story to Williams:

'I'm saying in the insurance claim that he'd parked on a double yellow line.'

'Doubt if that'll cut much ice, dear boy. Whatever the circumstances, you still backed into him.'

Six weeks later very early in the day, Williams left the office for an area organisers' meeting. Two minutes later he was back:

'Did you forget something Tom?'

'No, I've just reversed into someone's car.'

Gray looked out the window.

'Oh my God, Tom, it's the same car I reversed into a while back.'

'Well, serves him jolly well right. He was parked on that double yellow line.'

'What are we going to do?'

'Well, I'm off to my meeting.'

'You can't. What about the chap?'

'You'll think of something, John. Cheerio!'

Five minutes later the driver entered the office and aggressively pointed at Gray:

'You've done it again, haven't you?'

'What do you mean?'

The driver led Gray out to view the damage.

'Look for yourself,' said Gray 'there's no mark on the back of mine.'

'Well it must have been that weird old boss of yours, the one with the funny hat.'

'Not possible I'm afraid. He went straight to a meeting at Latham this morning. Why don't you try the social work office next door? Plenty of their staff park here.'

In the years leading up to Williams' retirement, he and Gray would share that story over and over again while laughing themselves to tears.

The second thing they had in common was that neither was ambitious. They were content to stay at a field level and work closely with the public. And whilst in the past they were entirely suited to the language of youth and community work, they were uncomfortable with the language of community education, the

new name of their profession The former was all about a partnership between the professionals and the community, both
bodies learning from each other. The new breed of community
education worker seemed to think he was in charge of something. Men like Williams and Gray would have been considered
soft if they hadn't started off with a ramshackle youth centre in
a depressed area. This new lot came out of college looking for
the best possible ticket and their ambitions didn't stop there.

And yet, in a situation where they now worked so closely,
the two colleagues remained laws unto themselves. Neither was
inclined to disclose to the other their histories or, for that matter, their emotions. Basically they were shy and private men.

Gray was wary of Williams and by now familiar with the
black dog which often as not lay across his brow when he arrived for work in the early morning. Like the former secretary
Mrs C, John learned to wait until 9.30am before engaging with
his boss.

In September of '85 Gray caught a dose of black dog for
himself, some sort of mild breakdown. Getting up in the morning was a Herculean effort, and when he took the family pet out
after breakfast, it seemed the animal was walking him. Julia, his
wife, hadn't a clue what was wrong with him, and the expres-
sions on his children's faces spelled out their feelings:

What's happening to our daddy?

Another kind of boss would have told Gray to snap out of
it. Not Williams:

'This is the sort of thing that follows you around, ye know.
And it usually happens years after whatever's caused it. Bet it's

something to do with that carry-on you had before you came here, you know, the thing you never talk about.'

Gray thought that last bit was rich, coming from a man who never spoke about his past. But it was helpful, and more than he felt he was getting from his GP who leaned over a tad too quickly for his prescription pad. And like all colleagues in his age group, Gray once more wondered how this single old man had come to be so informed about such things:

Has he gone through something himself, perhaps something much worse. And if so, what was it?

Williams felt that John's best cure was work. The *Big Summer Show* had once again been put to bed, so he landed him the job of compiling a complete and up-to-date list of Crack Willow's voluntary organisations. There were more than 200. Even so, there were times when Gray could be seen at his desk with his head bowed down, unable momentarily to carry on his work. Inevitably he was signed off by his doctor for two weeks. It didn't help. At home he was even more morose to the point at times of feeling suicidal. And then the doorbell rang.

Standing on the doorstep with a huge smile on his face was Tacker Taylor. Years before, Tacker, real name Colin, was a typical lad carrying around a troubled luggage from his childhood. In a state of unemployment he went to the West Street office and was first fascinated then uplifted by Williams. Gray then gave him a voluntary job with the *Big Summer* Show. His first task was laying an old carpet in one of the flats to be used by Gray's foreign volunteers who were due to arrive in a couple of weeks. In the middle of the job Gray was called away, leaving Colin to get on with it:

'If you need tacks, Colin, just bang a few in around the door. I'll be back in twenty minutes.'

When Gray returned, the whole packet of tacks had been used to fix the one carpet along its four sides and even diagonally across it. Gray was livid and the poor lad on the receiving end of a bollocking.

Later, and in front of the whole band of volunteers, Gray's Glaswegian humour dubbed Colin Taylor 'Tacker'. The name stuck, he became renowned for it, then he played the part for all it was worth – with friends, bosses and girlfriends alike. Tacker Taylor was a star.

Gray was delighted to have one of his old boys visit him, one of his successes. He was now a student in Manchester and was taking a week's break back in Crack Willow. They had coffee and a long chat together. When Tacker announced he was studying medicine with a view to becoming a surgeon, Gray almost choked on his coffee in his shock at the revelation, even joked later:

'Now remember, Tacker, don't use tacks when you stitch up your patients.'

The following day they booked a table and played snooker. Tacker duly returned to Manchester. And Gray duly returned to his work, refreshed by Tacker's unexpected and welcome visit.

'Tacker came to see me when I was off, Tom. Did you have anything to do with it?'

'He did call in here, but no, he must have gone on to yours on his own initiative. Lovely lad, eh? How thoughtful.'

Gray didn't believe him for a second.

As time passed, Gray began to feel he'd made the right decision, namely to stay with the old man when the office staff had split into two groups. He was beginning to like and admire Williams, for all his eccentricities. And when Gray was honest with himself, he realised, when it came to caring for people and personal integrity, Williams was in a league of his own. The boss also possessed a formidable strength of character:

Gray had become accustomed to the groups of unemployed youngsters huddled around Williams' desk. In fact he welcomed it, for most of them worked as volunteers on the *Big Summer Show*. As such they were a help to Gray, and he was able to practise his own brand of youth work on them. At one such gathering, Williams said:

'I'm just popping out to Social Work next door, John. They want us to be one of the placements in their new Community Service Orders Scheme.'

The young lads remained around his desk and one of them, Bruno, moved into the old man's vacant chair. Gray decided not to scold him, judging that Williams would not have minded.

Then in walked Williams' boss, the regional director. Charles Masterton was a portly and dishevelled man, full of bluster and self-importance, at the pinnacle of a non-essential service, in other words not really important at all. He was already displeased about something, and the sight of Bruno in

Williams' chair horrified him to the point of apoplexy. He stared at Gray:

'Where's Mr Williams and what's that boy doing in his chair?'

Fortunately, Gray did not need to answer. Tom Williams had returned:

'Good afternoon, Charles. How are you?'

'What's that boy doing in..........Oh, never mind, I want to speak to Roger Jenkins, he's been very rude to the management committee of Exodus Youth Centre. They've complained to me on the phone.'

'I'm afraid Roger's working at a new office in Winton Primary School, Charles. But it's only half a mile away.'

'Then get him on the phone and tell him to come here immediately.'

'Now Charles, why don't we relax, sit down, have a coffee, and you can tell me all about it.'

'I want to see him now!'

'Charles, this is my show here. If Roger's done something wrong, I'll be the one to deal with it, I'll be the one to saw his head off.'

'Don't talk to me like that !'

'Calm down boy, calm down.'

'Don't call me boy!'

'Then stop behaving like one.'

Five minutes later Masterton left the office with his tail between his legs. The lads had been right royally entertained and

Gray had a smile on his face for the rest of the afternoon, all the way home, and all evening until bedtime.

He had just witnessed something he had never thought possible. He had always been led to believe, no matter how wrong, no matter how stupid, people in high office were always above reproach. But more than that, there was a serious and meaningful message to be taken from this strange event. For years John Gray had been unable to trust any of his professional colleagues. Now there was one colleague he could trust – his boss. Here was a man who put his lads first, a man who was never afraid of his superiors, who more often than not got the best of them.

But turning the relationship the other way round, Williams was close to retirement and worried for his younger colleague. He could see that Gray was a very caring man and possessed considerable skills when it came to youth work. In fact there were times when Gray reminded him of himself. His concern was that the younger man lacked self-confidence, assertiveness, and an ability to work with colleagues in other areas of the region:

'You should really take part in joint initiatives, John. When I speak to your colleagues around Colliershire, they all sing the same song – oh no, John Gray? He's not up to much.'

Gray did not respond. It was of course true. Williams had an ability to feel comfortable with the truth and when he made a point to someone, he did not miss that person and hit the wall. But he wondered what he had to do to shake Gray out of his reticence. Gray was indeed sullen much of the time. He wasn't prepared to stick his head up from the long grass in case the same thing as had happened to him before would happen again and he'd be used as a fall guy. He considered his lot the lesser of two evils.

'John, why don't you at least throw your cap in the ring when chances for promotion come up? Take my job, for example, it comes up in a couple of years.'

Again, Gray did not respond.

By the summer of '86 Gray could see that the days of the *Big Summer Show* were numbered and he began to get tetchy with his voluntary staff, even those among them who were his guests from abroad.

Two lads, who came over from Belgium, got fed up with the *Show* and absconded taking with them some of the provisions in the foreign volunteers' flats.

Feeling miffed about this, Gray wrote a letter of complaint to their home addresses and asked for compensation. He received a reply from one parent in letter-headed paper, an official it seemed in one of Belgium's embassies. The content of the letter was non co-operative, the tone decidedly condescending.

Gray showed Williams the two letters:

'Hmm, he's probably a clerk,' said Williams dismissively.

'Is that all you have to say, Tom?'

'Look John, you should stop involving yourself in such inconsequential detail.'

'But Tom, this is theft.'

'Oh well, if you must. But of course, you are a psychologically obsessional creature.'

Gray was furious. It was 10 minutes to 5, so he stormed out early and drove towards home not knowing what speed he was doing and lucky not to be stopped. He parked at a corner shop for a paper, returned to his car, got into the driver seat and pulled the door shut so fast and furiously that the window shattered, as car windows do, into a thousand crystal pieces. Over the next 24 hours Gray had time to reflect on those inner rages of his. More importantly, he had time to reflect on the cost of this latest one – 60 quid to be precise. And most of all, he reflected on the unavoidable truth. Yet again, the old boy had been right.

In the months leading up to Tom Williams' retirement there were all sorts of background moves to ensure he was given the best possible send-off. When the time came there were in fact two send-offs, one from the region's professional colleagues and one from local voluntary organisations, so highly was the old man regarded. After all, he had helped a countless number of people.

David Samson, the lad whose talent Tom had noticed in the sixties, who had gone on to be his colleague in the seventies, and who also was an area organiser by the eighties, chaired the professionals' event. David and Tom were very close friends and would remain so.

John Gray chaired the event run by the voluntary sector and used his love of comedy to do a party piece – a caricature of the old man. Williams thoroughly enjoyed his night and when he smiled, there were those who swore they could see his bow tie twirling like a Catherine- wheel.

Williams had put it about that John Gray would shortly fill his shoes, he wanted that for John. But Roger Jenkins was waiting in the wings. He wanted promotion badly, had been preparing for it for some time, had made himself well-connected, and was looking forward to his interview with relish.

On his last day Williams avoided any fuss when he left. He wished the secretary well then shook hands with Wellsley and Jenkins. Gray noted that the handshakes were neither firm nor warm. The old man said nothing to Gray. There was no need. They had said all they had to say to each other over the past few days. And the younger man was pleased that the old boy would get some rest now, time to tend to his garden, one of his favourite passions. In the twenty plus years Tom Williams had worked for Colliershire's youth service he had never been known to take a proper holiday. Any holiday he did take, usually a few days, was spent on visits down south to his Quaker friends or on national business of Toc H or the YMCA. He did take a week every other year to visit an old army friend. John Gray could see that was special to him, but that was as far as he was likely to get. On his army experiences Williams kept the door closed.

Gray had come to regard his boss as a bit of a shaman. He had the ability to put in a nutshell all of work's, and life's, problems, irritations and absurdities, then make the vast majority of them seem trivial, while at the same time giving his all to people when he realised they were undergoing a truly hard time. He also had an uncanny knack of predicting things which would invariably come true. And he always framed his wisdom in a one-liner. On many occasions he would say to his colleagues:

You must remember, there are no friends in business.

Those who worked with him didn't always like that remark, but it was true, almost unerringly, true.

When Williams had gone, Gray returned to his seat and discovered there was another reason for the swift departure, and it sat proudly on top of his desk – a brand new state of the art briefcase with a short but telling note stuck to the handle:

Thanks for taking the brunt of it for my last five years

When Monday morning arrived, only Jenkins and Gray were interviewed for the vacancy. Always the opportunist, Jenkins had managed to be taken first. Gray had been more or less warned by David Samson on the Friday that the interviews would be difficult for him. Jenkins got the job. Gray would go on to hazard all sorts of guesses for why this had happened, but he had to be honest about the one, the only one, that mattered. Jenkins had a vision for the future of the profession. It was a vision Gray neither understood nor felt convinced about, so he wasn't exactly equipped to say great things about it at his interview. Although in some pain at the outcome, Gray got a pleasant surprise a few days later. He was taking a meeting at a local community hall, one that he visited every Thursday evening. Standing waiting on his arrival was his old boss.

Williams offered his condolences. Gray pretended to be okay and played the whole thing down. Williams thought he'd best change the subject:

'Now that we've finished our work together, John, we can be friends.'

Gray readily agreed and made a mental note of it. The two men would keep to the pledge.

With Gray's meeting imminent, Williams knew he couldn't hang around, so left his former colleague with an open invitation to visit him in the not too distant future. He switched his engine on but, before winding up his window, called out to Gray:

'Your help will come, and when it does, it will come from the least expected source.'

As it turned out for John Gray, Williams had just delivered his finest one-liner of all.

CHAPTER 3

Withdrawal

'SOME FUCKING KETTLE o' fish this,' grizzled Mad McKinlay.

'What's the score, Sarge?' Stork enquired, turning round from his cooking.

'Wan each and it luiks like we're aboot tae score an own goal.'

'How do you mean?'

'We're turnin roond is whit Ah mean. Attention! About turn!'

'We don't understand, Sarge.' Stork was now speaking for them all.

'Ah've jist been briefed by yon Captain Morris, ye ken, the wan wae the awfie yaw-yaw voice. Chins up, lads, and all that. Oniewey, Wingate the wunner boy has decidit we're no fit tae cairry on wae the job. So we're goin hame, well no quite, as faur as India, Ah mean tae say.'

The platoon was shocked at first but when they'd had a few minutes to gather their thoughts, they were not displeased. It had been a gruelling affair thus far. They had lost men to battle, to being left behind, to captivity, to disease. They were constantly starving, constantly sore with the marching, and now it had been raining for 36 hours.

'Ye needna luik sae pleased wae yirsels, that's no the hauf o' it.'

Bernard Markham very seldom spoke up but did so this time:

'Does the column stay together, Sarge?'

'A guid question Kiddo, you're no as daft as ye luik. Ach, eat yir grub lads, we'll talk aboot it efter.'

Wingate had been criticised by his senior officers, but not to his face, for his decision to cross the Irrawaddy. Now that the two divisions of his brigade had crossed and met up, he had assembled his column commanders again, for he himself was beginning to see that the final operation of the *Longcloth* campaign, namely the disruption of the main Japanese railway line from Lashio to Mandalay, was no longer doable. Some of his commanders were keen to press on, but apart from the weak condition of many of his men, one issue above all was making him turn. They had reached a point where air-drop supplies could not be made due to the brigade being now beyond the range of available fighter cover.

Markham had finished his meal, was growing in confidence in the wake of Mac's compliment, and was getting more impatient for answers:

'You were saying, Sarge?'

'Okay, okay, Kiddo, dinna fash yirsel.'

McKinlay took a minute to finish his own grub:

'Aa richt lads, gaither roond. Stork, ye'd better tak some notes.'

Stork struggled for pencil and paper.

'It appears the bastards are musterin tae baith the west and the east o' us. Thir plan is tae pit us in a vice and crush us. So oor column is splittin intae nine sma groups.'

'Does that not put us more at risk, Sarge?' queried Thomo.

'Quite the reverse, son. This wey the bastards dinnae ken what tae attack. Theh'll hae tae split up thimsels. As for us, oor platoon steys basically the sem.'

'But how do we get out, Sarge?' Stinker put in.

'That's the million dollar question, laddie. A'm fucked if Ah ken.'

All looked at him in horror and some gasped.

'Tak it easy, Mac's only jokin. And Goad alane kens, we need a laugh.'

McKinlay drew fresh breath and continued:

'Ther's wan hunner and twinty miles tae the Chindwin.'

'Was that the first big river we crossed on the way in?' It was Smudger's turn.

'Correct. But gien the up and doon wey we'll hae tae travel, ravines and that, no tae mention diversions tae avoid the bastards, ye can add anithir fifty mile.'

The platoon had not wanted to hear this and Mac could see it in their faces:

'Ach, smarten up for fuck sake, we're sojers efter aa.'

'What do we take with us, Sarge?' asked Stork.

'Maist things we can tak as before, but we ditch the heavy stuff, includin maist o' whit they mules cairry.'

'Do we keep the mules?'

'Oh ay, ther's a new life for thaim. A short wan. Theh've been divied up, wan tae each group. If we get tae starvation pint, we shoot him or, if they bastards are close, cut his thrapple, then we hae steak.'

This reduced Stinker to tears. He may have had his faults but when it came to animals, he was a big softie. And it got worse as Mac corrected himself:

'Ah should o' said oor mule's nem is Daisy. So it's her heid and her neck.'

'What about our rations, Sarge?' Kiddo cut in again.

'We'll no see a drop again till we're well ower the Irrawaddy, and even then we'll be lucky, whit wae oor new formation and the fact that the column's lost maist o' the wireless sets. Captain Morris has wan and that's oor lot. If we can rendezvous wae ither groups, mebbe, but we canna tak it for granted. Accordin tae wunner boy Wingate, we can live aff the land, or if we can fund villages, beg for some grub there. Maist o' the locals hate the bastards oniewey.'

'Can I help, my Sergeant?' It was Shankar.

His English wasn't good and he knew Mac's English wasn't much better, so he passed a little book to Stork. The big man studied it a while then exclaimed:

'This is brilliant, Sarge! It's a list of fruits native to Burma. There are sugar-apples, we've had them before, then there's durian, the book calls it a king of fruits, green or brown and prickly on the outside, and up to twelve inches long. It says here we'll know it because it stinks a bit, but once inside it tastes sweet and looks like butter. Then there's jackfruit, green and prickly, tasting like chicken and known locally as vegetable meat.'

'Ther ye are, lads, the Lord is with us and will provide. We'll dae jist fine.'

Thomo then added to the talk about menu.

'Sarge, have you noticed how the mules eat the bamboo leaves? If we're stuck for vegetables, they might do.'

'Ah dinnae fancy that, but as ye say, if we're stuck.'

'And there are always onions.'

'Oh Ay, Wingate's favourite. A while back Ah clocked him chawin wan o' them raw. He's a queer bugger and nae mistake. But that's enough. Coorie doon my lads, noo we sleep. In the mornin efter breakers, we luik at the maps and plan the wey forward.'

Fires were out soon after and although most of the brigade had mixed experiences of sleep, Mac's platoon slept soundly, dreaming of villagers who cooked warm meals, exotic jungle fruit and cool streams where they could bathe, slake their thirst and replenish water containers.

At dawn on the next day, Stork and Mac went around the groundsheets and nudged the men awake. All of them breakfasted on a modest amount of the K-rations still available and drank some water from their canteens, making sure they popped a Mepacrine tablet to suppress malaria. The tablets were in short supply and were now to be self-administered three per week instead of the normal one per day. Then they convened. McKinlay shared out the maps he had been given by Captain Morris and as instructed by Wingate himself, one for each man with directions and distances, and he made sure he had compasses. Maps were not always reliable due to the incredibly complex terrain, but compasses were crucial. The Sergeant began:

'The problem richt noo is we're in a dodgy triangle. Apart frae the bastards on baith sides, ther's the rivers, Irrawaddy tae the west, and the Smelly tae the east.'

'The Shweli, Sarge,' prompted Stork.

'Ay, that's the one. And as Ah wis sayin, the triangle is complete wae a motor road south o' us and runnin east tae west for transportin mair bastards.'

'That means we're shut in, Sarge,' said Kiddo. He was close to giving up.

'No necessarily, son. We'll merch, and sometimes mebbe trot, in a north-westerly direction, avoiding the bastards comin frae oor due west, then cross the Irrawaddy. Noo, get doon and luik at yir maps.'

He pointed to a spot on the Irrawaddy where they could rendezvous with Morris and his group, and where it was hoped they could find a friendly village.

'If the whole brigade's doing the same, that must be sixty groups,' said Stork.

'No no, at least wan column, mebbe twa, fancy thir chances makkin a run for China, efter crossin the Smelly.'

'Shweli,' prompted Stork.

'Ay indeed. Stork. Why do ye aye feel ye huv tae correct me. Ah ken fine whit Ah'm talkin aboot.'

'Yes Sarge.'

'If ye ask me, it's too damn risky, crossin the Smelly Ah mean. Ah've heard some nightmare stories aboot men droonin when theh try tae swim across. It's a fast river, even in guid weather.'

With their packs and rifles at the ready, they waited for the word of command. The groups were to move off one by one at intervals. When the platoon's turn came, it had seemed an eternity, the men were joined by a new Gurkha, Govinda, a mucker for Shankar who had lost his good friend Ganesh at the last Irrawaddy crossing. Mac was pleased about the addition. Gurkhas were invaluable, not just as soldiers, but due to their knowledge of the environment, their ability to forage, and their understanding of a little of the traditional Burmese language.

'Wan mair thing, ye're no gonna like this but it comes frae the supreme commander. If wan o' us becomes sick or wounded tae the pint he canny go nae further, then he's no tae be left tae the bastards. And it's up tae his mucker tae pit him oot o' his misery. Unnerstood?'

Mac's prediction was right, they did not like it. But what was the alternative in such a small group?

'Yes Sarge,' they all said, never believing any of them would have to do it.

Mac set off with his mind in a mixture of dogged determination and foreboding. What was he leading his men into? Realistically, what were their chances? Probably slim. Then he geed himself up by estimating, if it was to be done, it could be done in six weeks or less. He could well picture the re-crossings of the Irrawaddy and the Chindwin, but there were other rivers to cross, none of them easy. Where would he and Morris find boats? The Japanese were getting wise to the Chindits and had begun to commandeer boats belonging to the local villages. He needed a safety net, something to fall back on. Then he thought of making rafts from bamboo. Then he switched again to thinking the whole task was impossible, and cursed to himself at his predicament:

Ach McKinlay, ye should o' bloody weel listened tae yir uncle Willie when he asked ye tae jine him on the ferm and become a shepherd. Workin wae they braw dugs, whit a great life!

On the first days the weather was good and they made real progress. The two small groups kept in contact with each other by maintaining two parallel lines in a north-westerly direction. It wasn't always easy, because this steady direction meant as often as not they drifted off pathways into thin jungle. They had only two small rivers to cross which they negotiated by wading up to their waists most of the time or in the case of smaller soldiers, up to their chests. Wingate had advised his men not to go too far out of their way to avoid the Japanese, lest they increase the chances of drowning or running out of food and water. But luckily, none of the enemy appeared in those early days. His men got buoyed up by this but McKinlay remained cautious:

'Jist ye wait and see, dinnae count yir chickens yet. The bastards wull be waitin for us wance we're ower the Irrawaddy. That's whaur theh are.'

'How long till we reach the big river, Sarge?' asked Stork.

'We should crack it in three days, auld fella.'

'Thank God.' Stork was a religious man, but not normally outspoken, a member of the Quakers back home in Blighty.

'Ye mention that chap quite a lot, Stork. Is he real?'

'Oh yes, Sarge. Since you ask, his son Jesus died on the cross for us.'

'Ach weel, Ah widnae ken aboot that. Ah wisnae aroond at the time.'

Stork changed the subject:

'What about the ammo, Sarge? Only twenty rounds per man.'

'It's enough, long as it's no wasted, made tae coont.'

'And the K-rations?'

'Ah wish ye widnae go on aboot them, Stork. We're aa in the sem boat. We'll run oot o' them in a few days for shair, then Ah guess it's plan B.'

'Plan B?'

'Dae Ah huv tae spell everythin oot? For wan thing, Daisy the mules's days are numbered.'

This had the desired effect. Stork's stomach had turned and he decided it better to shut up for a bit.

That evening they came upon a small lagoon and decided to bivouac. Some men replenished water carriers, some chose not to, thinking the water rather still and possibly contaminated. Just before dawn they were wakened by screaming. At first, in their half-conscious state, they thought the enemy had found them. Then they saw it was Stinker. He was covered head to foot in leeches.

'Ya bloody scunner, Ah tellt you no tae crash sae near tae the watter.'

Stinker was shaking all over with chills, despite the humid atmosphere:

'Sarge, there's fifty of them.'

'Mair like a hunner, son. Noo, haud still.'

Mac grabbed a dah and prized off the small ones, occasionally and unintentionally cutting Stinker's skin. Stinker cried out some more.

'Oh, dinna be such a big baby. Mind you, ther's a cracker doon here.'

He was referring to the big one, six inches long, having engorged itself on blood. Stinker wasn't quite sure what Mac was pointing his blade at.

'Wha's the smoker here? Smudger, gie's twa fags.'

'Sarge, I've only got one packet left.'

'Gie me twa fags Ah said !'

Smudger obeyed. Mac lit two cigarettes and gave one to Thomo. They burned off Stinker's monster, but he still shook with the shivers for another ten minutes.

A mixed progress was made until they reached the banks of the Irrawaddy – up and down, and circuitous at times. Mac knew that once they'd arrived, his platoon only had to turn north and follow the east bank until they met up with Morris' group who would hopefully be waiting for them. As it happened they rendezvoused two hours later and there was good news. Morris intimated there was a village settlement only two miles further north. The men were uplifted and began to forget their hunger and sores. However, Bernard Markham was becoming worried about Smudger. During their customary game of chess at the last bivouac, he had noticed Smudger didn't look himself and had developed a rasping cough. But these thoughts and those of the others were suddenly of no matter when they came under fire from the opposite bank at a point where the river narrowed and passed through a bottleneck.

It soon became clear that the Japanese riflemen couldn't hit a barn door from ten paces, as bullets thumped into trees and bamboo above and behind the heads of the joint platoon. McKinlay confidently stepped forward and raised his Enfield at the first enemy soldiers to take to boats.

'Okay ya bastards, let's see if McKinlay's still got it.'

Two of Morris' marksmen stepped on either side of Mac. Like everyone else in the brigade they knew of his fame as a crack shot and were proud to stand with him.

They fired and hardly a round was wasted. The figures in the leading boats had slumped over. The dinghies swung round to point southward and aimlessly followed the current. It made the remaining Japanese think again and they backed off into cover.

'Well done McKinlay, your reputation goes before you,' commented Captain Morris.

Strangely, Mad Mac went quiet and simply said:

'Sir.'

When they entered the village, they received a welcome fit for conquering heroes, and there were stories of how the

Japanese had shot three of their young men for hiding boats. The young women looked beautiful with white shining teeth and shapely legs below their short sarongs. Soldiers who had not seen a woman for some time began to feel a surge in their hormones.

'Are ye all right noo, Stinka?" queried Mac.

Stinker looked puzzled. Mac went on:

'Jist you watch him this time, lads. He'll be washin his feet and the rest o' him, cheyngin his socks, combin his hair and shavin, then dancin wae the lassies come nightfall.'

The whole company howled with laughter.

After a well cooked meal of rice with vegetables followed by plenty of fruit provided by their hosts, the soldiers bedded down in the stables along with the domestic animals. It was a bit noisy from hour to hour but the men didn't care, they were tired and slept like logs.

Morris and Mac were woken early by the headman who had something to tell them. In turn they awoke Govinda for his powers of translation. The headman told them to go with his two teenage sons to a hide-out less than a mile away. When they got there, the boys pulled away loose bushes to reveal a cave. Hidden there from the Japanese were boats and provisions, mostly rice, and loads of it. After breakfast it was all hands to the pump. The men busied themselves with transporting the dinghies and stuffing as much rice as they could into their spare socks. The headman had told them to take as much as they needed. It was just as well, the K-rations were now out. And Daisy the mule, it was decided, was left with the villagers as a thank-you. She was not to be executed after all. On one return trip McKinlay and young Markham were at either end of a boat:

'Sarge, can I ask you something?'

'Acourse, Kiddo, fire away.'

'When Captain Morris paid you that compliment, you know, after you shot the Jap soldiers, why didn't you say anything?'

'Listen son, a sojer only kills if he has tae. It's a terrible thing tae kill a man. And wance ye come tae likin it, it's time for ye tae get oot.'

Morris and Mac discussed the next move. It wasn't wise to cross the river in daylight and neither was it to cross directly from the village, in case the enemy on the west bank would be expecting them. They decided to carry the boats and their packs to a point well north of the village. It would be quite a haul but by the time they got there, much of the day would be gone and they could bivouac, eat and drink, then wait for night-fall. The two teenagers begged to go with them as far as the crossing point, for they saw the whole thing as an adventure. Morris refused but the headman, their father, told him to take them, they would be a help, an extra pair of hands.

'We go chaung?' one of the boys asked.

Morris nodded and made the sign of a wave with his hand to mimic a river:

'Yup, you go chaung with us.'

On the trek upstream, Mac and Stork couldn't help but notice the change in Smudger. It looked for all to see he had the typical symptoms of flu – sweating profusely, headache, coughing and several bouts of vomiting.

When they finally reached their goal, they hid the boats well back from the bank and rested. They cooked some rice and vegetables from the supplies they'd received from the locals and brewed cha. Ten minutes after consuming the meal Smudger brought the lot back up again.

'Why don't you let young Wilson have a look at him?' asked Morris of Mac.

Wilson, although not fully qualified, had studied medicine for several years. Mac agreed and after a cursory examination of Smudger, Wilson whispered to the two commanders:

'I don't like the look of him, I think he has typhus.'

When the light faded, the joint group embarked. Smudger had to be helped into a boat. They would cross in two phases, there were not enough boats to do it in one go. It meant a few of the stronger men would paddle and have two trips. The crossings were smooth, but occasionally in the distance the unmistakable voices of Japanese soldiers could be heard echoing up and down the river.

The two teenagers waved to the stragglers and kept waving until the boats were mere dots in the darkness. They had been given silver rupees by Morris and they vowed to hold on to them along with their story of adventure.

Once on the other side, the soldiers heaved the boats into the jungle and covered them with loose bushes and branches, and then they scrubbed over their tracks, so as to leave no evidence of their crossing. They decided to keep going as far as they reasonably could into the night. There was a full moon and little cloud, so enough light not to get lost. As they went, Markham had to support Smudger, and at one point the sick man stopped his mucker and muttered:

'Promise me, Bernard, you won't leave me to the Japanese.'

'Don't be silly, Smudger, you'll be better in a few days.'

It was all that Markham could think of saying.

Dawn rose the next day with a gorgeous sky which under normal circumstances would have been welcome. Now it only served to make the men more visible. The order was given for absolute silence and Morris and McKinlay went into hushed debate about breaking up again, for the area was crawling with Japanese patrols. It had become more necessary than ever for men to move in small groups. Morris wished Mac and his men the best of luck, before moving off first. He left word, if he could negotiate an airdrop of supplies, he would somehow get in touch.

It was dreadfully slow for the platoon, the entire day spent in silence, every footstep planted with care. When they bivouacked later, they counted themselves lucky not to have been discovered. That night was Smudger's worst, he groaned and havered throughout, and Markham was at his wits end, unable to sleep.

All of the buddies had heard it and took their breakfast in a huddle of grim faces. McKinlay had a terrible duty on his hands:

'We hae tae face it, lads, that young doctor Wilson tellt me afore he left, when theh gan intae delirium, it's ace king queen jack.'

He made a sign of the cross.

'Oh no Sarge, no, we can't,' said Markham, second guessing his commander.

'Ther's nae treatment, son. Smudger's gonnae dee, either theday or themorra. An' if he gans on groanin' and callin' oot the day long, the bastards will fund us and we'll aa be deed.'

Stork, always the sober one, intervened:

'There's not much morphia left, Sarge. Most of it's been used up by wounded men two tablets at a time. But there's enough for one lethal dose. Don't worry Bernard, he wouldn't know anything about it.'

'Thank Christ for that. Ach weel, so be it, we cannae use a gun. The bastards wull hear us.'

McKinlay looked down with his hand on his brow:

'Poor laddie.'

The tablets were dissolved in water and Mac moved towards Smudger:

'Time for a drink o' watter, son.'

'No Sarge, it's my push, I'm his mucker.' It was Markham.

McKinlay handed the mixture to the boy.

And it was all over quickly. As Stork had predicted, it was peaceful. Smudger was buried in a makeshift grave marked with a bamboo cross. His bush hat was placed on top and a map reference was taken. At Mac's invitation Stork led the platoon in a short prayer.

Following the eventual defeat of the Japanese in Burma, the allies attempted to find the graves of fallen comrades. Some searches were successful, but some not. As is the case with many allied regiments, Chindits still lie in Burma where they died.

Chapter 4

Changing times

IN THE WEEK that followed Tom Williams' retirement, Roger Jenkins moved back to the West Street office as the new boss, and after tut-tutting his way through all the files to intimate his disapproval of the way they had been kept, he turned his attention to impressing on John Gray just who was boss. His first tactic was to look for faults in his subordinate's work:

'John, I've just been looking at your expenses claim for last month. You've put in two return journeys to Kingrennie and back. One is for nine miles and the other is for ten miles.'

Gray thought to himself:

Is this guy serious or what? He wants to make an issue of one mile? Maybe it's a joke.

Realising that Jenkins was indeed serious, Gray responded:

'As you know, Roger, Kingrennie has two of our community halls, half a mile apart from each other. Does that answer your question or do you need me to explain the maths?'

Having failed at being petty, Jenkins went for the shock tactic on the Friday:

'John, if I were you, I'd be very unhappy right now, in fact I'd be searching my conscience to see where I'd gone wrong.'

Having satisfied himself that he had heard the remark correctly, Gray's first instinct was to break Jenkins' nose. But no, that wasn't the way, a tempting thought, but not a good move.

As it happened, Gray decided to do nothing but treat it as something the younger man had obviously learned from a textbook as a student.

What concerned Gray more was that the open door policy of Tom Williams, allowing unemployed young people to gather informally in the office, was now history. Jenkins had shut that door in their faces. This rebounded two weeks after the new regime when Gray arrived at work, first man in as usual, to discover the office had been burgled and trashed. Gray knew this was no co-incidence. The kids had vented their spleen. When Gray confronted Jenkins about the wisdom of his new policy, Jenkins had the perfect answer:

'We're living in a changing world, John.'

Gray responded with a cliché of his own:

'Maybe so, Roger. But that doesn't mean to say we have to throw the baby out with the bath water.'

But as the following year panned out, Gray had to admit that Jenkins was a prodigious worker, and more importantly, a good leader. He convened regular meetings of the area staff, came up with new initiatives, and delegated duties to individual colleagues which gave them opportunities to stretch themselves. He made arrangements around their work to enable them to retrain, and in turn they were able to retrain their fleet of part-time youth workers. Gray also had to admit that the new relationship between himself and Jenkins had been uncomfortable for both of them.

This awkwardness was considerably reduced when the council's plans for demolishing the West Street office, in favour of extending town centre parking, were realised in 1989, sending the two colleagues into the Winton Primary School office along with Mike Wellsley and the rest of the area team. The school roll had continued to fall, so with a bit of invention and negotiation, a second classroom was handed over to the community education staff. They now had two sizeable rooms.

But there would never be a bond between the two men, they were vastly different. Jenkins was always ambitious and would go much higher in the years to come, albeit his colleagues sometimes questioned the methods he employed to get there. Gray never trusted Jenkins, he was no Tom Williams.

By 1992, Gray had decided on his way forward. He had fifteen years to go to retirement in a non-essential service, one that his whole experience had told him was highly corruptible. When it came to advancement, it seemed to him that it mattered more to the prevailing powers whether or not you were well connected politically than whether or not you were a person of skill, intellect and integrity. In the same year, the service in Colliershire came up with a new professional structure. Gray had never seen the like before. To him it was a piece of pure careerism, and had little to do with public service. He made a token gesture of an application for promotion but didn't seriously expect there would be a place for him. There wasn't.

A year later he started to study and write poetry and it wasn't long before he was getting published. It had come a bit late in life, he was pushing 50 now, but it thrilled him to be a success at something again.

Jenkins had moved onward and upward, and there was a new boss, also ambitious. Gray thought:

More of the same.

In time he found that he could write a report with his left hand and a poem with his right simultaneously. Gray was right-handed. When on one occasion a young female worker complained about this to his boss, a boss for whom she had taken a shine, Gray merely had to say:

'Is there anything wrong with my work?'

'Well of course not, John, it has always been excellent.'

Gray had become supremely confident, so went further:

'Yes, you bet, and it's done in half the time it takes anyone else in here to do theirs.'

'I know, John, but we have to be careful.'

'Don't worry, I've not been around five minutes, I can handle it.'

Gray was developing a sharp edge, just like his old boss Williams. And also like his mentor, an ability to get his way with his bosses. He had missed Tom Williams, hadn't really been to see him often enough, and when he learned that the old fellow, now in his mid-seventies, was suffering from cancer, he phoned him and arranged a visit.

'John, come in, how are you boy?'

It tickled Gray that Williams still saw him as a boy.

'I'm fine, Tom, but more importantly, how are you?'

Gray was shown to a settee next to the old man's armchair.

'Oh, it's a bit of a carry-on. You know my adopted son, Gerry. Well his sister, Aileen, has been ever so kind. She drives me through to the hospital in Edinburgh every other day, and they fire this gun into me. X marks the spot !'

Gray marvelled at his old friend's pluck. Williams proceeded:

'It's like a circus, you have to laugh. They come in dressed all in white, put the gun in position, then scurry away, shut the door, then set the gun off. They repeat the performance twice, so that I get three doses at each visit. I've only got another nine visits to go.'

Williams was amazing. Gray could see the treatment was taking a lot out of his friend, but to be able to poke fun at it? And Williams wasn't finished:

'Once they knock the tumour down to size, they'll operate. I'm going to beat this, John.'

Gray didn't doubt him for a second. During their conversation, which was warm and full of each other's news, Williams noticed a sea change in the younger man. He was confident and self-assured, articulate, and fascinating when the subject of poetry was raised. Not like the colleague he had known previously.

'I've been reading about you in the newspapers, John. A nationally recognised poet, indeed. Steady now, I wouldn't want you to eclipse the old boy.'

Gray laughed heartily. When they parted, Gray promised himself he would visit Williams on a more regular basis. Not just to keep in touch with his friend's health, but because this visit had been a thorough tonic. Gray was refreshed. The visit had re-assured him of his stance on his job. There were more important things in life than ambition and promotion. He would carry on with his writing, perhaps get better at it. And at his work, he would keep the faith with the public, maintaining the routine practices while always making sure he had one new project on the boil at any given time. This would make any boss happy, and as far as the wider profession was concerned, he would keep it at arm's length. But one thing still puzzled Gray, the same thing that still puzzled the other close friends, the few close friends, of Tom Williams:

How does he come to have this remarkable strength of character, and this genuine love for mankind. It can only be that he's suffered in some way. Is it anything to do with his army service during the War?

Williams was a shaman, of that there was no doubt, for Gray and the others had amassed a wealth of wisdom from him, but the man himself remained a mystery and backed off from any curiosity as to his life prior to coming to Colliershire.

CHAPTER 5

A place called Hell

'IF THIS GOES on, it will shortly be every man for himself,' said Stork.

'Ach, the trouble wae you lad is ye think too much, it's jist the wey things are.'

Stork and his sergeant were taking stock of their situation. When they'd crossed the northern railway line a few miles west of the Irrawaddy, they had rendezvoused with Morris' party again. The news from Morris about future air-drops of supplies was not good, although an attempt was in the offing to land a Dakota and take out the seriously ill and wounded. Morris had also been instructed by Major Bissett to draw off some of Mad Mac's men to lend firepower to an assault on the railway, a bridge and a viaduct. This left Mac and Stork with less than twenty men. Wingate had told his commanders, prior to the break-up of their columns, not to remain in a totally defensive mode, and if the opportunity presented itself and few casualties were forecast, then they should take the risk and attack.

Stork resumed:

'I'm worried about Bernard, Sarge. He hasn't spoken for two whole days since we lost Smudger. He won't do anything silly, will he?'

'He micht luik like a boy, Stork, but he's a sojer efter aa's said and done.'

'I know that, Sarge, but just look at him, sat against that tree with his head in his hands. He hasn't eaten any breakfast yet, you know.'

'Leave him alane. He'll come roond in his ain guid time.'

'Sarge?' It was Thomo.

'Ay?'

'What about Bernard?'

'Jesus Christ, am Ah runnin' a lanely herts club here? Wull the hale bloody lot o' ye leave Kiddo alane?'

Bernard Markham had cried himself to sleep the past two nights. He cursed himself for what he'd done. Smudger was his best friend. He had done it in the line of duty, but as far as he was concerned, it was murder. In Hampstead, where he'd been brought up, murder was unknown, and the regular Sunday mornings he had spent in church with his family had clearly spelled out *thou shalt not kill*. He cursed Burma, he cursed the Japanese. He cursed Wingate. He had never wanted this war. He was supposed to have become a piano teacher. And then, because his fiancé stood him up, he'd gone and volunteered for this insane campaign. He was a damn fool and a contemptible killer.

Stork turned to more pressing matters:

'Sarge, we really need to think about our food. Thankfully, there are plenty of rivulets and waterfalls in this area, so we won't go thirsty. But we don't have a lot of that rice left, the load we got from the locals way back.'

'Noo let me see, we can mak the Chindwin river in three, mebbe twa weeks, aa things remainin equal.'

'There won't be enough, Sarge.'

'Weel, we're aaricht for a couple o days. Thommo clubbed a watter buffalo, jist last nicht afore lichts oot, then he cut his thrapple. He's slicin the beef up the noo intae steaks. We can hing them ower oor bag packs and theh can dry in the heat as we merch. Then we roast them the nicht.'

'What about fruit and vegetables?'

'For the time bein, they bamboo leaves wull dae, mixed in wae the rice. Itherwise, we huv tae rely on Shankar and Govinda.'

'It's dangerous for them, Sarge. All this foraging off track.'

' Stork, will ye jist jist? When it comes tae this kinna thing, theh're the best. Huv faith, eh? Ye ken, faith, that thing you're an expert on.'

Stork had to smile.

McKinlay wasn't letting on, but he was worried. He could see the weight of his men dropping by the day. There simply wasn't enough to eat, and when it came to rice, he knew he would shortly be imposing rations. Fish was always an option. Men could sharpen a piece of bamboo and use it as a spear, but they weren't much good at it, not as good as the locals who had learned as children. And when there was some success, invariably the fish were small.

When next they bivouacked, McKinlay gathered his men around him and they consulted their maps. Going in a northwesterly direction was certainly avoiding many of the Japanese patrols, but at the expense of encountering hilly terrain which slowed them down, using up their energy and increasing their hunger. So, glad to rest, they roasted their steaks over their fires and had boiled rice with bamboo leaves. Once they were satisfied, McKinlay convened another meeting.

'Listen up, lads. Oor chances o' gettin tae safety are no great, no much better than fifty fifty. Whit we huv tae consider is the chance o' bein captured by the bastards.'

'We won't be taken, Sarge,' said Stinker.

'That's the spirit, son. Nanetheless, we huv tae talk aboot it.'

Stork broke in with his usual candour:

'It's not the capture or being put to labour that worries me. Likely we'll be interrogated, possibly tortured. They're an evil race.'

'Jist whit Ah wis goin' tae tell ye. If theh ask ye aboot locations o' oor ither units and thir plans, then tell them the opposite o' the truth. If units are goin west, then tell them east, if north, then south. We ken aareddy that some o' the brigade are makin' for China and some, like us, for the Chindwin, so ye've got some slack, ther's ivry chance the bastards wull believe ye.'

Bernard Markham decided to break his long silence:

'But Sarge, with all this breaking up of the column, we really don't know anything.'

'Oh Kiddo, you are brilliant. Jist you tell them that then, and we'll hae bets wae each ither on whether the bastards wull let ye live for five minutes or ten.'

There was a moment's laughter then total silence as the reality of the discussion sunk in.

Suddenly there was a movement in the bushes. Whatever it was, they were, could only be fifty metres away at best:

'Fires oot,' commanded Mac. 'Hush noo.'

The men could feel their hearts thumping at their chests. Then Thomo appeared, large as life.

'Two wild boars, that's all. I was looking for more water.'

'Ay, and you maist likely set them aff. Dinna you ever dae that again, laddie.'

'Yes Sarge.'

'Whadayamean Yes Sarge?'

'I mean No Sarge.'

'Jesus Christ ! Whit a bunch o' dumplins.'

Stinker thought he would cheer Mac up:

'Don't worry Sarge. We'll all look out for you.'

'Dinna worry aboot me, son. They bastards wull nivir tak McKinlay alive.'

The following night a hungry and exhausted group of men limped their way into a local village. It heartened them. The hills' people had a reputation for warmth and kindness. Realising the bad state of the soldiers, they fed them well and showed them to makeshift sleeping quarters with little or no ceremony at all.

It was 4am when McKinlay was shocked out of a deep sleep by a hand over his mouth. It was Shankar and he whispered:

'It's a trap, my Sergeant.'

Shankar had overheard a conversation between the senior men among their hosts. Mac had always admired the ability of a Gurkha to sleep with one eye open and one ear cocked. Shankar warned:

'Enemy come at daybreak, one hour.'

It only took five minutes for the group to be wakened, packed and off. Shankar made a slight detour for a further two minutes. They were being watched by one of the head villagers. The spy was quickly despatched in silence by a kukri. They decided to continue on the planned route but for a marginal adjustment to throw their pursuers. They had no track of time as they jogged with as much speed as the jungle would allow. Finally, when he could see his men were out of breath and felt the Japanese had been shaken off, Mac gasped until he'd recovered his breath:

'We'll rest here a bit. Jist a bit, mind.'

Two hours later Stork awoke to find they had all been so exhausted they had fallen asleep. He shook Mac.

'Jesus Christ ! Gie yirsels a shake. Quick as ye like noo. At the double!'

They had gone on less than a mile when Markham tapped Mac on the shoulder. He tried to speak but put his hands on his knees instead and struggled for the breath.

'Whit's the matter, Kiddo? Come on, spit it oot.'

'Stinker and Thomo, Sarge. I can't see them.'

Mac called a halt and searched up and down his men. Kiddo was right. They weren't there.

'The stupit buggers must o' slept in.'

McKinley had a crucial decision to make, Learned from last year's special training school in Burma, there were only two options for such an eventuality. Leave them to their fate or send a party back allowing it a set and limited time to re-join the group.'

Stork spoke up:

'They might catch up with us, Sarge.'

'No if theh're still in the land o' nod, theh'll no.'

Mac decided to go back with Markham, Stork and Shankar, leaving instructions for the others to wait no longer than half an hour for their return. A few minutes later he was regretting having selected Stork. Not only was he a senior man who would have been a boon to the main body in the event of separation, he was limping again and having difficulty keeping up. Even a great soldier like McKinlay was human under pressure like this. His brains were turning to mince.

Mac and the other two turned a corner to find Stinker who was crying. When he saw his buddies, he started to blubber. He was making no sense at all, and then he became hysterical.

He needn't have bothered. The reason was starkly evident. Thomo had been tied to a tree and ruthlessly bayonetted through his neck. And his buddies were now surrounded by Japanese soldiers. The action on Thomo had been taken to make Stinker talk or suffer the same fate. He had told them his buddies would probably return for him. All the Japanese had to do was wait. The three allied soldiers were relieved of their arms. The Japanese had only a few words of English, but enough for a working knowledge:

'Hands behind your heads.'

They were interrupted by Stork who had limped into the net as well. The Japanese officer resumed:

'Now march ! If you try to escape, we shoot you.'

Five buddies then began a long march south to what Stork believed would be a Japanese outpost. But he wondered why McKinlay had managed to place himself at the rear. The answer wasn't long in the coming.

'Aw Christ !' Mac had stumbled.

One of their hindmost captors prodded him with his rifle:

'Up Tommy!'

In a flash he was grabbed around the neck by Mac and dragged into the first trees. His sidearm was removed, then his neck broken. Having served his purpose, Mac let him drop and lunged into the jungle, quickly followed by three Japanese soldiers who fanned out to make his recapture, and inevitable execution, easier. It was probably less than a minute, but to Stork, Markham, Shankar and Stinker, it seemed an eternity. A single shot rang out. The four men recognised it as a pistol, not a rifle. The trio of Japanese soldiers returned without Mac. The Aberdonian had kept his promise to his men:

They bastards wull nivir tak McKinlay alive.

In the three hours that went by before the Japanese outpost was reached, the four allied soldiers were never bothered by the pain of having to march so long with their hands behind their heads. All they felt was a horrible emptiness in their stomachs. Their grumpy, mad, incomprehensible, foul-mouthed Sergeant was gone and wasn't coming back. And they were missing him, in the same way as they would have missed a father. The future, the immediate future, was unimaginable without him.

What they walked into was a Japanese outpost with a section which functioned as a holding post for prisoners of war. And it was the custom, when marching allied soldiers into them, to frighten the living daylights out of them.

Bernard Markham turned to Stork:

'What are the soldiers using for bayonet practice? They don't look like stuffed bags.'

'They're our boys,' said Stork, clasping his hands in prayer.

And he prayed that the two men had been executed before being hung up, as they had been, by their heels. They were American airmen, and airmen were the only service in the allied force who could drive fear into an all-conquering Japanese Army. When such men were captured, they were dished out the worst treatment of all.

'No talking!' commanded a Japanese guard.

He gave Stork one blow of his wooden sword across his back which completely winded him. He sank to his knees for which he sustained a second.

The four soldiers were assembled in front of a couple of Japanese officers. The junior officer spoke first:

'Good evening gentlemen. My name is Captain Akio Kobayashi. I am your interpreter. This is the camp commander, Major Daiki Yamada.'

The major bowed and said one word of Japanese. That was all he said.

Captain Kobayashi continued:

'You will be our guests for the next few days, until we decide what to do with you. The cookhouse will be serving food in one hour. Meanwhile you will receive some water and you will join our other guests.'

He pointed to a cage where three other allied soldiers were detained. Kobayashi wasn't finished:

'Any prisoner attempting to escape will be beheaded. At all times, in the days to come, when you pass a Japanese soldier, you will bow or salute. If you don't, you will be beaten. There are latrines to your left. When you need to go, you will ask permission. A guard will go with you. Tomorrow you will learn Japanese for *I have come for my food* which you will say when your turn comes at the cookhouse. If you don't say it right, you will be beaten. That is all, gentlemen. Follow the rules and all will be well.'

Stork was still recovering from the two blows he received earlier. When they'd all been watered and put in the cage, he collapsed and without any apparent concern from the three Japanese guards. In fact, their gaolers began to giggle and swap jokes with each other at their captives' expense. Then they hooted at them:

'Tommies, hey Tommies!'

When they had their attention, they made gestures with their rifles to make the incarcerated men think they were going to be bayonetted. One of the buddies' new friends spoke up to comfort the new arrivals:

'See the fat one at the end. If you're close to him, he smells like a dead rat. And when you look into his eyes, they've got no pupils, they're all white. He's had a frontal lobotomy.'

'Really?' said Markham.

Although still in a heap, Stork had overheard:

'No, Bernard. He's only pulling your leg.'

'I'm telling you, he's braindead.'

It was Corporal Bill Carruthers and he introduced his new mates to his old ones.

'Looks like we're all in the same boat, eh? I mean the same cage. Sorry, bad joke.'

'How did you get here?' said Stinker.

'Our engineers fired a line over a fast river. As we were crossing, it came loose. Those who weren't drowned were washed up well downstream, straight into the welcoming arms of the Japanese Emperor. Now, we are at his Majesty's pleasure.'

He saluted then spat with as much force as possible. It was time to eat. They queued up at the cookhouse. This being their first time, they were excused from asking for food in Japanese. Not so their new friends, and one of them got it wrong. Stork, Shankar, Stinker and Markham had the dubious privilege of trying to digest rice through a stomach which had been turned by the sight of a fellow prisoner being beaten senseless for nothing.

The four buddies had by now received the message loud and clear, and they could only see things getting worse. Their first night in captivity went by in restlessness, few opportunities for sleep, and not helped by Bernard who whimpered about what he'd done to Smudger.

Carruthers asked Stork what it was all about, and when told he said:

'Jesus, he's only a boy. He'll never get over it.'

In the morning before queuing for breakfast, they were relieved of their new buddies, only hours after meeting them. Carruthers turned to them as he left the cage:

'Don't worry guys, we'll be okay. They put the stronger ones to work on their railways.'

That left the buddies wondering what happened to the weaker ones. Then Kobayashi appeared:

'Good morning, gentlemen. I hope you slept well. Now, this is the Japanese for *I have come for my food.*'

He handed them a note with it spelled out in capital letters.

'Enjoy your breakfast, gentlemen.'

Thankfully, all managed to get it right, even Stinker who wasn't the brightest of sparks. The rest of the morning was spent with a session in house – the cage, and a session being allowed to stretch their legs in the grounds. However, Stinker forgot to either salute or bow to Carruther's 'braindead fat guard' and received the same thumping Stork had been given the day before.

What the four didn't know was, in the nearby officers' quarters, they were being assessed by Kobayashi and Major Yamada. Kobayashi had introduced himself on the arrival of the four as the interpreter. He was also the interrogator. In Japanese Kobayashi gave Yamada his opinion:

'The tall man they call Stork is a very religious man, unlikely to break under questioning. He is not strong physically, but would be a calming influence on other men. I suggest we send him to the maintenance and repair work on the northern railway. The Gurkha is a very strong man. I suggest railway as well.'

'And the other two?' replied Yamada in Japanese.

'The man called Stinker is a fool. Do what you like with him. But the one called Bernard is the one who interests me. He speaks with a very proper English accent. He's very young but I don't believe he's a private. I would really like to question him.'

Yamada nodded, but intimated that Kobayashi should question the other two British soldiers as well, not the Gurkha, and dismissed his advisor with a wave of his hand.

A pleasant morning turned into a hot and gruelling afternoon, and stifling in their cage, the four buddies longed for more exercise and more importantly, an evening meal. The portions dished up to them were meagre, about half of what was given to the guards. At about 3 o'clock they were distracted by a piece of macabre theatre.

A guard had committed some sort of unforgivable offence. He was dragged out into the centre of the compound, for clearly he'd been beaten and couldn't stand up. A hose was forced down his throat and water poured into his stomach until it was full to bursting. Then he was tied down on his back. A board was placed across his stomach, and two morons, standing on either end of it, took great pleasure in playing at see-saw. The game was stopped when it became clear the man had haemor-rhaged and died.

Shankar stood grim-faced and silent. Stinker was bubbling again. Stork was on his knees:

'Poor boy. May God save his soul and give him peace.'

Bernard Markham blurted out:

'Fascist bastards!'

'No talking!' shouted the guard.

In the evening they stood waiting for their meal, still shell-shocked by what they had witnessed. Surprisingly, the assistant cook who served them put more rice than usual on their plates. He remained inscrutable throughout, only looking around to see if any one of the other guards was watching.

'I heard the cook call him Katashi,' said Stork.

Shankar made one of his few contributions:

'Not all Japanese bad, my Corporal'

It was a small gesture by Katashi, but in this hell-hole it mattered a lot.

Dusk had already fallen when two guards approached the cage and unlocked the door. One pointed his rifle at Markham:

'You come, Tommy.'

Bernard had a dreadful feeling in his water as he was led to Kobayashi's quarters.

'Please sit down, I have a few questions to ask you, it won't take long, but first, you seem very young to be in this war.'

This was designed to make Bernard feel comfortable. It worked:

'Well, I didn't really want to be a part of the war.'

Kobayashi queried why that was and Bernard explained about the loss of his fiancé and his resultant volunteering for the campaign:

'It was stupid of me, really it was.'

'Who do you think is going to win the war?'

Bernard saw a chance to win favour:

'I don't think the Japanese can be beaten, they are too strong and determined.'

'Yes, you are right. Now, just a few questions and you can return to your friends.'

Kobayashi spread a map of Burma in front of Bernard:

'Now here is where we are.' He pointed. 'Tell me where your unit is.'

'That's just the thing. We were all split up into small groups. I don't know any longer.'

'But surely you have communications?'

'Before the split many of the wireless sets were lost. There wasn't one left for us.'

'Point to the area where your next air-drop of supplies was to take place.'

'I don't know, I was never told.'

'Just one more question.'

Bernard heaved a sigh of relief.

Kobayashi raised himself from his chair and stared at Bernard:

'You're not a private, are you? You're an officer. Your English is too good.'

Bernard panicked:

'No, no, honestly. I've always been a private.'

'I think that will be all for the time being. We will talk again. Don't worry Mr…eh?

'Markham, Mr Markham.'

'Don't worry, Mr Markham. The war will soon be over. Then you can go home.'

Bernard was escorted back to the cage where his buddies were unable to even think about sleep:

'Well Bernard?'

'It wasn't too bad really. Kobayashi is very polite. He asked me questions and I gave him honest answers. He's going to talk to me tomorrow or the day after, I expect.'

The buddies asked him about the questions and the answers he had given.

Stork then said in a quiet voice:

'Whoever among us is questioned, I think we should give them something, however false, and we should all sing from the same song sheet.'

All agreed and they went into a hushed huddle of discussion, once they felt the only two guards weren't close enough to hear the details.

The buddies had been asleep for only an hour when the guards burst in and grabbed Bernard. He was in that awful state that everyone experiences when wakened up shortly after falling asleep. In a flash he was before the interrogator again, only this time his head was pressed on to the table and his arms, extended above his head, also pressed down. He felt a searing pain as a shredded piece of bamboo was whacked at the backs of his hands and forearms, again and again until they bled. Bernard thought it would never end. He wished he could pass out. He had been corporally punished at school, but never like this. When it did end, he was allowed to collapse into his chair.

Kobayashi waited a few moments then spoke:

'Now, Mr Markham, we will begin again.'

He went over the same questions again and this time Bernard decided to be devious, as agreed by the buddies. It was hard because of the pain. He was given a drink of water.

'After the crossing of the Irrawaddy, most of the brigade went eastward with the intention of crossing the Shweli and making for China.'

The interrogator didn't believe him. He knew about the move for China, but not by most of the brigade, they were headed for India:

'You said, once you crossed the Irrawaddy on the way back, your group was divided again by your Captain Morris. Where is he now?'

'He was always going parallel to us, just a mile or two to the south.'

Most of that was true. Morris' direction was a lie. He was always north of them.

'Now, Mr Markham, what is your rank?'

'I promise you, I'm a private, I've always been a private.'

'I am not satisfied, Mr Markham.'

At the interrogator's command, Bernard was secured flat on his back to a board, and his head also secured so that he found himself staring upwards at the mouth of a tap. The tap was turned on just enough to drip on his forehead every few seconds.

'Goodnight, Mr Markham. We'll see how you feel in the morning, and what you would like to tell me.'

And they left him to the dripping tap.

The use of a dripping tap as an instrument of torture had been invented by the Chinese in medieval times. Being a traditional enemy, the Japanese had in a sense stolen the idea. Nobody other than a victim can explain what it's like. It's not a painful physical torture, but the effect on the nervous system of the constant drip on the centre of the forehead will drive a man mad if unstopped. Bernard howled all night, begging someone, anyone, to stop it. His three buddies, especially Stork, went through agony wondering what was being done to him.

And just as it had started, it did stop. The sun had risen and was shining into the dingy wooden hut. Nothing happened for a while and slowly, very slowly, Bernard came to his senses.

'Good morning, Mr Markham.'

Kobayashi was back. His guards restored Bernard to his chair.

Yet again the interrogator asked his questions, and yet again he wasn't satisfied with Bernard's answers:

'Today, Mr Markham, you will rest while your friends are questioned. Tomorrow I will give you one more chance to give me the information I need to know.'

Then it was Stinker's turn. Kobayashi dispensed this time with the opening niceties, and went straight into the beating of Stinker's hands and feet. Stinker howled and blubbered throughout. The interrogator thought to himself:

This is a total waste of time. He won't say anything because he knows nothing. He's an idiot.

Stinker was returned to the cage. All Kobayashi had to decide was whether to shoot him or send him to forced labour. Then he turned again to his work:

'Bring the holy man to me now.'

Stork wasn't exactly a holy man, certainly didn't see himself as such. But the Japanese did and they were a superstitious race when it came to philosophy and religion. To strike a prisoner on first acquaintance was one thing, but to find out he was a holy man and continue to strike him was entirely another. It could result in your own misfortune and possibly a horrible death.

Stork was invited to sit down by Kobayashi.

'Good morning. Or is it good afternoon, Stork? Your friends call you a shaman.'

Stork saw an opportunity here. He would scrap what he'd agreed with his buddies:

'Oh, I wouldn't go as far as that. I did do a bit of hands-on healing back home, that's all really.'

That was a lie. But Kobayashi swallowed it hook, line and sinker.

'Do you have the power to foresee the future?'

'No, I take whatever my God has in store for me.'

'Do you convert others to your faith?'

'No, everyone is entitled to their own faith. But I do think it is good for all human beings to believe in something.'

'I am a Buddhist. But Buddhism is not a religion, that is to say we don't worship a heavenly god.'

'No, but you believe in his teachings.'

'That is true.'

Kobayashi thought in silence for a moment then proceeded:

'I don't suppose there is any point in me interrogating you?'

'Absolutely none. If you want to question me, I'll answer you, but it won't do you any good. If then you want to torture me, go ahead. If you decide to kill me, then I have made my peace with God. I am prepared.'

'That will be all, Mr Stork.'

'Taylor.'

'Pardon?'

'Taylor, my name is Taylor.'

'Then that will be all, Mr Taylor.'

Stork was led back to the cage where he found the wounded Stinker and the half-dead Bernard. Only Shankar was able to ask him how on earth he was still in the one piece.

'I guess I was lucky, Shankar.'

Later the four buddies queued up as usual at the cookhouse, with Bernard supported by Stork on his left, Shankar on his right. His arms and hands still ached from his beating and the weals were threatening to become infected. His head still pounded from his night under the tap. Stork told him a good meal would help. Stinker just about managed to look after himself.

As Bernard moved forward for his share and spoke the appropriate Japanese, he was given an extra helping, and quite unashamedly so, by Katashi. He looked at Bernard a long time as if he wanted to tell him something. After food there was twenty minutes of exercise. When they'd completed the first lap, Stork spoke in a measured tone:

'We're leaving, Bernard. We're being sent to work on the railways.'

Bernard struggled to take it in. He was losing everything – his power, his mind, tomorrow quite likely his life. He needed Stork right now, more than ever.

'Have courage, Bernard. I have prayed to God and I just know that you and I will survive all this. Help will come to you, my dear boy.'

When morning came, Bernard hugged his buddies and watched their backs as they were led out of the compound. He was alone and his life was hanging by a thread. Within the hour he was back in the company of Kobayashi.

'Good morning, Mr Markham. Now that you have had time to consider your position, are you ready to talk?'

'No, I'm not. You can do what you like, I don't care. Kill me.'

Kobayashi wasted no time:

'Hole! Now!'

Bernard was beaten and dragged to a pit which had been dug to hold just one person. He was thrown in and a latticed wooden caging put on top of him to act as a trapdoor. The caging was sturdy and secured on all four sides. Kobayashi looked down at him:

'Mr Markham, in your country a man can survive without water for a whole week. In this country it's three days, and where you find yourself now, in this heat and humidity, probably less than two. At first you will get dizzy with terrible headaches, then you will pass into delirium, then your body functions will break down and you die. Good luck, Mr Markham. Let one of my guards know when you feel like talking.'

Bernard sank back into the coolest corner of his pit. He had made up his mind. He was going to die and hoped it would be quick and painless as possible. But as midday arrived, the sun beat down on him and he was soon in distress, By mid-afternoon he was begging for water, for it seemed his throat had become so dry it would close up. At mealtime he could hear other captives who had been brought in that morning being told the rules by Kobayashi. He prayed to God to give him just one chance to kill that man before he himself perished. As night fell so did the temperature, giving him a little relief, but he knew that tomorrow would be his last day. Somehow he fell asleep.

He was wakened some time later by a crashing noise. The caging above him had been smashed with the butt of a rifle. Looking down on him, through the darkness, was one of two guards on night duty, the unmistakable figure of Katashi. He lowered one arm and, despite his debilitated condition, Bernard grabbed it firmly and climbed out. Katashi led him behind the latrines, handed him a sack and pointed to the best way ahead. Had this been one of the prisons used by the Japanese in Burma, there would have been a high perimeter fencing. This was only a temporary holding station.

Bernard looked at Katashi.

'My dear fellow, thank you. But what will happen to you?'

'No time, Bernard. Go! Go now!'

Bernard ran as fast as was physically possible.

Katashi knew that the other guard at the far end of the compound would now be alert. He charged towards him shouting:

'Leopard ! Leopard !'

Then he charged past him and fired twice into the trees.

The second guard 'was allowed' to discover in his own time the damaged caging and the now empty hole. Other guards were stirred and a search party quickly put together, but not quickly enough. Bernard was free.

The clouded leopard was native to Burma and had a habit of crouching in trees until an unsuspecting rodent wandered along below. The leopard would dive from his hideout on top of his prey.

In the morning Katashi told the story of the leopard who could not have expected to crash into the caging when he dived. Kobayashi believed him but put him on half rations for three days with a warning to be at all times vigilant.

Katashi had been brought up by enlightened parents who had encouraged him to learn English and study the cultures of other countries around the world. He was unlike many of his countrymen at that time, had a keen sense of justice, and the treatment of Bernard had been abhorrent to him.

When he had no energy left, Bernard sat down at the base of a teak tree. He already had a good idea what was in the sack Katashi had given him. They had made familiar sounds as he rushed along – a canteen of water and a mess tin. Careful not to drink too fast, he took his time. Even although water has no taste, he thought this water tasted sublime. And there was a bonus, in fact two – a paper bag with some rice and a box of matches. He rested a few minutes before realising he'd better get on. He was starving, hadn't eaten for long enough, but a meal could wait until he was far gone. As he moved sideways to get up on to his legs, he felt something hard pressing into his buttock. Something else was in the sack. Glory of glories, it was a compass.

Having travelled a further three miles, he was stopped by a rustling in the bushes to his right. His heart missed a beat, he reckoned it had stopped. He imagined the unthinkable:

Surely not, after all I've been through, it's not those bastards again.

He didn't notice that the foul language of his old Sergeant, Mad McKinlay, had rubbed off on him.

In seconds the prowlers revealed themselves, just a single wild boar. This relieved him mightily at first, before his thoughts strayed to his old friend Thomo, who had incurred the wrath of McKinlay for setting two of the same species off and scaring the whole platoon to death. Remembering his old buddies inevitably brought up Smudger. And then the worst thought of all:

Oh God, all three of them are dead, and killed in no time at all.

In a gamut of emotions, ranging from anguish at loss and base brutality to euphoria at his escape from torture, Bernard collapsed in a heap and sobbed uncontrollably like a small child.

CHAPTER 6

A woman's world

AT LAST THE year 2000 arrived, a new millennium, and in Crack Willow, all the usual fireworks normally reserved for Guy Fawkes' night – bangers, rockets, Catherine wheels and more – went off around the town between 12 midnight and 2am, and the town's children, old enough and allowed to wait up for it, whooped with delight in time with the whistling whizbangs.

John Gray's 18, 19 and 23 year old sons were out on the razzle, so he and his wife Julia were content to stand in the conservatory and watch the night sky light up with all kinds of patterns. Just three miles away, an old man stood by his window and celebrated with his adopted son Gerry. Gerry's wife, Laura, and their three small children were at home, tucked up in bed.

And well might the 77 year old Tom Williams celebrate. He had beaten cancer, and now, after spending the first sixty-two years of his life as a confirmed bachelor, he had a family. The fact it had been achieved through adoption was neither here nor there, they were his family and all five of them loved him. He was good to them, and they were fascinated by his voice, his knowledge of music, literature and life itself, and the caring way in which he related to all kinds of people, particularly the young. And now his telephone was ringing:

'Hello, Tom, it's John here. Just phoning to wish you a happy new millennium.'

'And a happy one to you too, John. Mind you, I'm not intending to be around for the next thousand years.'

'Get away, Tom. I've told you many a time, you'll outlive us all.'

Williams laughed:

'Oh well, we'll see. Bye now, John, my love to Julia and the lads.'

'Cheers, Tom, see you soon.'

The following Monday morning, Gray drove into the third office he had used in Crack Willow since his arrival there in 1980. In a former life it had functioned as a school for handicapped children. Now it was a singing and dancing affair, the many rooms all needed for what was now a multi-disciplinary service covering aspects of youth work, adult education and community service. And adult education was very much the in-thing. All sorts of courses were needed for people who had lost their original employment and needed to be retrained, or for people who wanted to return to learning many years after leaving school. Youth work was no longer a priority, very much the poor relation.

Gray found the office even quieter than usual for the first working day of a new year, and chuckled at the likelihood some of his younger colleagues would be suffering hangovers. Nonetheless he wanted something done quickly:

'Margaret, I'm going to tidy up my report for that new out-door facility in Carriston. I should be finished by 10 o'clock, and I'll need it for the end of the day.'

Margaret looked at the schedule on her computer:

'John, I haven't got time to do it today.'

'Helen then, can you do it?'

'No chance.'

That was clear enough. Gray decided:

'Thanks anyway, girls. I'll do it myself.'

Like everyone else in the office, Gray had his own com-puter now.

But he did wonder at the let-down by the young secretar-ies. He couldn't imagine Tom Williams' old secretary, the loyal Mrs Crossley, having to do something at the drop of a hat and refusing to do so. Far less did he imagine Williams having to request it of Mrs C. Gray sighed. This was the way of it now. Due to their in-depth knowledge of computers, especially when the blasted things weren't responding of a morning, clerkesses had power, incredible power. John Gray could be forgiven for believing they were the bosses of the whole show.

He sat down at his desk and brought up his new e-mails, 90 percent of which he consigned to the e-bin. Billy Watson, his latest young colleague seated at the adjacent desk, was giggling:

'How do you manage to do it, John?'

'Most of them are a load of nonsense, Billy – mission state-ments for the umpteenth time, health and safety twaddle, and a few written in Swahili.'

'Swahili?'

'Well, it's an attempt at English, but the writers clearly can neither spell nor punctuate properly.'

Billy giggled some more.

'Oh, of course, you would say that, being such a great poet.'

The speaker bowed before Gray satirically.

It was Irene Ramsay, ages with Gray. They didn't have a lot in common.

'And good morning to you too, Irene,' said Gray.

Gray hammered on with the report he needed for the management committee of Carriston Community Hall. Occasionally, he stopped to look across at his other three young colleagues who had finally managed to stagger into work:

Look at them, hard at it as usual on their computers. Likely they'll be sat there until lunchtime. I thought they were supposed to be community workers. You'd think that maybe one of them would go out for a bit, into the community as it were.

Again, Gray sighed.

'John, could I see you for a minute?'

It was Gray's new boss, his seventh in thirty years, and the first woman to be so, Melanie Paton.

'Whoo-ooh!' It was Billy. 'Mr. Gray is being called to the headmistress's room. What delights are in store for him?'

Gray knew that the others saw him as an oddity, a dinosaur from the halcyon days of youth work, the late sixties to the late eighties. But he was happy to play the part for them, for they found him a very funny man. They also had great respect for him. They knew his track record as a published poet.

'Good morning, John, have a seat,' said Melanie.

Melanie Paton was 30 years old, Gray now 54. She had a background in adult education and was one of the many young women now asserting herself in what had previously been very much 'a man's world'. She was married with a 2 year old son who was looked after during her working hours by a childminder. Gray liked her, not least for her good looks and slim figure. There were times when the younger lads got quite aroused in her presence. Even Gray could feel that old itch on occasion. But he also liked her honesty. She was at all times herself, an irresistible mixture of feminine vulnerability and the determination required for an upholder of women's rights. There were times when she reminded Gray of his mother who had campaigned for justice for women during the fifties. With the exception of Tom Williams, his former bosses had been full of themselves, possessed of egos far in excess of their abilities. Without doubt, Melanie was the best boss since Williams in John Gray's book.

'John, I'm just looking at your application to go on a job share. I fully understand your reasons for wishing to do that, what with your writing being so important to you, but I'm afraid it's not up to me. You need permission from the Head of Service, Roger Jenkins.'

'Don't worry, Melanie, I can handle him.'

Melanie was faintly amused:

'Oh really? What makes you say that?'

'We go back a long way, Roger and I. But let's not go there for now.'

'Okay, John, I'll flag it up to Roger.'

On the way back to his desk, he was stopped by the younger secretary, Helen:

'There's a man here to see you, John. He's in the tearoom.'

Gray went in to the tearoom and found Bob Muir who had applied for a post as a part-time youth worker.

'Hello Bob, what brings you here this morning?'

'John, it was nice of you to send me that letter asking me to come for interview, but I'm sorry to tell you I've changed my mind.'

'Why so, Bob? This is a surprise.'

'It's too risky, John. I've got to think about the day job, and then there's my family.'

'That needn't interfere with it.'

'It's not that. Things have changed, John. At one time you could give a difficult laddie or lassie a row. Nowadays they go home and tell their parents you've done all sorts to them. And they're believed whether it's true or not. Only last month a youth worker was suspended for touching up a young lassie. He didn't lay a finger on her, I know the guy, he would never do that.'

Gray knew there was no point trying to change Bob's mind. It had become an all too familiar pattern. Today's young men were avoiding youth work. It had taken a downward trend since the tragedy at Dunblane. The murders by Thomas Hamilton, onetime boys' club leader, had inevitably tainted the regard the public held for youth organisations.

'I'm really sorry, John.'

'I'm the one who should be sorry, Bob'

The two men shook hands. Gray wished Bob well.

Later in the day, Gray said to Melanie:

'That's another one slipped through the net.'

'You mean Bob Muir? Yes, I heard.'

'We have, and always have had, about fifty part-time youth workers under our wing in Crack Willow. When I came here, eighty percent of them were men. Now, eighty percent are women.'

Melanie gave Gray a stare:

'Do you have a problem working with women, John?'

'Melanie, you know very well I don't. You also know why we can't attract men into youth work.'

'We can't do anything about that, John. And if we tried, we'd be swimming against the tide of progress, and of course the new legislation on childcare.'

'I know that, but the kids these women are working with.'

'What do you mean by that?'

'To most of our female youth workers, it's their second job of the day, after working on a pre-school playgroup or an after-school club. They see evening youth work as a natural extension of the first job, and their programmes reflect that. So the age group they attract is between eight and thirteen. That's not youth.'

'Well, you'll just have to train them in youth work.'

Gray knew, if he attempted to do that, many of his female youth workers would leave. They had no desire to work with youngsters aged 14 to 17, many of whom were going through any number of adolescent problems. At least he could reflect that work with that age group still went on in the voluntary sector. The YM/YWCA had satellite organisations for homeless young people, and there were new projects coming on stream to help young people who had become addicted to drugs. Gray thought:

Thank goodness for that. But I'm too old to move into the voluntary sector now. Apart from anything else, I'd lose a whack of my pension entitlement from Colliershire Council. I couldn't afford that. Oh, I need this job share, it's time for me to wind down and go.

In 2001 Bob Muir's fears came back to haunt John Gray. He had made his usual Thursday night visit to Caddick Community Centre's youth club. The programme was in full swing when two former members, now years older than the kids in the club, turned up at the door wanting in. They were drunk, and Gray suspected they'd taken some other substance as well. He decided to stand by the door and talk to them, explain that they couldn't be allowed entry. But before he did, something in his gut told him to ask one of the female youth workers to stand with him. Eventually, although the two youngsters were beyond reason, they were persuaded to go home. Next morning Gray's phone rang:

'Hello John, this is Karen Drummond, Mr Sutherland's secretary. He wants to see you right away.'

David Sutherland was the top man, Director of all community services in Colliershire Council.

'Well, does he now? And what does he want to see me about?'

Ten seconds silence while Mrs Drummond put her hand over her phone.

'You'll find out when you come over, John.'

'I think you'll find I'm entitled to know now.'

That caused a longer silence this time.

'A lady has made a complaint that you struck her son last night, then tore his jacket.'

'Oh, I see what it's about now. That lady has a drink problem herself. I certainly did no such things to her inebriated son, and I have a witness who was standing beside me the whole time I spoke to him and his girlfriend. Why don't you get Mr Sutherland to tell the lady that?'

Gray had learned how to deal with his bosses long since when he worked with the master craftsman, Tom Williams. He heard no more about the incident. Nonetheless it had taken its toll of the ageing professional. Now he was really looking forward to a reply to his application for a job share. He had waited a long time and was beginning to think it wouldn't happen. His luck changed:

'Hi John, it's Rhona here. You know, from Links Lane Youth Centre, Kirkleonard?'

'Yes Rhona, we met a year or two ago at the regional seminar. I remember you.'

'I heard you were looking for a job share partner.'

'But I thought you and your hubbie were expecting a new addition.'

'Well, the new addition arrived last year, a boy.'

Gray pinched himself for allowing time to pass him by.

'Oh, that's great Rhona. And how's he doing?'

'He's fine, a bit of a handful, but fine. I've just returned to work from maternity leave.'

Again Gray pinched himself.

'I see. Well, we'd best meet up, eh?'

Rhona and John duly met up and worked out a plan to make the job share function in a fair way. It only required rubber-stamping by Roger Jenkins. For two or three weeks there was a lull, an uncomfortable one for Gray. He had thought it would be straightforward. So had Melanie, his boss:

'John, haven't you heard yet?'

'Nope.'

'Well I'm sure it's just bureaucracy.'

Ironically, Gray's phone rang out ten minutes later, and it was Roger Jenkins.

'Hello John, I'm afraid I've got bad news for you.'

'I've never had good news from you, Roger.'

'The thing is, Rhona's husband has just been transferred by his firm to France. It's a great opportunity for them. However, it rather puts the kibosh on your plans.'

'I'm afraid you're wrong there, Roger.'

Jenkins was stunned:

'What do you mean?'

'Well I never. Roger Jenkins, of all people, hasn't read up on council policy.'

'What policy?'

'Colliershire Council, Equal Opportunites Policy, paragraph 239c.

In the event of a job share not working out, the applicant partner will be offered what would have been his or her job share hours as a part-time job.'

When the call was over, Gray tickled himself at the thought of Roger frantically wading through council policy to check it out. Triumphantly he knocked on Melanie's door to give her the news. She had a puzzled frown on her face:

'Well I knew that. How come His Highness doesn't?'

A few days later, Melanie was on the ball again.

'John, I'm bringing in a young graduate to take up the hours you drop when next month you go part-time. Her name is Mandy Tait. I take it you'll show her the ropes.'

Gray was quite happy to do so. He had known Mandy years before when she did voluntary youth work. She was made of the right stuff.

A year later John Gray had an important poem to write It was for Tom Williams' 80th birthday. He knew it would be a big event, for there was so much love and respect for the Shaman of the Service. He also knew it would have to be good.

It turned out a very successful night. Old friends paid tribute to Williams and there were hundreds of anecdotes swapped between them. John Gray recited his poem and to laughter from his old boss, joked that he would do a poem for his 90th. It finished with a typical flourish from the old master, thanking everyone for making his birthday so memorable.

After the ceremonies were done and dusted, Williams chatted with his close friends, David Samson, Malcolm Ingles, his adopted son Gerry and John Gray:

'How's the work going, John?'

Gray described the two main projects he was heading up, then talked about his part-time hours.

'What made you go for that?'

'Oh, it's all very different, not like the old days, too many systems and people falling over each other.'

He went on to highlight the sea change that had taken place in the gender of workers.

'Goodness me, you don't mean to tell me women are running the show?'

'It's just the way of it, Tom. You get used to it. You get used to anything in time.'

'Well, I don't know if I could. A woman boss? Blimey!'

During the school summer holidays which followed, Mandy Tait got the job of organising day trips away for some of Crack Willow's children. One Monday morning Gray found her in tears at her desk:

'Dear dear, Mandy, what's happened?'

'The Sunday bus trip, it was awful.'

'Tell me about it.'

'It was all that health and safety stuff. Some of the parents hadn't filled in their forms. I had to hold back the bus and get them to do it. It took ages. The driver lost his temper and said I'd have to do a whip round to compensate him for his extra time'

Gray could see Mandy was beginning to hyperventilate:

'Take a deep breath, Mandy. It's not your fault, you know, you've done nothing wrong.'

'That's not the worst thing. Three of the parents got pissed off. They took their kids off the bus and went home with them. The children were crying. It spoiled the rest of the day. I hate that Health and Safety department.'

Chapter 7

A soldier on his own

BERNARD MARKHAM CROSSED the Mu River in the twilight before dawn. He had no idea what date it was nor even which day of the week. The Mu was a tributary of the Chindwin but didn't join its parent river until a point one hundred miles to the south. At Bernard's chosen crossing point, the Chindwin, his first major goal, was still a good seventy miles away.

During captivity Bernard had been parted from most of his belongings, including his map with directions, the one he got down to with his buddies and Sergeant McKinlay when brigade began its withdrawal. But he was able to remember enough of it to make it work in tandem with his compass and enhance his chances of getting back to India.

He had worked out that his southerly forced march into captivity had taken roughly three hours. With a rest break in the middle of fifteen minutes, this could not have translated into more than six miles and had probably placed him near the town of Wuntho. If he maintained a north-westerly heading, he could reach the Mu somewhere between its source and the town of Pinlebu. He had also remembered from chit-chat between Stork and Mac that the Mu needed the monsoon season to reach its full level. This was mid-April, three weeks before the anticipated monsoons.

When he eventually crossed, he was able to wade between waist and chest deep, holding his sack above his head. In mid-river he lost his footing and had to swim for a bit, using one arm and kicking for all he was worth, the other arm fiercely clutching his sack. Luckily, when he reached the western bank, he had only drifted south by 200 yards. He thanked his lucky stars his sister Cynthia, 14 years his senior, had taught him to swim when little. And two months back, when the campaign was on its outward journey, he had been amazed that quite a number of Chindits couldn't swim at all.

The only downside was the loss of some of his rice. He had less than half a packet left now and decided he would only eat once a day until he reached the Chindwin. His diet was not great. He mixed boiled rice with bamboo leaves. He didn't know enough about Burma's natural greens to augment his food with any sense of confidence. He remembered the book given by Shankar to Stork, but any durian fruit he'd come across was not near ripe and would have given him stomach pains had he eaten it. As for the other fruits, he never seemed to come across them. He would have loved jackfruit. It was the biggest and heaviest of the fruits, was in season, and tasted like a mixture of apple, mango and pineapple. Just thinking about it made him hungry.

Like it or lump it, whatever scant comfort was to be derived from his larder, he was tired after crossing the Mu and decided, once he'd covered a respectable enough distance from the west bank to dismiss thoughts of a Japanese presence, to sit down and light a fire. That was one of his positives. The weather had been warm and dry, perfect for kindling.

As he polished off his ration of rice, his thoughts were all about Katashi:

I'm alive because of him. Shankar told me, not all Japanese are bad. Why did he do it? And what has happened to him? He must have been punished, surely. If Stork was here, we could pray for him. I hope he had a way of explaining how the trapdoor was broken. That's it, the prisoner got hold of something and set himself free. That has to be what he told Kobayashi. Maybe he's still alive. Maybe one day we'll meet again, long after this insane war. I would like that. Yes, we'll meet again. We must.

Bernard took a long draught from his canteen. Thankfully, there was no shortage of water. It coincided with the hilly environment in which he was travelling. There were numerous streams and occasionally small waterfalls and rock pools.

His main problem, apart from constantly keeping eyes and ears alert for the enemy, was food. He reckoned he would only have enough rice for four days, and he had no idea how he was going to kill a substantial animal like a water buffalo without a dah or kukri or some other sharp instrument. He worried too about his feet. His boots were slowly but surely coming apart. One Chindit, who had survived a previous long march in a different theatre of the war, spoke of having to discard his boots in favour of tearing a spare pair of shorts into strips and binding them around his feet like rags. Bernard didn't fancy that at all. He didn't have a spare pair of shorts. There was no-one around. He felt alone on the planet. But no way was he going on naked.

Two days later he was brought to an abrupt halt. He could clearly hear a Japanese patrol and as the volume of their voices continued to rise, he realised they were walking in his direction. He took cover behind a bush.

Why do these bastards always make such a noise? I'll bet it's because they've never been beaten. They probably think they're invincible and immortal.

He watched them marching past and was just beginning to take his first real breath for a while, when the last man stopped and shouted something in Japanese to those ahead of him. To Bernard's horror the man was in need of a pee, and he moved towards the Englishman. There was nothing Bernard could do but remain still. The soldier selected a tree, then relieved himself against it. It seemed an endless stream during which he spat and made all sorts of disgusting noises. Bernard could hear his breathing and smell his water, he was that close.

When the Jap re-joined his comrades, Bernard was certain he hadn't been well enough covered for the soldier not to have seen him, had he looked at the right bush.

The young British soldier was discovering qualities in himself he never thought he possessed. He had done very well for a privileged Hampstead lad. He had gone through a place he had come to know as Hell and survived, and he had managed on his own for a week now in one of the remotest places on Earth. He now felt he could manage without buddies and on the other hand not be a burden to them either. He was developing strength of character, and a strong survival instinct. He was determined to reach India. After all that had been thrown at him, nothing was going to stop him now.

As he jogged along, he thought he'd keep himself sane humming some of his classical music. He had played Beethoven on the piano, so the *Eroica* was followed by the *Pastoral*. He imagined his finger placements on the ivories as he hummed. In lighter moments he opted for the popular rhyming music he had learned as a small child in his home city:

London Bridge is falling down,
falling down, falling down,
London Bridge is falling down,
My Fair Lady.

But Burma had one more black card to deal him.

When he reached the nursery slopes of the highlands between himself and the Chindwin, he felt he was catching a cold. He had a headache and was shivering. When he threw back up much of his next meal, he reckoned it was flu. That evening he shook uncontrollably for what must have been an hour with a penetrating cold he had never known, and he was unable to cook far less eat. As night fell, his temperature went from one extreme to the other. He was consumed by a raging fever and sleep was nigh impossible. When daybreak came his stomach retched and retched in a vain attempt to be sick. There was nothing to bring up.

He didn't need a doctor to tell him what it was. He had seen enough of it in the British Army, not only in Burma but in other countries where he had served. Kobayashi had failed to break him. The tiny female mosquito looked likely to have succeeded. Bernard Markham had caught malaria.

He made an attempt to move progress once the first fever had subsided, but it was hopeless. A healthy lad weighing in at 11 stones at the start of *Operation Longcloth*, he had plummeted to something between 6 and 7. And his strength was fast ebbing away. Lucky to have travelled a mile, he literally stumbled into a stream, hoping to at least take on some water. He managed to drink a little and dip his canteen to its neck and get a refill. Then he moved to the bank and reached for his sack. He put his canteen inside it and struggled out and upright, but when he threw the sack over his shoulder, his knees gave way and he collapsed.

There he lay in a cold sweat for some time, unable to do anything but take in the surrounding scenery. It was certainly the most beautiful spot he had seen during his spell in Burma. And birdsong was just reaching its zenith for the morning. Feeling that his time had come, he experienced a moment of calm, and imagined Stork was standing above him in prayer:

Don't be afraid, Bernard, it's only one step from this life into the next, where the Lord awaits and will bring you his eternal peace.

And before he knew it, he was asleep.

'Aakuuaanye r swarr par!'

It was Burmese for 'Go and get help!'

A Burmese woman had come from her village with her two sons to wash and do her family laundry. She had only needed one look at Bernard to know the signs. Burmese villagers knew all about malaria. They kept supplies of quinine given them by either itinerant missionaries or visiting medics. It was not available in its natural state, coming from the bark of a tree native to South America.

Her older boy obeyed his mother and ran the half mile to his village like a wind. Bernard was brought to consciousness by the cool hand of a woman dabbing around his head and neck with a damp piece of clothing. She pointed to herself and said her name:

'Maya.'

Then she pointed to him with the obvious question in her eyes.

'Bernard, my name is Bernard. Thank you for helping me.'

She understood and conveyed it by pressing her palms together, her fingers upwards, and placing them against her forehead. In no time at all her husband had arrived with the village strong man. He was huge, weighed 17 or 18 stones, and in one movement, slung the 6 or 7 stone British soldier over his shoulder. Bernard was carried like a side of beef into the village.

Markham knew very little about the days that followed, and he cared even less. He was dangerously ill the whole time, so lacking in weight and energy that the malaria threatened his very vital organs. His legs were so weak when he tried to go to the latrine, they felt like rubber and gave way underneath him. Eventually, he allowed Indi, the strong man who took him from the stream to the village, to carry him every time. Indi had become his minder.

Meanwhile Maya tried to work magic with some of the village's supply of quinine, administering two strong doses morning and night. She abandoned her husband's bed night after night, maintaining a vigil by the side of the British soldier, waiting for just one sign that he might be turning the corner. The quinine certainly calmed the fever, but there was no miracle cure. Bernard's chances were no better than fifty fifty. Either he had chronic malaria, that is to say the type which would return again and again, if only reducing in potency over a long period of years, or he had its fatal sister. Only time would tell.

Almost exactly a week from the time he had stumbled into the local rivulet, Bernard awoke and said to Maya:

'I'm hungry.'

Word got around and a burst of cheering spread through the village.

'How long have I been here?'

Bernard had to back it up with a sort of sign language. Maya extended 7 fingers.

'Seven days?'

She nodded.

For a full 24 hours he continued with the regular water and quinine, accompanied by several small portions of food, very plain like chicken, fish, or just rice. On the second day his meals were more substantial, and by the third, he was on a diet of boiled rice with chilli soup, followed by chopped up jackfruit, something he only dreamed of before. The villagers clearly knew where to find the fruit trees. The fourth day brought steak butchered from a water buffalo. He was now gaining strength and walking around the village. He announced to Maya it was time for him to move on. She looked horrified:

'Not time, Bernard.'

In their days together she had learned a few words of English.

'But I must, Maya. I must.'

'Not time, Bernard.'

And she waved a reversed forefinger at him.

Bernard started to pack, then had his things taken from him by Indi and dumped back on his bed. The big man then stood across, and filled, the open entrance to the wooden hut with his arms folded and stared at Bernard. The message was clear, but the soldier pleaded with Maya. She made two signs with her hands around her waist, the first to mimic how Bernard looked now, still skinny, the second to mimic how he would look when he was really fit enough to go. Bernard understood and saw sense. He stayed for a further five days and ate like a turkey cock.

When well enough to leave, he washed in a rockpool and shaved with the kukri given him by Indi. He was given a wickerwork bag to house his essential bits and bobs, more rice and the kukri to keep. A makeshift rope functioned as a shoulder strap. Finally, he was given a strong pair of sandals.

Then he heard the voice of Maya:

'Indi and Chai come with you a bit of way.'

He didn't refuse. He knew, as Indi did, the most difficult passage would be through the hills which were looking like 2000 feet at their summit, but he also knew from his memory of the old map it wouldn't take long. He didn't know what to say to Maya. She was the second person to have shown him kindness and care in this war torn beleaguered country. And now he was leaving her behind forever, just as he had Katashi. He moved to embrace her. She took one step backwards and extending her arm, placed the palm of her hand against his chest.

'Oh, you fat boy now, Bernard !'

He laughed, but still wanted to hold her.

'Go now, Bernard. Maya always remember you for teaching her English.'

Walking almost backwards, he watched her until his last sight of her was the by now familiar pose of blessing, her palms pressed together in front of her forehead.

Chai turned out to be Indi's young brother, a smaller, much smaller, model. And he was quick on his feet. Bernard and Indi had trouble keeping up with him. They made steady progress until dusk, by which time they were in the hills. They settled down to cook a meal, and review the last two weeks of their time together with the help of hand gestures. This created much amusement, until they felt tired and lay down to sleep. Bernard used his rattan bag as a pillow. Indi and Chai needed nothing.

They rose at dawn and decided to make some headway before breakfast. Two hours later they were stopped by first the smell then the sight of smoke. Two Japanese soldiers were just ahead, eating breakfast and chatting. Bernard reckoned they were there as look-outs for retreating Chindits.

'Sssh.' It was Indi.

What happened next astonished Bernard. For a big man, Indi was remarkably sure-footed and fast over a short distance. He and Chai were upon the soldiers before they had time to reach for their weapons. One guard had his throat cut by Chai's dah. The other made a vain attempt to wrestle with Indi. He was upended and his head was smashed into a teak tree. Bernard helped them to drag the two bodies out of sight and cover them with loose branches from the surrounding area.

They had to move carefully now, yet maintain their speed. They decided to do so by keeping a gap of fifty yards between each man – Chai first, Bernard in the middle, Indi bringing up the rear. Breakfast, when it finally came, was very late that morning. The rest of the day was much less dramatic than they thought it would be, and as the sun began to sink towards the Chindwin, Chai stopped and waited for the other two. They were out of the hills.

Indi turned to the man he had protected for the last sixteen days.

'You okay now, Bernard.'

The young British soldier hugged him, then hugged Chai. His Burmese guardians had restored his faith in mankind. He owed them a debt he could never repay:

'I don't know how to thank you. You and Maya saved my life.'

The big man waved his arms by way of saying there was no need for thanks. They had done what they had to. Before parting, Indi amused Bernard by handing him a large jackfruit. Bernard worked out, as Indi was at the rear all day, he must have gone off track for a couple of minutes to cut it down. He knew how much his English friend craved for it. A refreshed but emotional soldier watched his guides waving to him all the time until he was gone.

He could see why Indi had chosen that time. The land had flattened out and the Chindwin was within striking distance. And the coming darkness would allow him the necessary cover to keep going in more open country.

By the following morning Bernard had slept for only three hours. He breakfasted on a large piece of Indi's jackfruit, opting to leave a cooked meal for later in the day. By his reckoning, there was only fifteen miles, twenty at most to the Chindwin. He was impatient but he was aware of the need for self-discipline. He would have to figure out a way of crossing the big river, and then there were more hills to negotiate before the Indian border. He ate and slept long that night, but was wakened by rain, the first for many a long day. He covered a further three miles before succumbing to a drenching and taking advantage of a cave half-hidden by undergrowth, where he could light a fire and hopefully dry out. When the rain abated he continued, but it wasn't long before he cursed himself. The change of weather had sparked off his shivering and shaking again:

Why oh why did I not keep taking the quinine? You're a bloody fool, Markham. You didn't even take any with you.

When by the following morning he had reached the eastern bank of the Chindwin, he was not in a good position. He was feeling sick and he could hear exchanges of gunfire on the other side of the river. As a soldier he had been alone for more than a month, but he hadn't been entirely on his own. With help and nursing, he had made it to his first goal. And now, in yet again a weakened state, he had to scour the bank of the Chindwin for a boat. No way could he consider swimming. This river was no small matter like the Mu.

He had gone only half a mile upstream when he spotted a boat. It had pushed off from the bank with four figures in it. Whoever they were, he had to take the chance. He shouted:

'I'm a Chindit, wait for me!'

He rushed into the water until he could no longer stand, then swam. A strong hand reached out of the boat and dragged him half in. The rest he managed for himself. He looked at the other two passengers in the middle of the boat. They were be-draggled and in a sorry state.

Good God, they look worse than me. Then again, maybe that's what they're thinking about me.

Until they had crossed, not a word was exchanged by the three British soldiers, they were beyond exhaustion. Bernard looked at the two bearded skippers of the craft, seated and paddling at either end. The insignia on their turbans was un-mistakable. They were soldiers of the elite Sikh Light Infantry, renowned for their extraordinary courage and determination.

Wingate had managed to convince his superiors that the efforts of his men to get as far as the Chindwin under their own steam was all that could be expected of them. Sikh regiments had served the British Raj commendably for a hundred years. They were ideal for going into Burma, helping out the heroes of *Operation Longcloth* and bringing some of them home.

When the three British soldiers beached on the west bank, they joined other comrades and went on to witness the Sikh regiment making short work of any Japanese attacks. It didn't take long at all for Bernard Markham to be over the Indian border and tucked up under clean sheets in a hospital bed at Imphal.

Operation Longcloth, from late January to early May, 1943, was deemed a military success. Orde Wingate had proved that jungle warfare tactics could disrupt the Japanese Imperial Army. A year later he headed up a second campaign with seven times as many men and better logistics. Despite Wingate losing his own life in a plane crash, the campaign played a major part in the defeat of the Japanese in Burma. But some senior officers felt that the success of *Longcloth* had come at too great a price. Of the 3,000 men who set out, almost 1,000 were lost, with a further 600 deemed unfit for future active service in the Army.

CHAPTER 8

India and Blighty

'HOW ARE YOU doing, old chap, any better?'

The MO, Lieutenant Cracknell, was at Bernard Markham's bedside.

'Better, Sir. Only thing is I'm so bloody tired all the time, and I've been here for a week already.'

'After all you've been through, that's to be expected. No point in rushing, that sort of thing takes time. While I'm here, do you mind if I ask you a few questions?'

'Not at all, go for it.'

'The scars on the backs of your hands and forearms are still new, have been there for no more than six weeks I'd say. They're regular in pattern, not likely caused by jungle undergrowth. Would you feel like talking about it?'

'They're courtesy of a certain Captain Kobayashi, Interrogator of the Japanese Imperial Army, or to put it more accurately, his thugs, those of the braindead variety.'

'Oh God, you poor chap.'

'I wouldn't say that. Some poor buggers got a lot worse.'

'Yes, I've heard some awful horror stories since I was posted here. Nevertheless, it's bad enough. Anyway, suffice to say they're well mended. You will have them for the rest of your life, but at least they'll fade in time.'

'My war wounds, you might say. Something I can use to break a lady's heart.'

Cracknell smiled:

'Listen, if you don't want to talk about this, I will fully understand, it's just what the night duty nurse was telling me about.'

'Oh come on, Doc, spit out.'

Bernard had a momentary image of himself as Sergeant McKinlay. He was definitely beginning to sound like him. Cracknell explained:

'She was saying there's a leaking tap in the toilet along the corridor. You shouted out about it in the middle of your first night, but she didn't take much notice of it. Trouble is she tells me that you've been shouting out a lot since, and generally having terrible nightmares.'

Cracknell watched as Bernard went tight-lipped at that, used his experience to manage the silence, and continued more informally:

'Listen Bernard, there are plenty of men in this hospital who shout out in the night, who like you have been through a living hell. If you don't want to talk about it, that's your business, but it's better if you do.'

Bernard remained shtoom.

'Tell you what, I'll come back and see you later, possibly tomorrow, or if things get busy, the next day. Don't keep the nurses off their work by chatting them up, now.'

Bernard spent the next hours trying to make conversation with a wounded soldier in the next bed. He never got as far as an exchange of names, the man being too far gone. Some consolation came in the evening meal as it had done for the previous six days, and this time it was steamed fish and vegetables. The cooking was Indian but it might as well have been pure Hampstead. Anything was delicious compared to the pap he'd been served up by the Japanese, or for that matter the K-rations he had marched on in one of Wingate's columns.

At 2 o'clock in the morning, Bernard woke up shouting:

'For Christ sake, will someone fix that bloody tap?'

Nurse Wilson tried to calm him down:

'Now Mr Markham, you know we're getting someone to fix it, but there's a war on, and as you can see around you, there are more important things for us to do.'

'Well, I'm in a cold sweat now, and I'm shivering.'

'That's got nothing to do with it, Mr Markham. It's your malaria. It's likely to do that from time to time.'

She stayed with him until he settled. It took fully half an hour but eventually Bernard drifted away.

He had to be wakened in the morning by the day nurse. He had slept in. The first thing he noticed was the empty bed next to him. He didn't really need to ask the nurse but did anyway. The incumbent had passed away in the night.

Bernard thought to himself:

The poor sod is just another statistic of this insane bloody war. And now there's another grieving widow, son, daughter, father, mother. When will it ever end?

When he'd been given his breakfast and washed, he stood by the window. Outside there were droves of casualties taking morning exercise, some of them under their own steam, some of them on crutches, many in bandages of one sort or the other, some of them supported by nursing auxiliaries or fellow soldiers.

'Jesus Christ,' he said, then returned to his thoughts:

What was it all for, that bloody campaign? There was no victory. The Japanese still occupy Burma. They're still invincible. And now, all those allied prisoners of war, taken on the fall of Singapore, are being worked to death on that hellish railway from Thailand through Burma. What good has Orde Wingate and Operation Longcloth done for the British Empire?

And finally, he got personal:

And now I'm one of the walking wounded, maybe for the rest of my life, and still only just 20 years old. Forgive me Stork, but I can't, I just can't, believe there's a God in heaven. What about Smudger, Thomo, Mad Mac and Ganesh? They gave their lives for this show.

As if that wasn't bad enough, Bernard wasn't even confident that Stork, Stinker and Shankar would still be alive.

After his evening meal that night, he had a visitor he was this time pleased to see. It was the MO Cracknell:

'Hello Bernard.'

'I didn't expect to see you until tomorrow, Doc.'

'I'm afraid for me it's non-stop duty here from dawn till dusk, and new casualties are coming in all the time.'

'I've had a think about what you said.'

Cracknell sat down and listened intently to Bernard's tale of capture, torture and escape. When he'd finished, and only when he'd finished, did the MO speak:

'It's just as well you had some help along the way, old chap. Otherwise, you'd be dead, or if not, completely round the bend.'

'That's what I've been meaning to ask you, Doc. Am I going mad?'

'No, it's trauma brought about by all you've been through. As I've told you before, there are loads of other blokes in here who have nightmares, but very few of them have gone totally mad. I'm afraid though, you'll have to carry some of those images for the rest of your life. But it will get easier as the years go by.'

'I suppose I'll just have to get used to it.'

'At least you won't have to think about future action in the Army.'

Cracknell had guessed that Bernard Markham was no hard man, no born and bred, dedicated soldier, and he was right:

'I won't argue with that, Doc.'

'Well, I've made a report which I expect they'll rubber-stamp. But you'll need to be seen by a colleague of mine as well. He's a psychiatrist. Don't worry, it should be straightforward. The malaria on top of your Japanese tormentors should be more than enough to swing it. That leaves just one question. What do you do when you get out of here?'

'I'm not thinking about that at all.'

'Well you should, Bernard. Your weight has gone up to more than eight stones, so you'll be well enough to leave hospital in a week or two.'

Bernard spent the following week exercising outside, making conversation with fellow patients and nurses, and reading from the works of the American poet, Robert Frost. He also saw the psychiatrist. He never gave a second thought to his future until Cracknell returned:

'It's all sorted. And there's something else, old chap. I've been speaking to my CO. He's coming to see you tomorrow. It seems they're looking for men with your background and education. There's a lot going on in India, as you know. The War won't last for much longer, and of course there's this Quit India Movement being headed up by Gandhi. The CO feels that Indian Independence is coming whether we like it or not.'

'What's all that got to do with me?'

'Paperwork, Bernard, and lots of it.'

'Paperwork?'

'A desk job, Bernard, a desk job. It would keep you in the British Army until the end of the War at least, maybe longer. Think of the regular pay, old chap.'

24 hours later and Cracknell's CO, Major Birrell, was at Bernard's side. It seemed the whole British Raj was interested in him.

Birrell looked at him through his walrus moustache:

'Well boy, have you made your mind up?'

'Sir, I..........'

'You can type, can't you?'

That was true. Before the war, Bernard had been trying for a place at University to study music while working as a clerk to help his father's business.

'Yes, Sir.'

'Well then, bit of tap-tap and zing, some filing, keeping our boys' records up to date, that sort of thing. Here are the details of the H/Q address and living quarters, I'll see you in Poona a week on Monday morning, sharp.'

Major Birrell had been in and out like a breeze.

For the next year, Bernard Markham tapped and zinged away in the army office at Poona, going through a forest of pulped wood in the process. Compared to what he had gone through in Burma, this was easy street. But not quite, for two further bouts of malaria hospitalised him for a total of three weeks, and each time he returned to a mountain of new work.

On his days off he wandered the vast myriad of bazaars, thoroughly amused by the haggling and general banter of the traders. He would stop occasionally to watch and listen to the music, usually delivered solo or in small bands of two or three, most commonly playing hand-drums, sitars and bagpipes. As a keen player of classical music on piano, he appreciated the depth and feel of traditional Indian music.

In due course he was transferred across country to Bombay, India's busiest city. He was awestruck by the crowds. He had never seen anything like it. It was particularly hectic at that time due to the growth of the new Quit India Movement. But what really moved him was the scale of poverty. Late one afternoon, he stumbled on a hovel which barely passed for a family home, and noticed what he first thought was a pet animal crouched outside the door. At second glance, he could see it was a man with no arms or legs. He had a tin into which passers-by threw whatever they could afford.

Instinctively, Bernard bent down to talk to him.

'He can't hear you, Sahb, he's deaf.'

It was a neighbour. Bernard made signs to the beggar.

'He can't speak to you, Sahb, he's dumb as well.'

As it turned out, the beggar was the main source of family income.

Whether it was the terrible sights he saw, or the memories he had of Burma, Bernard was never sure, but it didn't help his nightmares at all. He longed for an end to the War. He longed for an end to his service in the British Army. He wanted to go home.

By the end of 1944, the Japanese were on the back foot in Burma. In the early summer of that year, they had opted to change from a defensive strategy of holding on to Burma to one of all-out attack on the cities of Kohima and Imphal, in an attempt to seize India from the British Raj. It was a bridge too far for the fascists, just as it had been for Hitler in Russia. They lost, severely.

Bernard didn't know it but by 1945 he was entering his last months in India. A further bout of malaria together with panic attacks convinced the Army they were done with him. Plans were put in place for his discharge as soon as the War was over.

During those last months, Bernard was uplifted by one thing, or rather one small man. Mohandas Gandhi. He looked like a skeleton, and walked around in a kind of beggar's mantle, an Indian dhoti and shawl woven with yarn on a spinning wheel. And yet, he was head of the Indian Independence Movement which he ran along the lines of religious pluralism and by non-violent disobedience. This remarkable little man, who physically couldn't swat a fly, was feared by the entire British Raj, even imprisoned by them many times to no avail, and worshipped by an Indian race which amounted to nearly a quarter of the Earth's population. Bernard sometimes thought him the only man who could bring peace and harmony into an ill-divided, shell-shocked world.

The Third Reich fell in May and the Americans dropped their atomic bombs on Japan in August. Days after the atrocities, which millions in the allied world simply viewed as payback, the Japanese Imperial Army surrendered to Louis Mountbatten. World War Two was over and Private Bernard Markham was duly demobbed.

His father had died in 1941 just after he'd been called up. So he wrote a letter to his mother and sister one week before joining a liner coming from Rangoon packed full of demobbed veterans of the Far East conflict. He vainly hoped to pick out Stork and Stinker in the crowd but knew the chances would be very slim. But he did take the opportunity to chat with the soldiers who had slaved on the infamous Burma Railway. The liner made for the Suez Canal, then The Med, at last at peace from German subs and fighter planes, passed the Bay of Biscay and finally reached Blighty.

The whole thing took ten days, including stopovers and his train connections from Liverpool to London and Hampstead. It was 3 o'clock on a fine September day when Bernard stood at the front door of his Hampstead home. Before he rang the bell, he experienced that strange feeling all servicemen feel when they return home after years away – a feeling of:

Is this really where I was brought up?

He was embraced by a tearful Cynthia. She looked so much older to him now. She was 14 years older than him anyway, but clearly the War had taken a lot out of the people back home as well. She led him through to the kitchen as he took in the furniture, the old pictures and photos hanging on the walls, the glass sideboards full of the best china, the patterned carpets, the mantelpiece clock tick-tocking away. Nothing had changed. Cynthia boiled the kettle, the only thing new about the house. They sat down to tea and some baking Cynthia had been holding on to for days.

'Oh Bernard, it's so good to see you, we thought you'd been killed until we got your first letter from the hospital at Imphal. Mum was so relieved when she heard you were on the way home.'

'Where is Mum?'

'She's upstairs in bed. I'm afraid it's not good news. Cancer struck her a year or two ago. She beat it but this second round is bad.'

'But why…….?'

'How could we tell you, Bernard? You weren't well yourself, after what those hideous people did to you. I hope they rot in Hell.'

Bernard climbed the stairs to the bedroom his mother had once shared with his father. His mother, propped up on pillows by Cynthia, extended her hand to him and they talked for a while in the half- light created by partially closed curtains. Sensing she had little strength, Bernard withdrew, telling her they would talk again later.

While Cynthia cooked an evening meal, Bernard went for a walk round his old haunts but didn't seem to recognise anyone he knew. After dinner he listened to the music on the wireless while Cynthia knitted, then he said goodnight and turned in early. As he moved from the living-room to the stairs, his sister called out:

'Your old room's ready.'

He was woken by Cynthia knocking on the door at 2am.

'Are you all right, Bernard?'

'I'm fine, Cynthia. Go back to bed.'

Clearly, a nightmare had made him shout out. For a while after the house had fallen silent again, he remained bolt upright and stared into the darkness. When, he asked himself, were these images ever going to end? One night it would be the sound of Mad Mac shooting himself, another night it would be Thomo tied to a tree with a bayonet through his neck, and then it would be his own turn being driven mad by that dripping tap.

When morning arrived, Cynthia drew him a bath, put out some towels and made him his breakfast, then shot off to tend to her mother. When she finally got a break, he spoke to her:

'You can't keep this up for long.'

'No, I can't. Mum needs proper care now, the kind I can't give her. She'll be going into hospital soon.'

Bernard attempted to offer help but Cynthia went on:

'There's something else, Bernard. You'd better sit down.'

Bernard did as he was asked:

'What's up?'

'After Dad died we discovered his business had piled up a load of debts. It was all to do with the War, I never really understood those things. Mum did but she's not well enough to get upset about it now. She believes it killed him.'

'No, I agree, best not to ask her.'

'Anyway, this is the shocker. We've had to sell the house to pay off the creditors.'

'You mean that SOLD sign outside is our house. I thought it was next door's.'

'It's ours all right. Luckily, the buyers have been really nice. Due to Mum's condition they've given us a six weeks extension to the time we have left here.'

Cynthia was relieved to see that her brother was more sad than angry. And anyway, after Burma and India, the last thing on Bernard's mind was money. He was just glad to be back in Blighty and have a life of freedom again.

Two weeks later and only days after her admission to hospital, brother and sister were at their mother's funeral. Bernard moved forward to the graveside and took a cord to help lower their mother to rest beside her late husband. That same week they consulted the solicitor about her will. It all seemed very straightforward. Once the house swapped hands, the debts were settled and the solicitor's fees deducted, there would be a fair split of the remainder between Bernard and Cynthia. Back home again, Cynthia made tea as she talked:

'It's not much for you, Bernard. Not if you want to go on and get married. I don't expect that army pension of a few shillings a week will keep you going.'

'Cynthia, how many times have I to tell you that Kathleen was the only one for me?'

'Well, she didn't hang around for you, that's for sure. Oh Bernard, there's more fish in the sea. There are dances at the local ballroom. You could meet someone.'

'No, I'm not interested. And anyway, what about you?'

'That's different. You're still young. What chance has an ageing spinster like me now?'

'You're not old, Cynthia'

'Well I look it and I feel it.'

Cynthia and Bernard saw sense and changed the subject in favour of what they were going to do about their future living accommodation. Cynthia had found a small flat to rent in Croydon where she had been offered a job as a shorthand typist. She gave Bernard the chance to board with her.

'No Cynthia, I'll get a place of my own nearby. We'll see each other from time to time.'

'Are you sure?'

'Yes, I have interests here in Hampstead. It's always been a great place for art, music and literature. The people are liberal, independent thinkers, the sort of people I like.'

Cynthia smiled:

'Oh yes, Bernard, you've always been like that.'

Bernard Markham spent a year after the War re-acquainting himself with Hampstead Village, and he bought a bicycle to get himself around. His immediate neighbours had taken a new interest in him. He wasn't a callow youth now, but a veteran soldier who had fought for king and country.

'Good morning, Mr Johnson. I picked up your paper for you.'

'Cheers Bernie. Heh lad, that was a right bashing we gave those Nippons, eh?'

'Yes, Mr Johnson.'

'Now I was in the Second Boer War. That was a right cock-up. Let me tell you…..'

'Sorry, Mr Johnson, gotta go.'

Bernard knew, if he stopped, he'd never get away.

Neighbours soon changed to housemates when he found digs only half a mile away. He got used to the times for breakfast and dinner, together with all the house rules laid down by Mrs Potter, the landlady. And the cost of his keep seemed reasonable to him. He was allowed to keep his bike in the back yard.

His early days were spent looking for a job. As Cynthia had rightly guessed, his army pension wasn't enough. But he did place an advert in the local paper for pupils, and two parents were soon hiring him for their children's piano tuition. While he kept looking for more permanent employment, he was a regular patron of Hampstead's Victorian Library and he visited other places like Hampstead Heath, and the house where John Keats had lived for a time and done his most productive work. Bernard had never been shown it as a child but he had pledged to Smudger he would make a visit. Never a day passed that he didn't think of his old buddie, nor how he'd been required to put him out of his misery. Following up Smudger's passion for poetry was one small token of atonement.

Mrs Potter had a piano in her living room, so it wasn't long before Bernard was entertaining guests after dinner in the evening with some of the Big Band numbers of the day. Glen Miller was the favourite, and Bernard lost count of his renditions of *In The Mood, Little Brown Jug* and *Moonlight Serenade*. Occasionally they allowed him to indulge in his classical pieces, but only for a few minutes. He didn't mind, he was making friends, albeit they were ships passing in the night.

He was looking for a vintage wine to share with Cynthia on the anniversary of his return from the War, when he passed the local music shop, stopped and retraced his steps. A notice in the window had caught his eye:

Shop assistant required, five days a week. Must have a background in music

Bernard pushed the heavy door which set off the now familiar loud bell, then introduced himself to Mr Walters:

'You're the lad who buys the classical stuff, right?'

'Yes, I've always played classical, but I can do other music as well.'

'And Mrs Potter tells me you're a dab hand at that an' all.'

'So you know Mrs Potter?'

'Everyone knows Mrs Potter, lad. And Mrs P knows everyone's business. Know what I mean? – nudge, nudge.'

Bernard laughed. Mr Walters got back on track:

'What about handling other instruments?'

'I've played mandolin, a little violin, mostly instruments my Dad had, not much really. But I can work out how they tune up when I'm handed them.'

'I bet you can, lad. Well, I've got another lad to see, and would you believe a lass with a degree from the Academy. I'll let you know by tomorrow.'

That last bit dampened Bernard's hopes. He felt sure the job would go to the Academician.

He was in the middle of his fiftieth or so *Little Brown Jug*, when Mrs Potter, who had just finished her dishes, tapped him on the shoulder:

'I've got news for you, maestro. You've got the job.'

Bernard was ecstatic, and told Mr Walters next morning about the doubts he had.

'No lad, that young lass was a high-flyer, she'll get something a lot better than this. Anyway, she wouldn't have stayed long, even if I had given her the job.'

Of course, as he'd given with one hand, he had to take with the other. He told Bernard he couldn't pay him a great deal. But Bernard couldn't care less, a job in music was right up his street.

On the face of it, Bernard had everything for his needs, but the shadows of Burma followed him around, and in 1947 he was again struck down by malaria. Mr Walters was very good:

'Don't be silly, lad, I'll manage fine on my own. I expect you won't be in hospital for more than a few days this time. The job will still be here when you come out.'

And he was as good as his word. So was Mrs Potter who would have to tell him that his nightmares were disturbing her other guests, but when he offered to leave she would have none of it:

'You leave them to me, Bernard. My first husband died in the trenches in France. Mrs P don't throw out soldiers just cause they 'ave a nightmare now and then.'

Nevertheless, Bernard felt he ought to go. He had a regular income now, so there was no reason why he shouldn't get a place of his own. He turned down quite a number of flats until he found the ideal one. It had an old piano which hadn't been played for many years. With Mr Walters help, they tuned it up into shape. The flat was two miles from his work so easily reachable on his bike.

But by 1948 Bernard was beginning to regret leaving Mrs Potter's digs. He had never lived alone in his life. On the face of it he had a decent life, but the quiet nights and the long shadows brought back his nightmares twofold. He stopped playing the piano so much in favour of records, and while he listened he could easily down a bottle of wine. He began to visit the off licence every other day. He believed the alcohol was suppressing both his nightmares and the malarial tendency on occasions to manifest itself in a fit of the jitters. Sometimes he got up in the middle of the night and drank two glasses. On some days,

Mr Walters could see he had a skinful the night before, but said little.

Bernard was still a young man. He couldn't see he was becoming an alcoholic. The odd day he either slept in for work or missed it altogether. He wasn't washing or shaving so much, or for that matter washing his clothes. He had a dishevelled appearance. When Mr Walters began to see that regular customers were making a note of it, he had to speak to him:

'Look lad, I know it's none of my business, but you don't look well. I think it's all that wine you're drinking these days.'

Bernard said nothing, and continued to say nothing every time Mr Walters raised the subject.

In the spring of that year there was a knock at his door. When he opened it, the light was blotted out by a huge man, 6 foot 3 and 15 stones at least.

'Don't you recognise me, Bernard?'

'No, I'm sorry, I……'

'Corporal Taylor reporting, Sir.'

The man stood to attention and saluted.

'No, it can't be. Stork?'

'The very same, my old mucker.'

How could Bernard have recognised Stork? During the jungle campaign the big man had gone down to 8 stones. The two former Chindits embraced tightly, much to the curiosity and mumblings of neighbours passing by. Bernard paid them no heed. He was overjoyed that the last words spoken to him by

Stork in the Japanese holding station had come true. They were etched in his memory:

Have courage, Bernard. I have prayed to God and I just know that you and I will survive all this. Help will come to you, my dear boy.'

CHAPTER 9

Catching up

'HOW DID YOU find me?' Bernard asked Stork.

'A long way round the houses, I'm afraid. I remembered you telling me the road where you were brought up, so I just knocked on doors there until a neighbour pointed me in the direction of Mrs Potter's. She knew where you were. Sounded to me as if she knew where everybody was.'

That evening after a light meal, Stork and Bernard made a deliberate effort not to broach the subject of Burma. Apart from Stork revealing he was now staying in Ealing, less than ten miles away, they talked about current British politics, arguing the toss about the wisdom of the electorate to put in a Labour Government after the War. They talked about rationing, the weather, Bradman's Australians who were on their way to England for the summer test match series, anything but Burma. They listened to Bernard's records for a bit then the wireless. They drank two bottles of wine between them. Then Stork dropped a bombshell:

'I've got something to tell you, Bernard.'

'You're not married or anything like that?'

Bernard was joking and more than a tad drunk.

'How did you guess?'

'You don't mean it? Well I never. Stork of all people. Who's the lucky lady?'

'Her name's Sylvia. She was a woman POW after the fall of Singapore. We met out in Thailand, just after the Japanese surrender.'

Stork stopped himself, realising he had trod on sensitive ground.

'Don't worry, Stork. We'll pick up on all that stuff another time. Anyway, what's she like?'

'Thankfully for me, she's tall for a girl, about five foot nine. She has auburn hair, done up, and green eyes. Main thing is she's a real nice lady.'

'That's great, Stork, I'm delighted for you. Let's have a toast. To Sylvia!'

'To the boss, you mean! Well, you must come to Ealing and see us. Make it soon.'

'You bet. Now, let's turn in for the night. No way are you going back this late.'

Stork made a call from the corner telephone box to let Sylvia know he wouldn't be back till morning. He spent the night on the couch under spare blankets but was dismayed when woken several times by shouting from Bernard's bedroom. The few words he was able to make out told him all he needed to know, so he thought it better to stay put rather than go through. These were all too familiar sounds to Stork and he didn't wish to make matters worse.

In the morning Stork got up first. He had a slight headache from the night before, but soon shook it off. He wasn't surprised that Bernard was still snoring. Stork had downed a few but Bernard had taken at least twice as much. The big man looked around for a kettle and had to wade through countless empty wine bottles. On his way to the bathroom near the front door he encountered even more, tripped over a loose one, then found a bag of them in the toilet itself which had obviously been placed there for chucking out later and had been forgotten. Stork was beginning to become concerned.

While he waited for Bernard, he washed and shaved, then put his things together. He intended to take a 10 o'clock train to Charing Cross, then one to Ealing. Bernard arrived, looking like he'd been dragged through a hedge backwards, sat down at table, hands in his hair, and obviously helpless. He gave Stork guidance on where to find food for breakfast.

Stork ate heartily, Bernard merely nibbled. Then Stork announced he had to go. The two men vowed to remain friends forever, a vow they would keep. Stork had written out his contact details earlier, so handed them to Bernard and told him to get in touch soon.

He had only gone yards when a woman crossed the road from the other side and stopped him:

'Excuse me, are you Stork?'

'Guilty as charged, Ma'am.'

'Mrs P told me you'd be here. Oh sorry, I'm Cynthia, Bernard's sister.'

'Pleased to meet you. Bernard's told me all about you. So sorry to hear about your mother.'

'Well I'm more pleased to meet you, Stork. He's been terrible recently. When he's drunk, I can't get any sense out of him. I come regularly on Saturday mornings, otherwise the place would be a hovel.'

'Yes, I've noticed that the......'

'You know, he thinks so highly of you, Stork. Could you do anything to help him? He badly needs a male friend, someone he can look up to.'

'I'll try, Cynthia. I promise.'

Stork lifted his hat to the lady and was off.

Bernard did as he was told. He phoned Stork and arranged to travel to Ealing on a Sunday three weekends later. As it turned out, it was a beautiful early summer's day in May. The cherry blossom was in full bloom, a sea of pink and white. Bernard was on his best behaviour. On his sister's instructions, he was washed, shaved, well-dressed, and hadn't touched a drop for two whole days. He had a touch of the withdrawals, but was determined to make a good day of it, for Stork's sake above all.

He sat down to a smashing meal cooked by Sylvia. She really was everything Stork had described, a lovely lady. Stork allowed the company one glass of wine each, before suggesting to Bernard that the two of them take a stroll along Mattock Lane to nearby Walpole Park. Sylvia declined, making outstanding housework her excuse. In truth she understood this was a very private time for the buddies.

Stork and Bernard eventually passed a Victorian lake and sat down by the side of a pond with an ornamental fountain. Despite the afternoon's warmth, there was a cool breeze stirring the surrounding trees. There were all sorts of species of waterfowl – diving, dipping, bathing, taking off. Stork could not have chosen a more idyllic place. The two Chindits sat for some time in silence, allowing the peace to wash over them. Bernard nodded off at one point. They could have been two old men. And in a sense they were. One was 25, the other 36, and yet they had gone through enough for a whole lifetime.

Without having to say it, they both knew why they were there. They glanced at each other, then looked away, glanced at each other again. It was just a question of who would make the first move.

'Ummh……..Ehh…..'

They both grunted simultaneously, then burst out laughing. Once they'd regained their composure, Stork quietly said:

'You go first, Bernard.'

It wasn't easy for him to get kick-started. He hadn't really talked about it since his spells in hospital in India. But in Stork's company he soon settled into it. He talked about his refusal to tell Kobayashi any more, his resultant incarceration in the pit to dehydrate him, where he was to die of thirst if he didn't talk, his sudden release at the hands of the compassionate Katashi, the attack of malaria, his fortuitous collapse in the lap of Maya who nursed him back to health, the warmth and kindness of all the Burmese villagers, the help he got from Indi and Chai in particular to get close to the Chindwin, and finally the escort of the magnificent Sikh Light Infantry back to India and freedom.

Stork had listened intently for almost an hour, only asking an occasional question for clarification. Then he spoke:

'God must have willed it that you live, Bernard, for all those people to come to your aid.'

'I can't say, Stork. I've never really believed in God. I went to church as a child, but it was more out of duty or fear of what would happen to me if I didn't.'

'Bernard, there has to be a reason for this. God has something planned for you. You just haven't discovered it yet.'

'How do you keep your faith, Stork? After all that they did to us, how do you forgive the Japanese?'

'I don't.'

'You don't?'

'How can you forgive people who tie prisoners to trees and bayonet them just for their own pleasure? Animals kill with more mercy, and for better reasons, than that.'

'Then, how do you square your non-forgiveness with God?'

'I ask God to forgive them. And then I ask him to forgive me.'

Before Bernard invited Stork to take his turn, there was something he had always wanted to ask him:

'Stork, back in the Army you were always Tiny Taylor or Stork. And I don't know if I should be calling you Stork now you've put the weight back on. I've never known your first name.'

Stork gave Bernard an uncomfortable look:

'Leonard, my name's Leonard. Well, actually it's Leonardo.'

Bernard managed to keep his face straight for some time during the ensuing silence, which was finally broken by Stork creasing up, his hand over his mouth. This released the tension in Bernard, who could hardly contain himself. Then they both let rip with laughter. When they had no strength left to laugh on, Stork explained:

'My father was an admirer of the great man, reckoned he was a polymath, whatever that means.'

'I see,' said Bernard, then started giggling again.

Stork decided to get on with it:

'After the Japs took Shankar, Stinker and myself away from you, we ended up on repair work on the northern railway. It was crazy really. Our boys had blown up parts of it, now we had to put it together again. Stinker was convinced we'd be shot once we'd finished.'

'Obviously you weren't, at least not in your case.'

'No. The three of us survived to be given the dubious pleasure of moving on to the Thailand-Burma Railway.'

'Not the Death Railway?'

'The same.'

'How did you survive that one?'

'To some extent it wasn't so bad for us. When we got there, it was in its ninth month of construction, and of course it was completed four months later. Some of the original workers were in a terrible state, many others had died already. The survivors were all skin and bone. I used to wonder how they could stand on their spindly legs, far less wield a pick-axe or a shovel.'

'What were the Japanese guards like?'

'They were a mixture, to be honest. Some were decent, others were brutal. The Koreans were worse. They were treated as inferiors by the Japanese but used as assistant guards. Sometimes they would beat a man senseless for simply working slower than the man next to him.'

'It must have been awful.'

'There was a Kiwi with us, Willy Tanaka. He was strong as an ox. He didn't salute this Jap officer one morning. The officer struck him in the face. So Willy punched him so hard, he fell back flat, unconscious. Then five of them beat and kicked poor Willy to death, right there in front of us.'

Stork had to stop. He pulled a handkerchief out of his pocket and dabbed his eyes. Bernard didn't speak. Stork took a while to recover and resume:

'The wild life around us didn't help either. Vultures who sat an eternity on the tree branches, prepared to wait for the next man to die. And there were monkeys, infernal monkeys, who screamed the whole twenty-four hours. It wasn't so bad in the daytime when we were working, we didn't notice them so much, but at night it disturbed what little sleep we got.'

'What was the work like?'

'It was back-breaking. The rails and sleepers were brought in by train. The sleepers were made of teak, very dense and heavy. It took two men, one on each end to carry one. Each rail required a number of men. The worst thing, though, was breaking up rock, sometimes sheer rock faces, with only pick-axes. The Japanese had no modern machinery to do the job quickly and efficiently. I don't know how they expected us to find the energy when they would only give us half the quantity of rice they enjoyed. I witnessed men die of sheer exhaustion.'

'Recent figures published in the newspapers claim that as many as one in four men died.'

'It wouldn't surprise me, Bernard. They should have added on the living casualties, the men who'll never be the same again, likely to be even more.'

'Were there other reasons for the high casualty rate?'

'Oh yes. Some men died from scorpion bites, from dysentery, from malaria, from beriberi. That last one nearly killed me.'

'Really?'

'Had it not been for the fact we had a wonderful MO. Tubby Andrews was a magician, considering what little medicine he had to work with. Beriberi is caused by a lack of certain vitamins. Tubby extracted them from the husks on rice which were normally thrown away by the Japs. It saved my life.'

'My God, it's a wonder you didn't die a hundred deaths, Stork.'

'I think the worst thing of all was the cholera. It was devastating. You could be chatting with a man in a bed next to you, and he was dead two days later. Sometimes, if it struck your own barracks of two hundred men, five or six men could die in the one day. And what was awful was that they had to be burned in an open pit. I was lucky. I wasn't selected to carry the bodies to the pyre. Nor did I ever watch the fires, I couldn't.'

Bernard could see how hard the memories were for Stork, so he got him off the subject of the Death Railway.

'What about Stinker and Shankar, Stork?'

'They weren't in my barracks during the construction, but I caught up with them later during maintenance.'

'Maintenance?'

'Yes, that wasn't so bad, maintenance of the railway line near Bangkok. It was closer to a normal day's work. We even had time for entertainment.'

'Entertainment? How on earth did you manage that?'

'The Japs allowed us to build open-air theatres of bamboo poles with palm fronds sort of interlocked to form a roof. It was amazing how much rainwater it could keep out.'

'What shows did you put on?'

'Sometimes plays, the odd musical, but pantomime was best. I played the dame.'

Bernard was beside himself again. Stork pulled a serious face:

'I'll have you know I was a very good dame. I got the most laughs. First off, I was just the right height for a dame, then there was my coolie hat, and of course the two half coconuts on my chest. The audience, and that included the Japs, were laughing even before I delivered my lines.'

Now someone else was laughing, uncontrollably so.

Time was getting on, so they decided to go back and see Sylvia who by Stork's reckoning would be preparing tea for them. On the way, Stork filled in the time between the period of pantomimes and the end of the War.

'Stinker, Shankar and myself thought it would never end, and then suddenly, like magic, the Japanese were gone. The atomic bombs had been dropped and Japan had surrendered. In no time we were shaking hands with American soldiers. The three of us ended up on the town in Bangkok. That's where I met Sylvia.'

'What happened to Stinker and Shankar?'

'I have a photograph of Shankar at home. He has a small-holding in the foothills of Nepal which he farms. He has a young wife and two children. Stinker is married and lives in Australia.'

'Just what Stinker needs, Stork. A wife to comb his hair and make sure he washes every day.'

The two Chindits were laughing once more.

After tea Stork walked Bernard to the railway station. On the platform, they had twenty minutes to kill.

'Can I ask you just one more thing, Stork?'

'Surely.'

'What about the atom bombs?'

'What about them, Bernard?'

'Well, what does your faith have to say about them?'

For once Stork was stumped. He was silent. Bernard was surprised.

'Bernard?' Stork asked, as the train drew into the station.

'Yes?'

'What I told you about my real name being Leonard or Leonardo. Just call me Stork, okay?'

Bernard smiled and nodded:

CHAPTER 10

A hint of disclosure

By 2008 JOHN Gray had retired from community education, or rather community learning, yet another new name for the youth and community service he had joined as a youngster. It amused him that, typical of that non-essential sector of local government, he had to go to the pensions' department and organise his own retirement. His bosses had told him he couldn't retire. Pensions told him he could have retired a lot earlier.

He finished at a time when unitary local government had created an all-embracing community services sector where all sorts of strange people from different backgrounds were falling over each other to pose as the one true expert in his field and trying to tell him what his job was all about. It was called the *multi-disciplinary approach* which sounded wonderful, the only trouble being that nobody had taken the trouble to research how it was actually going to work.

His most entertaining scenario was a bi-monthly meeting of at least twelve people comprising a representative of police, one from libraries, one from social work, one from locality management, whatever that meant, one from housing, one from welfare, one from community learning, so on and so forth. The company would sit down, take out their papers, and begin:

'Who's in the Chair?'

'I think it was Jim last time. He's on holiday just now.'

'What about Cathy?'

'Oh dear, well, okay I'll do it.'

Cathy moves to the top of the table and asks for a scribe.

'Oh for goodness sake, just do it yourself, Cathy.'

'Right then. Does everyone have a copy of the minutes of the last meeting?'

'I don't.' 'Neither do I.'

'Who took the minutes?'

'Bill, but he's not here.'

'Well, we'll just have to share one copy between two. Would anyone care to move them? Thank you. A seconder? Thank you. So moved'

Cathy continued:

'In the absence of last time's Chairman and Secretary, we don't seem to have an agenda.'

The locality manager intervened:

'We were talking about the number of disaffected young people between sixteen and twenty-five who went through our hands in the last year. The Scottish Office needs those figures urgently.'

John Gray looked at his watch. Twenty minutes gone already. He looked around the table. Not one of them had a clue how to conduct a meeting, far less had they any knowledge of how to do group work. Three decades ago, he could have done the job standing on his head. He could perhaps have spoken up when they raised the issue of number-crunching, if only to remind them they were talking about individual young people, all unique, each one requiring time to be understood, to develop trust for the professional, to learn, to gain knowledge and confidence.

What was the point? They wouldn't understand and anyway, they weren't going to listen to him, far less let him lead. He was yesterday's man. He was swimming against the tide. His best days were over. It was time to move on.

Nevertheless, his retirement went well. His colleagues of many years had brought a thoughtful touch to it by hosting it in Roundhill, where he had enjoyed success as a new professional in the seventies running his own youth centre. The presents and tributes were very fine, and he returned the compliment by reading his poetry to them. He chose poetry relevant to the work they had done together and some which took a satirical dig at the present day service. It made them laugh, which was what he wanted. Any disappointments he had sustained in his career were washed away. He had never lost his Glaswegian humour.

What he liked best was the fact that his wife and three sons were there. He was also pleased to see David Samson. And David had brought along the most important guest of all, Tom Williams. At the finish Gray went up to his old mentor:

'Thanks for coming, Tom.'

'Don't be silly, boy. I wouldn't have missed it. I liked the poetry best.'

Gray smiled to himself. Williams was going to call him 'boy' forever.

John spent the year after his retirement doing virtually nothing, apart from building a new garden shed and writing no more than five new poems. When he began to feel time heavy on his hands, he decided to go through fifty or so of his old poems and try to make them better. In 2010, having promised himself at retirement he would never join another organisation's committee in the rest of his lifetime, he found himself Vice-Chairman of not one but two. They were Colliershire Book Association and a campaign to raise a memorial to the victims of a railway disaster which had taken place in Scotland in the middle of the 20th century. Nobody knew why a memorial had never been raised before. Suffice to say it was an oversight badly needing to be corrected.

Like most committees, the members were a mixture of those totally committed to the task, those who were committed but didn't really have the time due to other concerns, and those who were doing nothing. After a time it became clear to Gray that he was, to all extents and purposes, leading both groups, but he wasn't sure of how to proceed. The group work experiences were different to those he had encountered in his career, where voluntary adults and young people looked to him for guidance. He was now just one of a number of older people now retired from their careers. He decided to pay Tom Williams a visit.

'Hello, boy, nice to see you. How are you enjoying the pensioner's life?'

'It's fine, Tom. Surprisingly enough, I have plenty to do.'

On his recent visits, Gray had noticed that Williams was changing. The spring in his step had gone, he'd put in a stair-lift some time ago and he needed a motorised scooter to get around Crack Willow town centre. And when they said their good-byes, the old man only came to the door, not to the road at the end of the garden as before. He was, after all, 88 years old. However, when it came to his reasoning, the shaman was as sharp as ever. Having listened to Gray intently, he gave his judgement:

'Well John, it seems to me you have a decision to make. Having two major projects like that is one too many at your age. You should choose between them.'

'And how do I do that, Tom?'

'Weigh them up in your mind and decide which of them is doable. Which of them is the more likely to succeed?'

Gray didn't like it, but he had that old gut feeling that Williams was right. Hadn't he always been?

A week later he had made up his mind. He resigned from the Book Fair Association to concentrate on the railway campaign. It was a decision he did not regret. He was able to give it his whole concentration, and the committee whittled itself down to a hard core of six dedicated members.

Gray was in his element. For the first time in almost twenty years he was doing quality group work again, a job which was more in keeping with the skills he had learned and become good at as a young man. It was just a pity it had come at such a late stage in his life, and after his retirement.

Williams was philosophical about it:

'It's the way of things sometimes, John. Life is nothing if not ironic. And anyway, it's never too late to do something special.'

Before that year was out, John Gray received the strangest letter of his life. It was from Tom Williams. In it he talked about a war memorial in Kohima on the border between India and Burma. Enclosed was a map of the western half of Burma. He was inviting Gray to read up on it and write some poetry. Gray wondered if at long last the shaman was feeling he should talk about his army experiences in World War Two. Perhaps he was feeling his great age, perhaps that he had little time left to live. The younger man made a special visit.

'Tom, about your letter?'

'Did you find it inspirational, for your poetry that is?'

'That's the thing, Tom. I was never a soldier. It doesn't really work for poets, or at least not for those who are worthy of the name, to write about something they know nothing about, something they haven't lived in themselves.'

'Ah, I see. Fair enough.'

But Gray could see the disappointment in the old man's face:

'Tell you what, Tom. You can tell me what you feel you want to tell me, then we'll do something together.'

Williams nodded, but there was a reticent look in his face, as if Gray had misunderstood. He had been thinking of fallen comrades, not himself. He diverted:

'Perhaps later, John. Tell you what, why don't you tell me about your early days, before you came to join me at Crack Willow?'

'If you mean the debacle in the west of Colliershire, I'd rather not harp back at that, Tom.'

'No no, I fully understand, but tell me about your voluntary work in the Mission Society in the east end of Glasgow. You once said it was a lot of fun. You were happy there.'

'Oh dear, we're going back more than forty years. Well, you've asked for it, Tom.'

Gray painted a picture of the old church which was known in the local vernacular as *Pisa*. It had been abandoned for its traditional use due to subsidence, and looking about to fall over anytime, was only good enough for a rough and tumble boys' club.

'Who were the boys, John?'

'A mixture of catholics and protestants between the ages of twelve and seventeen. They called each other *proddies* and *carbolics*. That was the amazing thing. Unlike some of their parents, the two different sects got on well together. They ribbed each other rotten of course, but they got on. There was never any violence, just loads of volatility.'

'That's the innocence of youth, John. What did they get up to?'

'Football, always football, in the downstairs hall. It was twenty-five a side.'

Williams laughed:

'That's almost impossible.'

'Even more impossible was the ball they played with. I swear it was the same one every time I did my voluntary stint on a Wednesday evening. It had burst months before but still did the job.'

'It's a wonder they didn't knock each other out.'

'Glad you mentioned that. The old pews had been removed yonks ago, but the end pillars had been left in. I suspect because they helped support the ceiling. So not only had the lad on the ball to twist and turn to fool an opponent, he had to watch he didn't knock himself out for being too clever.'

This was almost too much for Williams. He had his hand-kerchief out to stem a tear.

'Anything......?'

He could hardly get the words out. He coughed to clear his throat:

'Anything other than football?'

'Oh yes, table tennis upstairs. There were four tables and eight bats, half of which had broken handles. And a number of ping pong balls, some of which had dents in them.'

'It must have been difficult for them to play.'

'Not half. And bear in mind this was the *Pisa Palace*. As they played, the tables drifted southwards, so to speak, until half of the players were pinned against the wall. So half way through each game, the tables were lifted and put back at the top of the slope.'

Williams was back in his handkerchief:

'I don't think I can take any more, John.'

Undaunted, Gray continued:

'They had a great time. But by ten to ten the volunteers were knackered. Then we had to get the boys to go home.'

'GET them to go home?'

'Well most of them toddled off okay. But some didn't want to go home. We used to puzzle over what sort of homes were waiting for them.'

'What did you do?'

'Two of us would grab one lad, throw him out, then lock the door. Then we would repeat the process until the last one was out. The boys treated it like a game, they enjoyed making it as difficult for us as they possibly could.'

'Surely there was more than football and table tennis.'

'Oh yes, twice in the summer holiday from school we ran camps in Perthshire. They were a laugh. I got the job of taking the catholic boys to chapel on a Sunday morning. Like, 8 o'clock on a Sunday morning! The first time, I got the shock of my life. Our leader, the young minister, poked his head round the tent flap and said: *Gonnae take the carbolics tae pineapple?*'

Gray could see the puzzled expression on Williams' face:

'Catholics to chapel, Tom. Get it? He was a very unorthodox young minister.'

Williams had to pull out his handkerchief once more. Gray resumed:

'This tiny chapel was eight miles away. I took six boys there in the mini-bus. The mass was starting as we went in. Seated were four nuns and a local farm labourer. He had an upturned cap on his knee. It functioned as a collection plate.

The nuns were delighted. The boys and I had more than doubled the congregation.'

Williams face began to run with tears:

'I really don't think I can take much more, John.'

'I'm almost finished, Tom. The priest arrived, then left again for a couple of minutes. When he returned, it was clear he'd forgotten some of his vestments. I was sure he was hungover from the night before.'

'Oh stop, John, stop!'

'Almost there, Tom. The singing was terrible, especially the nuns. They sounded like violins out of tune. The whole thing was so confusing I ended up taking communion along with the boys. I'd never been a catholic in my entire life.'

Gray was done. Williams dried his eyes:

'That was marvellous, John. I haven't enjoyed myself so much in ages. It doesn't half make a change from us talking about poetry and classical music. Oh my!'

'Okay, Tom, I've done my bit. Now it's your turn.'

'What do you mean, boy?'

'We were going to work on those experiences of yours. Have they got anything to do with India or Burma?'

'Oh, all that jazz?. That's a long story, if ever there was one. I don't think......'

'Come on, Tom.'

'No John, no. Really, it's been great, but I'm tired. The old man is in need of his beauty sleep.'

Gray felt guilty:

'Of course, Tom. I wasn't thinking. Got carried away I expect. I'll see you soon.'

Gray made off, and as it had become Williams' custom in recent years, the shaman said good-bye to him by placing his palms together, fingers upwards, against his forehead.

Gray was no fool. He knew, if Williams was ever going to talk about it, he would do it in his own good time, and even then, it might be too late. And the younger man had been raised by a father who had also known the atrocities of war. Gray well remembered the long silences and dark brows he witnessed as a child. The veterans normally spoke about it only to their former comrades in battle.

CHAPTER 11

Bottle, Bedlam and Belief

As STORK PUSHED the door of the music shop open, the bell attached to the door-spring rang and resounded.

'I'm sorry, Mr Walters. I know you're busy just now, but I'm worried about Bernard. We usually get together today, the first Saturday of every month. You always give him that day off.'

'You'll have been to his house then?'

'Yes, but I can't raise him. At first I thought he'd gone to the corner shop for bread or milk. But I must have waited almost an hour. No sign of him.'

Stork detected that Mr Walters knew something.

'Wait just there, lad, while I serve this customer.'

When the customer left, Mr Walters closed the door, put up a sign saying *back in ten minutes*, and pulled down the roller blind:

'I don't rightly know how to say this, lad. You're his best pal, eh?'

'What's happened to him?'

Stork was imagining the worst.

'He was doing his best an' all. He'd been dry of the bottle for a whole week.'

Stork was now grinding his teeth, wishing Mr Walters would get to the point.

'His sister found him when she went in to do her weekly cleaning. There he was, lying on the floor. He'd collapsed.'

'Well, if he hadn't been drinking…..?'

'Exactly. But apparently, he was shaking all over. Cynthia called an ambulance. They took him to the General Hospital.'

Stork took out a diary and pencil:

'Do you know what ward he's in, Mr Walters?'

'That's just it, lad. It's a few days since it happened. They've transferred him now.'

'Transferred him?'

'Like I say, lad, there ain't no easy way to say this.'

Mr Walters bowed his head:

'Bernie's in the loony bin.'

'Surely you don't mean Bethlem, Mr Walters?'

'Ay, that's right, lad. Bedlam, God help him.'

The decade of the 1950s had started with a fresh feel in the air. There was a massive re-building programme on the go in London, the destruction caused by German bombing having been largely cleared by demolition and disposal. A new National Health Service was in place, removing worries about costs for working class families. British Rail had taken over the country's complex railway network. There were many changes, giving rise to a feeling of new beginnings, a better standard of living, and hopes for a better future for the Nation's children.

In that respect Bernard was like everyone else. He welcomed the changes, thinking in his liberal mind they would create a fairer society, one unlikely to see yet another World War. He had made new friends and neighbours. He had rediscovered an old friend who was more than a friend. Stork had become his confidante and mentor, had even managed to convince Bernard he should at least attempt to regulate his drinking. On the morning of his collapse he knew nothing about it. It started with tremors in his arms. He dismissed it.

Oh oh, it's the old malaria again, he thought.

Then he couldn't feel his legs. The room seemed to spin and move in on him in ever decreasing circles. His heart was racing to what seemed an impossible rate. And then came oblivion.

Having trained as a volunteer nurse during the War, Cynthia did what she could to make him comfortable from what little she could remember. She went with him in the ambulance and followed him to Bethlem Hospital a few days later.

Having left Mr Walters, Stork phoned Sylvia from the corner telephone box, brought her up to speed on Bernard, and told her he'd decided to go first to Cynthia's at Croydon, then on to Beckenham and the Bethlem.

Mr Walters had called it Bedlam, as did the majority of English people. And depending on how local people viewed institutions for the mentally ill, they regarded Bethlem as either an invaluable asset to the advance of medicine or a place of horror to be given a wide berth. Bethlem had been on the go for many centuries, if only to change sites several times until its present one at Beckenham. It had gained an international reputation for excellence in mental health care, but try telling that to local residents. Sadly, medieval attitudes to such illnesses were still alive and kicking in 1950s' England. To many, the patients were inmates and the hospital a madhouse.

Stork was at Cynthia's within the hour. She looked haggard:

'I'm so glad you've come, Stork. I'm at my wits end.'

'Have they told you anything?'

'Oh, you know what doctors are like. Well, psychiatrists are much worse. They gave me a load of mumbo-jumbo. about trauma, alcohol dependency, even his early upbringing. What a thing to ask me about? He and I had a happy childhood.'

'Don't upset yourself, Cynthia, you'll make yourself unwell. And that's not what we need right now.'

Cynthia went off to the kitchen and made them both a pot of tea. She talked as she waited for the tea to infuse:

'The visiting hour in the afternoon is three o'clock. But you won't be able to talk with him, I'm afraid. He's been heavily sedated since he arrived. He's in what they call narcosis.'

'That's okay. I just want to see him.'

After tea, Stork caught a train to Beckenham. Despite its much rumoured reputation, he was impressed by the aspect of the Bethlem building and the very fine and substantial grounds. Only when he had been permitted through reception and was half way to Bernard's ward did he realise what sort of a hospital he was in. The sounds of troubled people could be heard echoing around the corridors. He was met by the ward nurse:

'Are you a relative?'

'No, but we served together in the British Army in Burma. We're close friends.'

'I'm afraid he won't be able to speak to you, he's not at all well.'

'I'll just sit beside him a while, thank you.'

In total silence Stork looked at the almost motionless Bernard for some considerable time. He was flat on his back, eyes closed, and the only thing moving was his chest, up and down in a steady metronomic rhythm. But Stork had an ulterior motive for coming. He knew it wasn't just the alcohol had put his friend there. Eventually he turned to the duty nurse:

'Nurse, could I speak to his doctor?'

'Well, it's not normal for a non-family member. Is it important?'

'Very.'

It seemed an eternity before the young Doctor Crawford arrived and introduced himself.

'Sorry to keep you waiting. What can I do for you?'

'I realise it wouldn't be ethical for you to tell me about Bernard's condition, Doctor, but there is something you should know, something he wouldn't have been able to tell you, and I'm quite certain he wouldn't have told his sister.'

'She did talk about his interrogation by the Japanese, if that's what you're driving at.'

'Yes, but he won't have told her the full horror of it. I was there when it happened.'

'I see. Well, let's sit down and talk. He won't hear us. '

For the next ten minutes Stork went over the beatings, the water torture and what he had gleaned from Bernard about 'the hole'. He also talked about the terrible things Bernard had witnessed and his ordeal through malaria on the escape to India.

Doctor Crawford listened throughout, then said:

'Thank you so much. I'm sorry, your name?'

'Taylor.'

'Well, Mr Taylor, this puts a whole new light on things, and certainly, although I shouldn't really mention this, it squares with some of the things he's been saying in his sleep. I'll speak to my senior about it, and I do thank you, you've been most helpful. And don't worry, your confidence is safe with us.'

Crawford and his senior convened and decided to review Bernard's case:

The senior, Doctor Salt, began:

'Our difficulty is the complexity created by three different illnesses – the soldier's heart, the malaria and the alcoholism.'

Doctor Crawford was puzzled.

'Soldier's heart?'

'Oh of course, you'll be too young to know that one, Doctor Crawford. In the First World War it was called shell shock. That was because most of the trauma in soldiers was caused by the non-stop shelling of the trenches. We now know that the trauma can be due to all sorts of war experiences. Even the term soldier's heart is dated now. Just shows up my age, I expect. Let's just call it war trauma.'

Doctor Crawford thought for a moment:

'Dr. Salt, I'd like to gradually reduce the doses we're giving Mr Markham until he comes round, then if he looks like he'll make it, try counselling and milder drugs. As for the malaria, I don't think it's a relevant factor in this case.'

'That's a bit risky, he could relapse. However, in the light of what you were told by his friend, you're obviously committed to this patient. Go ahead Doctor Crawford and good luck.'

As Crawford reduced the high intensity of the drugs, Bernard became more agitated. The young doctor bit down hard and persevered, even when the night nurse's notes revealed an increase in ramblings due to nightmares. And exactly three weeks after his admission Bernard Markham woke up to the land of the living. It took him the best part of a day to orientate himself. The nurse kept checking on him every half hour until she could get some sense out of him:

'Where am I, nurse?'

'You're in Bethlem Hospital, Mr Markham.'

'Oh God no, not Bedlam!'

Bernard started to become agitated again.

'Now now, Mr Markham, that's just a rhyming slang coined by insensitive people who have no idea of the good work that goes on here. Just calm down, you're in the best possible hands.'

After a while the young nurse could see he was still jittery, so she brought him a pile of newspapers. He read for a few minutes then called her over again:

'Nurse, these papers are dated the twentieth and twenty-first. This is the first of the month.'

The nurse explained he'd been in a bad state when he arrived. So he'd been heavily sedated and had remained under for three weeks:

'But that's over now, Mr Markham, you're with us again. You can concentrate on getting better.'

'Well I don't feel right at all.'

'You'll feel much better once your strength is built up. In an hour and a half you'll get your first proper meal for some time. Meanwhile there's a mug of sweet tea on its way.'

Over the next week Bernard had plenty of time to reflect that this was the strangest place he'd ever known. He couldn't get a word out of his nearest fellow patients who seemed to wander around in a daze with nowhere to go. The reality hit home when he realised he was doing the exact same thing. And the only contact he seemed to have with staff was the regular checking of his vital signs, the administration of his drugs, and the bedside delivery of his meals. He longed for the visits of Cynthia and Stork, his sister every other day, and Stork twice a week, in the evening midweek and on Sunday.

Cynthia was convinced about the reason for Bernard's collapse:

'I can't say as I'm surprised. If I told you once, I told you a hundred times. Even your GP told you about the danger of liver damage if you kept at the bottle so hard.'

'Cynthia, for goodness' sake, give it a rest.'

'I'll give it a rest when you see sense. I don't know what your father would have said.'

Bernard enjoyed Stork's visits better. The big man didn't lecture him. And to Bernard, those moments were sacrosanct, a man kind of thing. On one Sunday visit Bernard was ready with a question:

'Stork, you never mentioned whether you were still with the Quakers or not, the people you used to call The Society of Friends.'

'Very much so, since you ask. We have a weekly branch meeting in a local community hall, and we send a delegation to the yearly meeting of the London Regional Group.'

'Not in a church, then?'

'No. We don't have a minister, or a priest or rabbi. No pastor at all.'

'So, how does it work?'

'Quakers don't believe in institutionalised religion. We believe in the right of the individual to commune directly with God through his son Jesus.'

'But don't you still have to worship together?'

'Not necessarily. Our branch meetings are not programmed, but if one of us feels strongly about something or is undergoing a personal crisis, he or she may ask for help in the way of a prayer or hymn. If so, all of us will join in.'

'Don't you get criticised by other worshippers, like those in The Church of England?'

'Oh yes, but we have an argument which stands up very well in the face of it.

Quakers believe that a religion where worship is the all important element is a dead religion. The Friends go out into the community and, without preaching, do what they can to help people in need.'

'That's fascinating, Stork. I had no idea. But it all makes sense now.'

'What do you mean, Bernard?'

'The way you handled yourself in the Burma campaign, supporting Sergeant McKinlay, and all of us really. You kept a cool head through all our troubles, praying to God on our behalf, but never preaching to us. You were a rock.'

'Well thank you, Private Markham.'

As Bernard began to feel a bit better, he was desperate to get out of Bethlem. The days dragged and the nights were restless. Troubled patients wakened him at all hours of the morning, and when he did sleep, Burma came back with a vengeance and he would sit bolt upright for up to an hour before sleep's veils returned. In his last weeks he was thought to be making such good progress, he was allowed to walk in the grounds, provided somebody was with him. On a fine Thursday evening, Doctor Crawford stopped by his bed:

'No Stork tonight, Bernard?'

'I think he's on a night out with his wife. Shame really, last week we enjoyed a walk down to the pond to feed the ducks.'

'Tell you what, Bernard. I'm off duty shortly. I'll go down with you.'

Doctor Crawford and his patient were soon seated together by the pond:

'Seriously, Doctor, when do you think I'll get out?'

'Oh, I think we should see the back of you by this time next week, Mr Markham.'

'That's great, Doctor. I am grateful for everything you've done.'

'No trouble, Bernard, all part of the service. But the main challenge for you will be making sure you don't come back.'

'How can I be sure of that, Doc?'

'Well, if you continue as before, we'll definitely be seeing you again.'

'I suppose you're hinting at the alcohol.'

'Spot on, Bernard. It makes you think it's suppressing the nightmares, but the benefit is only immediate. The nightmares just come back later, only this time they're worse.'

'You reckon I should quit altogether?'

'At least get it down to a weekly limit, or if you want to stop entirely, you could join Alcoholics Anonymous. They started in America before the War, and now they're starting up branches in this country. We have their number.'

'But even if I collar the drink, Doc, what can I do about the nightmares?'

'I'm afraid I can't help you with that, Bernard. They're based on what you went through against the Japanese. They're deeply personal, so you'll have to find your own way of dealing with them in the future. I'm sorry.'

The two men were distracted by the sound of laughter coming from patients on the other side of the pond. It surprised Bernard. The only laughter he'd heard from patients during his stay had been caused by hysteria:

'Who are they, Doc?'

'They come here from the General, due to shortage of beds there. They're the terminals.'

'Terminals?'

'Yes, their conditions are incurable. They've only got weeks left, in some cases days.'

When the time came to pack his case, and Cynthia arrived in a taxi to take him home, Bernard thanked Crawford and all the nurses who had helped him in the previous three months. He was still a frail man and had been told by Crawford it could be the best part of another year before he was fully fit. He was given a small bottle of pills and told that a letter had been sent to his GP advising a course of continued medication for the foreseeable future. Crawford called out to Bernard as he climbed into the taxi:

'Remember now, old fellow. Go easy on it'

He put his hand to his mouth and made the sign of some-one drinking from a glass.

Bernard gave Crawford a thumbs-up:

'You bet your life, Doc.'

In the weeks that followed, the initial joy at release from Bethlem was replaced by a feeling of isolation. There were a number of people looking out for Bernard, but he was missing the one major influence in his life. Stork had been working for a year now with The Ministry of Defence, and to some extent Bernard put that down as an excuse for why the alcohol had got the better of him. Contact between the two veteran Chindits had been markedly reduced, and now that Bernard was in the crucial post-hospital recuperation phase, he was missing Stork even more. While in hospital, Stork had made a special effort on his behalf. But Sylvia was now expecting a first baby, so between work and a growing family, Stork could only manage to visit Bernard once a month.

Occasionally Bernard gave in to the bottle, with just one image to stop him from taking too much and pull him back from the brink. The sight and sounds of the terminal patients at the duck pond seemed to have a sobering effect on him. When they did, he would think to himself:

I'm never going to feel sorry for myself again.

On Stork's next visit, Bernard had made a special effort. The house was clean, with no empty wine bottles, and this time Cynthia hadn't been within miles of the place. Buoyed up by the improvement in Bernard's condition, Stork had a suggestion:

'Bernard, why don't you come along to one of our Quaker meetings?'

'I don't know, Stork. I've rather gone off religion in these last years.'

'But I've told you before, the meetings are not like that. They're rooted in mutual need and friendship. Two chaps have alcohol problems just like yourself.'

Bernard relented and the following Sunday was with Stork at the community hall in Ealing. Although surprised, Bernard discovered Stork had been true to his word. There were no hymns or prayers at all that afternoon. More importantly, he was introduced to Ralph and Eddy. Ralph was the first to raise the subject of alcohol addiction.

'How long have you been an alcoholic, Bernard?'

'I don't think of myself as an alcoholic, really. My GP does. I suppose I've been drinking steady for three years now.'

It was Eddy's turn:

'I joined the AA three weeks ago.'

'How did you get on?' Bernard was interested now.

'It was hard at first, embarrassing. I had to stand in front of the whole group, say my name and admit I was an alcoholic.'

'That's awful.'

'At the time, yes it was. But when it was done, I felt a sense of relief. I'd got it off my chest.'

Bernard continued his visits to the Ealing branch of the Quakers. And the fact that there was an occasional communal prayer or hymn did not deter him. He was fascinated by what the members got up to in what they called their community service. Two of the women, Miriam and Betty, visited very elderly people who lived alone and were no longer able to get about. They helped with cleaning and doing messages for them. At Christmas time they organised hampers filled with a mixture of essential foods and seasonal goodies. This was a world apart from his childhood experiences of Christianity, when he never saw the church congregation from one Sunday morning service to the next. And it suited his unorthodox and independent thinking perfectly. In his heyday Ralph had been a good footballer. Bernard asked him about it:

'Oh, that was a long time ago. However, I do a favour for the local minister. I take his boys for football once a week.'

'His boys?'

'Not his own boys. He runs a boys' club for youngsters who lost their dads in the War.'

'Is it only for boys like that?'

'No, of course not. But that's why it was started. There's been a movement across the whole country to do this. The powers that be feel the boys are missing out on guidance and that some of them are turning to crime.'

'That sounds a very worthwhile thing to do, Ralph.'

'Why don't you come along, Bernard? We need more volunteers. The lads can be a handful and they don't all play football. We need people with other ideas.'

Bernard felt this was more up his street. It was something practical for him to do. And a month later Ralph introduced him to the volunteers and lads of the boys' club. Bernard enjoyed his first time, and spent it on light duties, serving tea and soft drinks while getting to know the boys. They were very forward and wanted to know all about him. They were hyper the entire time.

'Ralph, the two in the corner, they don't say much.'

'That's right, Bernard. The terrible two are brothers Frankie and Paul. They sometimes play football, but a lot of the time they just sit in the corner and read their comics.'

'Do they never talk to the leaders?'

'We don't know how to handle them. Sometimes they lash out at other boys. They're on probation just now. '

'What did they do?'

'Stealing from shops, I believe.'

On his second visit Bernard made a point of engaging with Frankie and Paul. And he got his nose bitten off.

Frankie nudged his younger sibling:

'I wouldn't go near him if I were you, Paul. He's a homo.'

'Is he then? Yuch!'

'Yeah, just look at the bow tie he's wearin' and listen to his posh talk.'

Bernard made a tactful withdrawal. And whether or not that had something to do with it, nobody knew, but Ralph informed Stork at a Quaker's weekly meeting that Bernard had stopped coming to the boys' club. When he hadn't appeared at either the meetings or the club for a while, Stork made a visit to Hampstead. Bernard was reclining on his couch, surrounded by empty bottles. He looked as if he had neither changed nor washed and shaved for a week. Stork began with a sideways approach:

'How's work, Bernard?'

'Not much of it these days. Old Walters is winding down. His health's not good, so he wants to sell up.'

Stork could hear that his friend's words were slightly slurred. He decided to go for a more direct approach:

'Bernard, this has got to stop.'

'Oh, shut up, Stork. You're beginning to sound like Cynthia.'

'You know, Bernard, if I had a mind like yours, I'd consider myself a lucky man.'

Bernard was genuinely stunned:

'That's rubbish Stork. You're a very clever man.'

'I guess so, but you have a great intellect, Bernard. And I don't just mean your musical ability. The pity is you neither realise it nor use it to its full potential.'

Bernard switched to sarcasm:

'Oh sure, I'm a bloody genius, starting sun-up tomorrow.'

Stork persevered:

'Think, Bernard. Why did you survive what the Japanese did to you? Why did the Burmese villagers and the Sikh Infantry come along out of the blue to help you? Why was Doctor Crawford there at the right time to get you back on your feet after your breakdown?'

Bernard lapsed into a piece of pure Sergeant McKinlay:

'I'm fucked if I know.'

'Well, if you don't know, I do.'

'Oh, you always have the answers, Stork, don't you?'

'I know this much. God put you on this earth for a reason, Bernard. You just haven't discovered what it is yet. Find a passion to consume you, something that gets you away from your dependency on the bottle, something to stop the nightmares, something that makes a worthwhile contribution to people's lives.'

Stork was making a sincere and impassioned plea, and it was having an effect on his friend. Bernard started to cry:

'I can't, Stork. The bloody nightmares won't go away. I keep seeing Kobayashi's face and hearing him screaming at me.'

Stork decided to wind down:

'The boys at the club have noticed your absence, you know. You should go back.'

'What do I have to offer them? One of them called me a homo.'

'Let's go and see Mr Walters. If he's clearing up, he might be prepared to give us some old instruments, maybe a turntable record-player, at knockdown prices that wouldn't break the club bank account. Ralph has a Morris car. We could ask him to transport them.'

'It's no use, Stork. You've been a wonderful friend, but the drink is winning.'

As a last resort, Stork opted for a shock tactic:

'No it's not. It's you that's losing. However, if that's the way you feel, then I wash my hands of it. Good-bye, Bernard.'

Stork turned, walked out the door, and closed it behind him. And the whole way home, he prayed to God that he'd done the right thing.

After Stork's disdainful departure, Bernard was indeed shocked. He refused himself a nightcap and went straight to bed. But he didn't sleep until four in the morning, sitting upright with the covers around his shoulders, going over and over again what Stork had said to him. Two days later he went to see Mr Walters and they came to an arrangement. Then he phoned Stork:

'It's about those musical instruments and turntable record-player. I've done a deal with Mr Walters.'

'That's marvellous, Bernard. How much?'

'It's nothing, not for the club anyway. Walters is taking it out of my wages.'

'Are you sure, Bernard?'

'Sure. Ask Ralph if he could drive over next Sunday and pick them up. Then give me a time so I can make arrangements with Mr Walters.'

'Will do, Bernard. I'll be in touch.'

Stork was mightily relieved. And his relief was nothing to do with the money. He had taken a huge risk with the best friend he ever had.

At the next club session, there was an assortment of old instruments – two old acoustic guitars, a banjo, two triangles and not least, a saxophone, Bernard having picked up that Ralph had played at one time. There was an old piano in the community hall and Bernard had already okayed the club's use of it with committee.

The Chairman in fact had said:

'If you can get one right note out of that old banger, my lad, you're welcome to it.'

The boys who didn't care for football were fascinated by the collection, even more so by the turntable record-player which Mr Walters had thrown in for free. It was Bernard's intention to get a piano-tuner some time to fix the old bandbox properly. Meanwhile, he was able to get enough key notes to help get the stringed instruments into tune. Before the session was over, they had a semblance of a band. They made an absolute cacophony but it didn't matter. They were enjoying the new initiative in the programme. Apart from Paul:

'I'm no use at it. The music teacher who came to the school told me I didn't have an ear for music.'

'That's nonsense, Paul. Unless you're totally deaf, then you have an ear for music. Tell you what. Do you have a comb?'

Paul nodded but wondered where Bernard was going with this. Bernard then left the room, returning within a minute with a piece of toilet roll. Always the joker, Frankie saw his chance:

'You've forgotten to wipe your backside, Bernie.'

'Shut up, Frankie. Just watch.'

Bernard wound a piece round his comb and using his lips, made a humming noise into the improvised instrument. The boys, including Frankie, were both amused and amazed.

'Now Paul, here's another piece. Wind it round your own comb, make the same sound, and follow what we play.'

Paul struggled a bit, needed three attempts, but soon enough the band had another member.

As an alternative in the weeks to come, some members turned to the record-player. There were LPs borrowed from older siblings, a favourite one being *The Voice of Frank Sinatra*. Bernard wondered how to get Frankie involved. The lad always remained on the periphery of activities, and Bernard's musical prowess had done nothing to alter his summing up of his club leader's sexual orientation. He did however help out with moving things around or providing refreshments. What Bernard did notice were the bruises Frankie was regularly sporting when he attended the club. He asked Ralph about them.

'It's his dad, I'm afraid. He's a brute of a man. And there's nothing we can do about it.'

'What about the police?'

'Someone would have to make a complaint, Bernard. His mother gets knocked about, so she's scared. And neither Frankie nor Paul is going to shop their father.'

As the months went by, the band began to manage complete songs together, and it was decided to put a few together for a performance in the community hall at Christmas time.

Bernard, Ralph, and Stork, who was given the task of promoting the event, had to work hard with the boys over the advent period. And with only three weeks to go, Paul and Frankie suddenly disappeared. Stork, always the one with his ear to the ground, had the answer:

'They've been nicked, Bernard.'

'You mean by the police?'

'Yup. They've been stealing from a general store. It looks bad for them. They're still under a probation order.'

'What's going to happen?'

'They go before the juvenile court next week. And it's Judge Carter. He's no softie. We have to face it, they'll be going to an approved school this time.'

At the young minister's request, Stork, Ralph and Bernard debated which one of them should make himself available as a character witness.

Ralph had no doubts:

'I can't do it. I've had to suspend them from the club twice now. Nothing seems to work with those two. Maybe approved school is the answer.'

Stork was swithering:

'I don't really know the boys well enough, Bernard. I'd have to be less than truthful.'

Bernard could see where this was going. He made a special trip to the next street and rang on the doorbell of the Thomson household. Fortunately, the notorious Mr Thomson was out at the pub as usual. And Bernard was taken with Mrs Thomson. She seemed a nice person, only very timid. Like her older son, she sported the same tell-tale bruises. The house was in a terrible state. When Bernard asked if he could use the toilet, she told him it hadn't been working for ten days. The poor woman was worn out and in need of help. But she pepped up at Bernard's offer:

'Oh, I'm so grateful to you Mr Markham. They're good boys really. They just need a good man…..'

Realising what she was saying, she stopped herself.

'Don't worry, Mrs Thomson. I'll do my best for them.'

On the morning of the hearing at the juvenile court, the weather was foul. Snow had fallen deeply during the night and was now gusting to blizzard strength. The wireless was forecasting problems with public transport systems. With one hand tightly on the collar of his coat, the other on his hat for fear it might blow away any second, Bernard leaned into the wind and shuffled through the snow to the railway station. He had been standing on the platform for no time at all when a loudspeaker crackled into life and delivered the message he had hoped not to hear:

'The ten o'clock train to Charing Cross will be twenty minutes late.'

Bernard cursed himself for not leaving earlier. When he arrived at Charing Cross, he opted for a taxi. To have taken a bus would have meant he almost certainly would have missed the hearing.'

'Where to, me old cock?' the driver asked.

'The courtrooms, I'm due at the juvenile court. And I'm late, so please, quick as you like.'

'Gotcha mate. Hold on tight, now.'

The driver went like the clappers, all the time talking non-stop. For the second time that morning, it was something Bernard had not wanted to hear:

'If you ask me, they should never have banned the birch. It's the only thing these lads understand. Just look at the state we're in now. Old folks can't sleep safe in their beds, and when a policeman pulls one of the little sods up for bad behaviour, he gets a mouthful of cheek.'

Bernard did not respond.

Frankie and Paul were stood in front of Judge Carter as he began his summing-up. Immediately, he was interrupted by the bailiff:

'Pardon me, Your Honour, but Mr Markham is here now.'

'Is he now? Well, show him in.'

Carter was a stickler for punctuality:

'You're late, Mr Markham.'

'I do apologise, Your Honour, my train was late due to the weather.'

Bernard caught Mrs Thomson out of the corner of his eye. She was distraught but now relieved.

Carter continued:

'Well yes, I suppose. Mr Markham, it looks very much as if I have to impose a period of correction on these young men. Do you have anything to say that would change my mind? I understand you're a bit of a musician, a boys' club leader and served during the War as a private.'

Bernard detected a slight condescending tone in the judge's voice. But he had been up half the night practising what he was about to say:

'My name is Bernard Markham, Your Honour. I served as Private Markham under Orde Wingate in the 77th Indian Infantry Brigade in Burma in 1943. I was a Chindit.'

It was his last word that did it. The entire courtroom hushed so dramatically that the old wall clock could be clearly heard ticking, and loudly. For the rest of the hearing Judge Carter was no longer the main man in the courtroom. There was a war hero present. Frankie was in a state of shock. He could never have imagined Bernard to have been such a man. Mrs Thomson's cheeks changed from pale white to red. Suddenly there was hope.

In Bernard's post-war mind there was never any belief that he was famous. He felt that the Chindit campaign had been tragic in terms of the loss of so many comrades, and it had cost him personally in terms of his health. But now he had a good reason to proclaim it.

Judge Carter realised he'd better regain control:

'Thank you, Mr Markham, I'm sure we all appreciate the service you have given to your country. Now, what would you like to say on behalf of these young men?'

'If it please Your Honour, they have been working very hard in the club for months now. Paul is turning out to have a talent for music, and Frankie has been helping our Mr Taylor with local publicity for a Christmas concert. It would be a pity if they were sent to an approved school, because I have them down for community service to housebound elderly people during the Christmas period. As for the money they stole, I feel I could get them to repay the shopkeeper week by week over the next three months.'

'Thank you, Mr Markham.'

Judge Carter turned to the shopkeeper:

'How do you feel about that, Mr Wilson?'

'That would be very acceptable, Your Honour.'

'Very well then. Frankie and Paul Thomson, your probation officer will check out your repayments to Mr Wilson. But if you come before me again, you will definitely go to a residential place of correction. Do you understand me?'

'Yes, Your Honour.'

Bernard's piece on the housebound was a total whopper, but he'd been given the floor, indeed the stage as it turned out, and he'd decided to go for it. The word Chindit was legendary throughout British society and far beyond.

Mrs Thomson was the first to speak to him:

'Thank you so much, Mr Markham. You don't know how much this means.'

The father remained as he had been throughout, like he would rather have been somewhere else. Frankie stepped forward:

'I didn't know you were like that, Bernie.'

'I guess I should take that as a thank-you. Well, don't bother, there's a better way to thank me. You've got work to do. You and Paul WILL take part in Christmas help to the housebound elderly. You can help the two ladies who organise it. Don't you let me down now. Don't even think about it.'

Bernard then turned to their father:

'Mr Thomson?'

'What do you want, mate?'

'If I see one more bruise or split lip on either one of these boys again, I swear to God I'll go to the police and report you myself.'

Thomson grunted and pushed past him. He was in no frame of mind to attempt a reply, far less have a go at a war hero.

Bernard stopped off at Stork and Sylvia's later. He was full of the day's events and his two friends had never seen him so pumped up. They sat down to a meal and had a celebratory glass of wine.

It was quite late before Bernard got home. He switched on the wireless and listened to the comedy *Much Binding In The Marsh*, followed by classical music. He limited himself to one large glass of wine. The music, while soothing, was just a background sound. His mind kept going round and round:

That old mate of mine, Stork, was right. People do need something to believe in. Otherwise, what's the point of it all? The two of us went through Hell and back. But that's over. It's what we do from now on that matters. And there's so much that needs to be done.

Bernard Markham had tasted youth service, and he liked the taste. He wanted more. And one month later he did himself another favour. He went with Ralph to a meeting of the local AA and introduced himself in the manner of a Quaker:

'It's good to meet you, friends. My name is Bernard. I'm an alcoholic.'

CHAPTER 12

The guilt that never dies

THE RAIN WAS tin-tacking on the conservatory roof outside the spare bedroom John Gray had chosen to use that night. He had come in very late and hadn't wished to disturb his wife.

He couldn't sleep. His mind was like a hamster-driven wheel. Time and time again his eyes misted up. He'd just been told a story, a true story, which was horrific, which could never be matched by any fiction he had read or watched at the cinema or on TV.

And it had all started routinely enough only hours before. It was the run-up to Tom Williams' 90th birthday. Gray had promised his old friend he would write a poem to mark the event and wanted to get it right. Having pre-arranged a meeting, he rang the old shaman's bell. The door was answered by Gerry, Tom's adopted son.

'Hello, Gerry, I didn't expect to find you here.'

'Tom's not good, John, but come in, he'll be pleased to see you.'

Williams was lying back on his reclining chair. The long years were taking their toll and he wasn't getting about much at all. Gerry and other members of Tom's adopted family were taking turns to look after him.

Williams began:

'Gerry, if you don't mind, I'd like to have a talk with John.'

'Tell you what, the boss needs me to drive her to the late night supermarket. You guys can take as much time as you like.'

The beginning of the conversation between the former colleagues was light-hearted. Williams thanked Gray for the stories he'd told about the mission society in Glasgow. Then he returned the compliment by touching on some of the funny images from his own early youth work days in Lancashire.

Gray laughed on several occasions, but he was keen to get on with some content for his poem and of course, Williams knew that:

'Tom, about your ninetieth.......'

'To be honest, John, I'm not sure I'll live to see it.'

'Don't be daft, Tom. I've told you many times. You'll outlive me.'

'Oh John, you've never lost that sense of humour. It's a blessing, you know.'

'Tom, if you're not well enough, I can always try next week.'

'No no boy, go right ahead. What would you like me to tell you?'

'I'd like to explore some of the Tom Williams we know nothing about, the years when you served in the British Army.'

At first Williams played it down:

'I was just a boy, John. They put a gun in my hand and told me to shoot my fellow man.'

'But you volunteered for a special regiment, did you not?'

'Yes, but I didn't really know what I was letting myself in for.'

Gray, like all his contemporaries who had been pupils of Williams, had tried over countless years to get information from the shaman to confirm what they had all suspected, and they had tried every subtle tactic in the book, but to no avail, the old man had been wise to them every time. Now that Gray had become one of Williams' closest friends, a position granted to only the select few, he decided to come straight to the point:

'Tom, were you a Chindit?'

Gray was surprised at the sharp and honest answer he got:

'Yes I was. Under Orde Wingate.'

There was a momentary silence between the two men, before Williams took up again. And this time his tone changed. It seemed to Gray he was back in the old Crack Willow office and he was on the receiving end of it from his boss:

'Well, you've asked for it, boy, and you're gonna get it.'

'Just tell me what you feel you can, Tom.'

'No, I don't believe in half measures, but there is something I need you to promise me.'

'Of course, Tom.'

'I've never told this to anyone since I came to Colliershire in the early sixties. When I did, I shut the door on my early life. Gerry knows I was a marine commando in South-East Asia, that's all. And I don't want David or Malcolm to know either.'

'You mean David Samson and Malcolm Ingles?'

Williams' tone became softer again:

'Yes, they were my main lads when I took up here with the Union of Youth Clubs. Before Gerry came along, I thought of them like the sons I'd never had. I still think of them as my sons. Promise me, John. I know I can trust you. I need to tell someone before my time comes. My old friends knew about it, they were my buddies in the conflict, but they're all gone now.'

'I promise, Tom.'

'After I'm gone you can tell the whole world, but only after I'm gone.'

'It's safe with me, Tom. Mind you, that means I'm going to be holding on to your secret for a long time. And what if I predecease you?'

Gray's Glaswegian humour was always a support to Williams. And now it eased him as he began to unburden his soul.

As the story of Williams' ordeal in the Burma campaign unfolded, there were moments when Gray wished he had never put the old man under such pressure. He thought to himself:

I have no right to expect this. I'm not a man like my father or Tom Williams. I can't begin to imagine what it must have been like. If I had been in the Malta Convoy and had gone down with my ship, I could not have swum around in the water in the midst of flaming oil and dead bodies. Nor could I have fought in the jungles of Burma against the Japanese, far less have lived through the pain of being brutalised as a POW. Nor could I have held on to it like them for the rest of their lives without talking about it. I could never be the man my father and Tom became, not if I lived for another hundred years.

But told the story he was, and considering it a great honour he listened intently. He could hardly do otherwise. It was shocking. It was harrowing. It was mind-boggling. Tale followed tale of thirst, starvation, disease, beatings, torture, summary executions by bayonet and beheading, men buried in dirt up to their necks, men shot then hung up by their heels for bayonet practice with their severed testicles stuck in their mouths.

Suddenly it stopped when the old Chindit drummed on the wooden arms of his recliner and started to hum an old army tune to himself. John Gray didn't know what to say. And he was astonished that his friend had related it all without a hint of emotion. He had an urge to cry but stopped himself. If his old mentor could bear it, so must he.

'Well, boy, you wanted to know. Now you do.'

'It's terrible, unthinkable. How on earth did you survive it all?'

'I've asked myself that question every day for the last seventy years of my life. And I still don't know the answer. All I know is I did, and too many fine men did not. I think about them all the time. It makes me feel guilty.'

'Guilty, Tom? How can you possibly…..?'

'Because you do. You just do. You'd have to be a veteran to understand that, John.'

'What about your other buddies who survived?'

'I lost contact with many. But I corresponded with some on and off. Had one special pal, who remained a close friend until ten years ago when he died. His son wrote to me about it, then turned up here one afternoon.'

'Really? What a fine thing to do.'

'He had a special motive. He had his father's ashes with him. In accord with the last wishes, we buried him at the end of the back garden. There, next to the morning glory.'

Williams pointed out his window through the blue dusk to a spot where Gerry had set up artificial lighting to play on mature bushes. Gray commented:

'You must have been great friends.'

'He was a wonderful friend. He stood by me after the War when I was one of the walking wounded. I never really got round to repaying him.'

'It makes you wonder what the two World Wars were all for, Tom.'

'The World had gone mad. It was all about empire building, glory and domination.'

'And what stopped all that?'

'As you've heard me say to you often, John, life is nothing if not ironic.'

'I'm not sure what you mean.'

'The madness was stopped by the greatest madness of all – Mr Oppenheimer's bomb. He showed the madness up for all that it was. It had to stop then.'

Gray finally fell asleep that night at 3 o'clock in the morning, but he spent the following days piecing together a jigsaw puzzle. All the renowned one-liners delivered by Williams during his later career to his younger colleagues were at last making sense to John Gray. And the shaman's quiet, unobtrusive, Quaker faith became so absolutely understandable. But what was Gray going to do for Williams 90th? What would he put in the poem? He agonised about it for long enough, then opted for a compromise.

Come the night and Gray's contribution, the poem was a portrayal of the old man's dealings with his colleagues and friends over many years. It showed up his foibles, his sense of humour, his remonstrations with his juniors. It was light-hearted, went down well, and to his delight, Williams was presented with a framed copy. The old youth and community officer thanked everyone for their contributions and ended with a quip at John Gray:

'Of course, I shall expect an even better poem for my hundredth birthday.'

Gray was on the ball:

'I won't be around then, Tom. None of us will.'

But Gray hadn't finished. His compromise was to do an unexpected extra. With the permission of David Samson, who along with his wife had organised the whole thing, he was determined to say something about their old boss and Burma. And so he began with:

'Dear friends, now that Tom has reached this great landmark, I feel it's time to pay tribute to the Tom Williams very few people have ever known about, the Tom Williams there was before the man we knew in youth work.........'

Gray went on to outline the history of the opposition to the Japanese occupation of Burma by a special regiment which became known as the legendary Chindits.

And he finished with:

'………..Tom Williams was one of those Chindits. I know he wouldn't want me to single him out for a special mention, for too many of his old friends did not come back from Burma. So this tribute is for them.'

Gray looked over to where Williams sat, leaning forward, both hands on the crook of his walking stick. He was nodding. Gray was relieved. The shaman had approved of the way the disclosure had been delivered.

But the full and detailed horror of what had been told to him was a burden that Gray still had to carry until the old man passed on. One particular part of Williams' story weighed heavily on Gray:

'One of our group was so weak, there was nothing we could do for him. And we couldn't leave him to the Japanese. We had to kill him. I drew the short straw.'

Silence reigned, a long silence. Eventually, John Gray felt he had to say something.

'But Tom, surely that wasn't uncommon in that kind of campaign? From what I've read about it, lots of men had to be left behind. Some of them were given grenades, some of them enough morphia for a lethal dose.'

'It doesn't help, John. The lad was too weak for that. He was my friend, and I killed him.'

CHAPTER 13

Liverpool lads and lasses

'YOU'LL JUST HAVE to be patient, Bernard,' said Sylvia, 'your luck will change.'

Bernard Markham was on his regular monthly visit to Stork and Sylvia. Their 3 year old son Robert was playing at his feet with soldiers, a Christmas present. Sylvia had sensed the frustration in Bernard, and seeing his pleasure in Robert's company, went for a diversion:

'Don't you miss it, Bernard? I mean, not having a family life?'

'I don't know if any woman would put up with a man like me. I think the female sex views me as a bit of an oddity. And anyway, since Kathleen, I've never wanted another woman.'

Sylvia smiled in sympathy.

Stork appeared, having been next door listening to the wireless:

'The Hungarians have murdered us. They scored six goals. What a fabulous player Ferenc Puskas is.'

Bernard was never a football man. He showed little interest. Stork picked up on his friend's mood:

'Cheer up, old man. It was only one interview.'

'It's the fourth interview I've taken. I don't think they want my sort.'

'That's nonsense, Bernard. More like they already knew who they wanted. No reflection on yourself at all.'

'Well, maybe I'm not cut out for professional youth work.'

'Bernard, you're a real hit with those kids at the club, everyone knows it. You have a rare talent. It's only a matter of time.'

'But they seem to want the archetypal ex-army chap who *will instil discipline into those unruly youngsters.* I see each one as unique, an individual in his own right.'

Sylvia re-joined the discussion:

'You stick to your guns, Bernard. Times are changing. These interviewing panels won't always think the way they do now.'

'Have you thought about widening the net?' Stork queried.

'What are you driving at?'

'Well Bernard, up till now you've only tried the London area. What about the cities in the North? They have huge problems with young people.'

'But I have ties down here. I've made good friends.'

'You can't have it both ways, Bernard. If you want a career, you may have to travel.'

So Bernard applied for jobs advertised in the northern newspapers. He took an interview in Newcastle and came only close, which frustrated him. A month later, he was on steam trains once more, this time westward across country, first to Birmingham, then Liverpool. He got off at Liverpool Lime Street and hailed a taxi which took him in the direction of the River Mersey's Dockland. He arrived at Brewster Boys' Club, formerly Brewster Institute, a social and welfare institute for employees of the ship-building industry, and named after its benefactor. He was a half hour early. A young clerkess approached him:

'Would you like to wait in here, Mr Markham?'

She showed him into the office. She had put on her best English accent, but Bernard could tell from the timbre of her voice she was Scouse.

'Cup o tea, love?'

Out of earshot of her employers, she was now pure Scouse.

Bernard was given a generous mug of tea and a plate of chocolate biscuits. He whiled away the time reading the local paper, while listening to the sounds of Liverpool's industry, most significantly the hooting of boats on the Mersey. Then the door opened:

'Good afternoon, Mr Markham, I'm Bob Craig, Club Treasurer.'

The two men shook hands and Bernard was shown into the interview room for the day, which was, as needs must, the coffee-bar. A man and a woman were seated behind the table. Bernard was given the seat in front of them. Surprisingly, he felt no nerves.

Craig spoke first:

'Mr Markham, let me introduce you to Lady Blakeley-Hunsworth, our Chairwoman, and Councillor Lindsay of Liverpool Council, the body who would be employing the successful candidate.'

'How do you do, Lady Blakeley-eh......?'

'Cecilia is my name. Just call me Cecilia, Mr Markham.'

'Ma'am. Good to meet you too, Councillor Lindsay.'

Lindsay only nodded. Bernard instinctively felt the man didn't take to him.

Lady Blakeley-Hunsworth started the ball rolling:

'Mr Markham, you are the last candidate today. We hope you don't read anything into that. As you had the longest journey, we decided to give you time to get here.'

'Thank you, Ma'am. I appreciate that.'

'You have an excellent reference from the Minister of Ealing Church. Could you tell us something about your voluntary work there in the last few years?'

Bernard gave a brief sketch of the programmes he had led and the support he had given to underprivileged lads.

At that point Lindsay weighed in:

'We 'ave a lorra trouble in Liverpool right now. Loads o' scallies on the streets, frightenin' the lives out o' decent citizens. We're lookin' for an ex-army man like yourself who'll put a bit o' discipline into 'em.'

Bernard countered:

'I don't think that army type discipline is the answer in itself. Every lad is a unique human being, an individual in his own right. It's my job to find out what makes him tick. I have to find the right place for him in the club, one that gets the best out of him and makes a valuable contribution to the club effort.'

Bernard Markham was a man ahead of his time, but he'd just said the wrong thing to Lindsay.

Although, Lady Blakely-Hunsworth leaned forward:

'Oh I say, Mr Markham. That sounds splendid.'

Councillor Lindsay disagreed:

'Sounds to me like you got that outta the textbook, lad.'

Bob Craig said nothing at all, as he had done throughout all the interviews, content to be a spectator.

The interview took twenty minutes. The Lady Chairwoman concluded:

'Thank you, Mr Markham. I wonder if I could ask you to wait in the office for ten minutes?'

Bernard wasn't used to this from his previous interviews, but was happy to oblige. She appeared eventually, if only a little flustered, as if she'd been in an argument:

'We'd like to offer you the job, Mr Markham.'

Bernard could hardly believe it:

'I don't know what to say, Ma'am. Thank you so much.'

'Cecilia, call me Cecilia, Mr Markham.'

'I'm not sure that would be right, Your Ladyship.'

Lady Blakeley-Hunsworth rather liked that in a man. She thought it gallant of Bernard, and showed he was no fool. She continued:

'We'd like you to start on the first Monday of next month. Councillor Lindsay will make arrangements for your living accommodation. You can of course refuse it, but I wouldn't advise it, he's not a flexible man.'

'I'm sure it will be fine, Ma'am.'

'Don't underestimate the task ahead of you, Mr Markham. Some of what Councillor Lindsay said is true. There's a lot of friction between the native Liverpudlians and the immigrant West Indians, there's always been a Catholic-Protestant thing anyway, and now we have Teddy Boys copying their counterparts in London.'

'It's a challenge, Ma'am.'

'Good. I thought you'd say that. Good luck and I'll see you soon.'

Cecilia Blakeley had married John Hunsworth many years previously. He had made himself a millionaire through supplying parts for the railway industry. He was knighted in the late thirties and the couple had a large estate in Lancashire. Apart from managing the estate, Cecilia was involved in a number of charities, and was particularly concerned about the welfare of young people who had lost their fathers in the War.

She had taken to Bernard Markham immediately. Clearly, he was a man with his own mind, who could read young people and get the best out of them, who wouldn't be ruffled by them when they were confrontational. With Craig sitting on the fence, the decision was between Cecilia and Councillor Lindsay. There could only ever have been one winner, Her Ladyship. Only weeks previously, as a token of her forward thinking, Cecilia had donated a state of the art jukebox to the Club. The committee were nervous about that, the hard-liners among them suggesting it would cause riots. Cecilia called them old fuddy-duddies and got her way.

Back home in London, Cynthia was mightily relieved that her brother had at last established regular and secure employment. With his army pension as back-up, and not being a married man, he would have few financial worries. She did wonder how he would cope with rowdy teenagers every night, hoped he wouldn't get injured, but accepted that this was what he wanted to do in life. She spent the lull between his appointment and the start date helping him with clearing his house, and kitting him out with some new clothes.

'Don't make such a fuss, Sis. I'll be fine.'

'And who else am I supposed to make a fuss of, Bernard? And anyway, Mum and Dad would have wanted me to look out for you.'

Stork and Sylvia were expecting a second child. So Bernard had more than one reason to be pleased:

'Well Stork, great changes all round. But I'll miss you both. Sorry, I'll miss all three and a half of you.'

Stork laughed:

'We'll keep in touch, Mr Markham. After all, it's my job to keep an eye on you, young man.'

'How are you going to manage with four of a family, Stork?'

'We'll be okay. A couple of years back I took advantage of the Government's new scheme to award veterans like us the one hundred pound lump sum instead of the weekly pension. It paid off much of the house. Then there's my job with the MOD.'

On the last day of the month Bernard boarded a train at Charing Cross and waved good-bye to Cynthia and Stork who had accompanied him to the station. All of his bits and bobs were to follow in a lorry to the flat in Liverpool arranged for him by Councillor Lindsay. He was greeted at Liverpool Lime Street by Charlie Hutton, Brewster Boys' Club's caretaker. He put Bernard's cases into the boot of an old Morris and drove him to his new flat. His last act was to hand Bernard the keys, but his passenger insisted he come in for a cuppa.

'Have you been long at Brewster's, Charlie?'

Charlie pushed back his flat cap and scratched his head:

'Now, let me think, must be almost twelve years now. Right, since I were a riveter on the ship-building. Mind though, I liked the first ten year better.'

Bernard had picked up that Charlie was a Yorkshireman:

'What makes you say that, Charlie?'

'When the place was the *Tute...*'

Bernard had interrupted:

'You mean Brewster Institute?'

'Right. Back then the blokes were same age as mesel. And it didn't matter them were Lancs and I were Yorks. We'd give each other big licks, 'specially when the roses' matches at cricket were on. We had good crack, and nobody took the 'ump.'

'So it wasn't the same for you when it changed to a Boys' Club?'

'You're bloody right, lad. These kids are nothin' but trouble, full o' cheek. If I pulls one up for doin' summat he shouldn't, he calls me an old sod and tells me to take a hike. And that's not worst. I could understand their fathers and grandfathers. This lot speak wi' marbles in their mouths.'

'You mean Scouse?'

'Right. But this be a new version of their own makin'. And it makes no sense at all.'

Charlie finished by wishing Bernard good luck:

'And thou'll bloody need it, lad.'

Bernard arrived at the Club on his first morning to find it very quiet. Bob Craig was ensconced in the office, going over the previous month's accounts and giving dictation to Susan, the clerkess.

Susan heard him coming, so was ready with an appropriate greeting:

'Good mornin', Boss.'

'Morning, Susan. Morning Bob, busy I see.'

'Yes, Mr Markham. And I'm glad you're here. Your predecessor was a bit of a rogue, I'm afraid. It's taken me about six weeks to bang the Club to rights financially. I do have a full-time job to think about, so much of the Club's transactions can hopefully be handled by yourself now.'

'Well of course, Bob. While you're here, can you tell me anything about the Club's weekly programme?'

'It's not as good as it should be. Recently, we've only been able to open on Wednesday, Thursday, Friday and Sunday nights. No full-timer for a while, you see. There are volunteers on those nights, of course, but I'm not sure they can handle the roughest lads. It gets a bit ropey at times.'

Bernard could hear the scraping of a shovel nearby, so left the office to investigate. He found Charlie in the boiler room clearing ashes from the night before.

'Morning, Skipper.'

'What was on last night, Charlie?'

'They have a dance on Sunday nights. Dancin' indeed ! More like a bloody riot. They do all this new stuff, jivin' they calls it. What a flamin' noise. And the mess they leave at their backsides, blimey! You wanna see the work I've got when I'm finished 'ere.'

'I'm sure you'll manage, Charlie. By the way, what's this room through here?'

'In the days o' the *Tute*, it was packed wi' beer barrels and bottles o' wine and spirits. I guess it's a spare one for you, skipper, if thou thinks o' summat to do wi' it.'

'Thanks Charlie, I will.'

That afternoon Bernard spent time with an old folks' group who had permission to use the place on Monday and Wednesday afternoons. He found it useful, for not only did it pass the time while he waited for his baptism of fire at Wednesday night's youth session, the oldies had invaluable knowledge on the history of the local community. On the Tuesday morning, he spent time with Susan, laying the ground rules for how they would work together. He could see she was tidy with her filing and could type both quickly and correctly. He had learned the value of having someone like that from his days as an admin assistant in India with the British Army.

The new Warden/Leader of Brewster's Boys' Club, or at least that was the title written into his contract, made sure he was there half an hour before opening time on the Wednesday evening, 7pm. The first youngsters to arrive were a group of six lads about 16 or 17 years of age:

'You must be the new manager, yeah?'

Bernard was looking at the strangest lad he'd ever seen. He wore a long jacket in the American style of a zoot suit, high-waist drainpipe trousers exposing his socks at the ankles, an incredibly thin tie and crepe-soled shoes. His hair was combed back to a duck's arse and there was a quiff at the front. His mate, as it turned out sidekick, was dressed exactly the same. The other 4 wore ordinary dress.

'Yes I am. My name's Bernard.'

He offered his hand. The lad didn't take it:

'I'm Danny, this is Jimmy, and the rest o' me mates.'

They breezed past him in the direction of the coffee-bar. Clearly to Bernard, Danny was the leader of the group, and he and his mate Jimmy had to be Teddy Boys.

The three volunteers for the evening, Ron, Sandy and Gill who ran the coffee-bar, arrived at 5 minutes, 10 minutes and 20 minutes past the hour respectively. The new boss was not impressed, but decided not to make an issue of it on his first night. But he did note that Ron and Sandy made straight for the games hall and started kicking a ball around between them. Again, Bernard opted for discretion rather than valour for the time being. As more youngsters drifted in, he made for the coffee-bar.

Gill was busy arranging the soft drinks' bottles, chocolate bars and other refreshments on the counter. A kettle was boiling.

'Can I get ya somethin', love?.'

'Bernard, call me Bernard, Gill. But no, never mind that for now. Can I ask you a few questions first?'

'Sure ya can.'

'How many more are likely to come?'

'We ger about twenty on Wednesdays. Might be more tonight, cos they've all 'eard about ya.'

'That's not a lot for a busy area like this.'

'There's noralot for them to do, love. We ain't had a leader for more than six month.'

'There are four girls seated at the far table. What can you tell me about them?'

'They're the fellas' birds. They just come 'ere to listen to the juke box, have a coke, a ciggy, and talk about the fellas. The fellas sit on the other side of the room and do much the same. They'll go down later and play footie.'

'No other activities?'

'On Sundays there's a dance. It's great fun, but sometimes there's trouble, a lorra trouble. We 'ad to get the rozzers last time. They took Danny and a coloured fella away in the car.'

'No coloured lads are here tonight.'

'They come on Sundays, though there's one fella who trains in the gym, at the boxin' on Friday nights. He's the local champ.'

'What causes the trouble, Gill?'

'The West Indian fellas come over 'ere for jobs, mostly on the busses and trains. Bob Craig, the treasurer, says the Government wants to encourage 'em cos they'll werk for lower wages. Our lads don't like it, so before ya know it, there's a punch-up.'

Bernard joined in the football later on, but most of the time he just soaked in the atmosphere and what information he could glean from members and staff. He realised it would be some time before he could facilitate change, but he was certain about one thing, he hadn't come all this way to run a coffee-bar full time.

W. Green and Sons was a factory in Liverpool specialising in domestic crockery. Two stockmen were stood one morning at the deliveries' entrance, puzzling over the dapperly dressed little man who was loading plates into the back of his tiny van. One stockman said to the other:

'Search me, mate. He's runnin' a boys' club or somethin' at the owld Brewster's Institute. I get a sheet from management and hey presto, along 'ee comes and picks up plates from the pile o' rejects. Nobody knows warr 'ee wants wi' them. And nobody asks. If he didn't take 'em, they'd just get crushed at dump. Ee's welcome. Bernard gave them a wave:

'Cheers lads. See you next time.'

The new Leader of the Club got Charlie to help him unload the latest crockery into the old wine cellar next to the boiler room.

'I wish you'd tell me what this rubbish be in aid of, Skipper.'

'One of these days you'll find out, Charlie.'

Bernard was busy. Now he was off to a wholesaler to top up on goodies for the coffee-bar, and in the afternoon he was expecting Her Ladyship, the Chairwoman. He had been in post for six weeks and felt it was time to make his mark.

Cecilia was keen to know how he was coping:

'How are things, Mr Markham?'

'Not bad, Ma'am. But changes are needed.'

'Go on.'

The leaders don't seem to engage with the rougher lads. They seem to be frightened.'

'Well, they could hardly be blamed for that. Are you not frightened, Bernard? Oh, I hope you don't mind me using your first name.'

'Not at all, Ma'am. And I'm not frightened. I fought the Japanese in Burma in '43. Compared to that, Teddy Boys are pussy cats.'

'I bet they are, Bernard. But what are you going to do with them?'

'I need to find something for them to do other than stirring up trouble. The same applies to the coloured lads. I've been lucky so far but I can see a fight coming at one of those weekend dances.'

'What about equipment, Bernard, do you have enough for your programme?'

'Good point. I'd like to start a junior club on the nights when there's nothing on just now. We'd need a lot of new equipment to keep volatile juniors occupied.'

'You make up a list of what you need, Bernard, and we'll put it to the management committee.'

Bernard was thankful that he had at least one ally, and an influential one at that. A month later he had a second:

'Good morning, Markham, the name's Crichton-Smythe, Dickie, if you prefer. I'm Youth Service Officer for Lancashire.'

The speaker was British Army to the core. Bernard asked him further:

'I heard you were a captain in the War, Dickie.'

'More's the pity. Got the old left pin shot off at Kohima, hellish battle.'

The two men had very little in common but it was all that mattered. For a while they swapped notes on Burma:

'I say, Markham, you've taken on a whopper of a challenge here. How are you coping?'

'It's hard going but I'm getting there.'

'Not surprised, given that rogue of a predecessor. He was a member of the criminal classes, you know. Damn scoundrel. Anyway, sorry I couldn't make your interview, had to go to Ireland for a conference. If you need anything, give me a bell on the old dog'n'bone.'

Crichton-Smythe, rather like the major who had come to Bernard's bedside in the field hospital in India and offered him the desk job at Poona, had been in and out like a breeze. Bernard was grateful for his visit, but realised his superior was just going through the motions and likely wouldn't appear again for some time, unless of course the new Club Leader screwed up and the management committee complained about him.

A year into Bernard's tenure of office, there was a big dance at Brewster's to celebrate the birth of *Rock and Roll*. Bernard had his work cut out to persuade the management committee. They were worried about youngsters from other communities being drawn to it and the possibility of a riot, but with Lady Cecilia's support, he convinced them all would be well.

Beginning on the Saturday night at 7.30pm, it was quiet at first with the music mainly ballads. Susan had answered Bernard's call to help Gill at the coffee-bar counter. The tables and chairs had been removed for standing room only. But by 9pm a cat could not be swung, the attendance was in three figures.

The tempo of the jukebox changed to *Shake, Rattle and Roll* by Bill Hayley and the Comets. Danny Monaghan and his girl-friend Trish took the floor. Clearly, they knew how to jive and for a while the others were content to watch while clapping their hands in time to the music. Trish had a pony-tail and was dressed in a jumper, circle skirt, ankle socks and sandshoes. Danny was in his full Teddy Boy regalia with an extra help-ing of oil combed through his hair to make his quiff stand out. The pair were thoroughly enjoying themselves. With their right hands clasped together, Danny twirled Trish around then twirled her back, they changed positions, she went down on the floor and through his legs, then jumped up, he bent down and she leapfrogged over his back. They went through the routine again and again.

The company had seen enough to whet their appetite. Another twelve couples took the floor, as *Shake, Rattle and Roll* was followed by *Rock Around The Clock*.

Bernard was enthralled. For a time he forgot all about the hard work he had done to get the Club on its feet again. The sight of young people interacting with such enthusiasm gave him a warm feeling inside.

But he should have known the unpredictability of young people. Around 10pm, some West Indian lads, including Conrad, Basil and Rohan, went across the floor to ask girls to dance. Rohan, who was the local boxing champ, asked Molly, Jimmy Tait's girlfriend. The girls were okay about the coloured lads dancing with them. Their boyfriends were not. Jimmy made his feelings known. He pushed Rohan:

'Piss off, Blammo.'

Blammo was Liverpudlian slang for Negro, and the coloured boys hated it.

'No, yo piss of yoself, man.'

Rohan pushed Jimmy back, so hard he fell on his rear. Jimmy got up and took a wild swing at Rohan, missing by a foot. Rohan delivered a blink and you miss it right uppercut to Jimmy's left jaw. It was the last thing Jimmy knew for the next 5 minutes. He was spark out.

Danny and his four other mates, also dressed as Teddy Boys for the occasion, sprung to life and went for Rohan. Conrad and Basil went for them. The rest of the male company took appropriate sides. The boss was powerless. It was as if he was watching an old black and white Hollywood movie at double speed, set in a Wild West saloon where punches were traded cowboy to cowboy. A different sort of man might have called for the police. Bernard weighed it up in his mind. It was the first mass engagement he had witnessed since Burma, but hardly a war, and given there was no furniture available to be wrecked, decided to let it run its course.

And run its course it did. Jimmy was revived with a cup of cold sweet tea. There were a number of bloody noses and split lips. Many of the girls were tearful. The non-combatants had sensibly scurried off home long before hostilities ended. Otherwise, little damage was done, and even then it was only to pride. The pity was the dance was over. As the wounded staggered out, Bernard picked out Danny, Jimmy, Conrad and Rohan:

'If you four want to carry on as members of this Club, be here tomorrow night at 6.30pm sharp. If you're not here, I'll take it you won't be coming back.'

Bernard had chosen the Monday night because the new junior club intended for that evening was not yet ready to start. Danny and Jimmy met at their street corner, shared a twopenny single cigarette, and shuffled off towards the Club.

'Whadya think of Bernie, Danny?'

'Ee's a shirtlifter is our Bernie.'

'Never, he never is.'

'You've just gorra look at 'im. The clobber he wears, it's antwacky it is. And then there's his gabble, dead posh like. I'm tellin' ya, ee's a shirtlifter.'

'Look lively, Danny. Here ee's comin.'

Bernard motioned them ahead of him into the Club:

'Good evening, Gentlemen. Rohan and Conrad are already here.'

After they sat down in the office, the four lads eyed each other up and down in silence, as if they were preparing for another punch-up. If they had expected a lecture from Bernard, they were surprised by what he said:

'Follow me, lads.'

He led them down the basement stairs, through the boiler room and into the old wine cellar.

'Now, as you can see, there's a mountain of old crockery stacked here, more than you could count. I want it smashed up into bits. Throw the plates at the far wall. That should do it. When it's all in bits, I want you to put it in those sacks over there, so that Charlie and I can take it to the dump. If you do a good job, you can keep your memberships.'

The lads hadn't a clue where Bernard was going with this, but they didn't care. They were excited and they went at it like dogs to mince. The Club Leader sat in his office for twenty minutes listening to the smashing, the laughter, the hooting, the yelling. When it all quietened down, he realised they had begun the less attractive job of filling the sacks. Danny was the first to surface:

'We're done, Bernie. It was great, super!'

Bernard went down for a look:

'Well done, lads, that's a big help. I'll see you at Club on Wednesday.'

And he watched the four of them go down the road together, shoulder to shoulder, reliving their latest experience as they went, and still blissfully ignorant of what he had done.

Bernard smiled. There was still a long way to go, but this was a start.

The following day Bernard had another problem on his hands. From a distance he could see Councillor Lindsay approaching with purpose in his step. When he was close, there was a look of self-satisfaction in his face:

'Well lad, I won't say I told ya so.'

'Everything's fine, Councillor Lindsay. Nobody was seriously hurt, and the lads have made up.'

'That's as may be, lad, but I've got complaints from neighbours that some of 'em were drunk when they went into Club last night. That's under-age drinkin', lad.'

'You're absolutely right, Councillor.'

Lindsay straightened in triumph like a peacock:

'Well then, lad, at next committee meeting...........'

Bernard interrupted him:

'Those lads came to the Club drunk, and I turned them away, drunk. So they went off home, drunk.'

Lindsay was stunned. That possibility hadn't even entered his head. And he sloped off sullenly. But Bernard was now aware that he had a natural enemy in the Club, and a powerful one at that. He would have to tread carefully, but nevertheless the main thing on his mind was to encourage integration between the different factions among the senior boys. In the future, textbooks would be written about social group work, but Bernard was an original. He had worked out these principles for himself. And he chose his moment only weeks after the great punch-up.

'Danny, Jimmy, Conrad. Please come into the office.'

Danny quipped to Jimmy:

'Told ya. Ee's lookin for a shirt ta lift.'

'Give over, Danny.' Jimmy was tired of hearing this from his mate.

Bernard gave them seats and began:

'Listen up, lads. We've got a junior club to get started for the new Club year kicking off in September. Some of them will be your younger brothers and sisters. I'd like to start a members' committee, made up of our seniors, and I want you three to be the first. Your job will be to come up with a programme and resource it.'

They were astounded. They had been led to believe by their school teachers, neighbours, even their parents, that they were the biggest dimwits and scallies in Dockland. For all that, they were genuinely flattered by Bernard's faith in them. So they went for it. And it didn't seem to matter to them any longer that some of them would be white, some coloured.

The meetings were held weekly and comprised three Scouse lads, two West Indian lads, and a girls' representative. Bernard chaired the first ones, to make sure they got used to democratic debate. They were rowdy at first, but settled down eventually. When Bernard felt they were ready, he allowed them to elect their own chairman and left them to get on with it. Once they had made their decisions, all they had to do was report back to Bernard through their chairman, and he would try to find the necessary finance to back up their ideas. There were times when he had to say no and send them back to think again. But that wasn't important. At school they had been academic failures, and now they were struggling to find and hold on to decent employment. Bernard had given them an opportunity to learn essential skills in terms of day to day planning and working in a team. He was confident, by the end of their years with the Club, they would be confident young adults with enhanced self-esteem and regard for their community.

Not surprisingly the next Club year was hectic. The members' committee became leaders in the junior club and with only Saturday night vacant, the Club ran with full houses six nights a week. The Treasurer was happy, the whole management committee was happy, and Bernard enjoyed what was by far the best time of his life to date. When the year finally ended, Bernard felt that the young people who had helped to run the Club deserved a reward:

'Jesus, Bernie, whadya wan' us ta do now?' It was Danny.

'I just thought you lot would like a special trip, a long weekend away, somewhere nice.'

Conrad was interested:

'Yeah, man. We nevva get away from this domp.'

The others nodded.

Bernard had been thinking of a hill-climbing holiday his late father had taken him on during the thirties when he was just 14.

'Okay then, we're going to Arrochar.'

'Souns like a place Conrad comes from.' said Jimmy.

'It's at the top of Loch Long in Scotland. We're going to be climbing mountains.'

Danny couldn't resist it:

'Are we goin' sheep-shaggin' as well, Bernie? Ya know what they say 'bout the Jocks.'

'You'll get your face punched by a Jock if you don't mind your tongue, Danny.'

It was Basil's turn:

'What like da climbin', man?'

'Well, we'll be threading the needle for one.'

'Warriz that?' said Danny, 'Me Nan threads needles all the time. Are we goin' sewin' then or what?'

'The mountain is called Ben Arthur, but is known as *The Cobbler*. That's because the top of it is like a cobbler's last. There's a passageway like a hole through the last. To get to the summit, you climb through the hole on to a ledge which is narrow and can only take one person at a time, then you go up the ledge and take a final step on to the top. Going through the hole is known as *threading the needle*. It's very scary. Locals maintain only the brave can do it.'

Bernard could see by their faces he had hit the spot. Just the idea of it was making them excited.

Normally the quiet one, Basil piped up:

'Bernard, how we gonna get there?'

'I haven't figured that out yet, but I will.'

It was a good question. Since his appointment, Bernard had been rolling around Liverpool in a small van. For this project, he needed something more substantial.

On the next Monday morning he approached Charlie, who was clearing up the coffee-bar after the previous night's dance.

That was something Bernard didn't do as a rule, knowing Charlie's mood at such times, but he had plans to get on with.

'Charlie, I have a favour to ask.'

'Oh ay, what might that be, Skipper?

'You know Simpson's, the old garage two blocks away?'

'Sure I do, Wally and I were workmates on the ships.'

'Yes, he said he knew you well. Thing is, Charlie, he's got an old army transport lorry I could use to take the lads of the members' committee on the Arrochar trip. Trouble is he won't let me drive it.'

Charlie could see where Bernard was going with this:

'No Skipper. Take those nutters to Scotland? You has to be jokin'

Bernard had great powers of persuasion. 24 hours later, Charlie had come round:

'Okay Skipper, I'll do it. I'll tak ye all there, I'll even come back for ye. But mind this now, if I gets one bit o' trouble from those nutters, I swear I'll dump the lot o' ye in the middle o' nowheres and go 'ome.'

Bernard had his transport and his driver. His next move was to borrow a patrol tent and a two-man leader's tent from the local scout troop, along with groundsheets, sleeping bags, guy pegs, a wooden mallet and dixies which curiously reminded him of old army mess tins. He then issued the lads with a list of the clothes and other items they should take with them. Like a good soldier, he made sure not to forget matches. It only remained for him to approach Bob, the Treasurer, to sort out the finances.

Bob was very obliging:

'You've done great here, Bernard. How much do you need? Just name it.'

The big Saturday arrived. And Bernard smiled to see Danny Monaghan and Jimmy Tait turn up dressed in outfits other than those of a Teddy Boy. There were six lads altogether, an even split between coloured and white.

Bernard and Charlie had chosen an early departure, 8am. It would take them the best part of the day to get there in the old lorry, plus the fact they would need time before dusk to pitch camp.

Danny complained at the outset:

'There's no seats in this old banger, Bernie.'

'Well, just think what soldiers in the War had to put up with. When I served in Burma, I remember being transported in a light bomber plane which didn't have any seats either. That was a rough journey I can tell you. Then I had to parachute out and land.'

'So how do we do it?'

'Sit on your bottoms with your backs against the sides. Now, no more moaning.'

Charlie drove to Carlisle where they went into a café for a bite to eat. Then he took the A7 to Langholm and turned left on to B roads which were slow but the best route towards Glasgow. They were into late afternoon when they got past Dumbarton, so they stopped at Arden at the start of Loch Lomond for a second break. Charlie was tired and there were six sore bottoms in the back of the vehicle. There was time to stretch legs, go for a discreet leak and take refreshment, before covering the last miles through Luss and Tarbet to their destination just beyond Arrochar where the lads got their first view of Ben Arthur.

'Jesus,' said Jimmy, 'we got nothin' like this back in England.'

Bernard re-assured them:

'We'll knock it off tomorrow no bother, lads. But for now, we need to offload and carry everything to a good campsite. Look sharp, we've only got two hours to sunset.'

The Club Leader couldn't help thinking of Mad Mac when he heard himself speak. Only, Sergeant McKinlay would have qualified it with a few choice adjectives.

Bernard chose a flat piece of grass, two hundred yards above the road and next to a flowing mountain stream. Once they had dumped all the equipment, they watched Charlie and his lorry roll down the valley and disappear from sight.

'We're on our own now, boys. Look sharp, no time to feel tired, you've got a patrol tent to pitch.'

For the next half hour, Bernard was thoroughly entertained by their first attempts at raising a tent. Quite deliberately he allowed them to make mistakes, intervening only when necessary. First they got it the wrong way round, then they got it twisted. Then they got the main guys wrong, and when they were finally hammering in the short guys, Basil tripped on a main guy and the top half of him ended up immersed in the stream. Once they'd all had a good laugh at Basil's expense, Bernard felt some sympathy:

'I'll get you dry, Basil, then you can help me with my own tent.'

The boys marvelled at their leader's skill at lighting a fire, using dry grass first, then brushwood, then more solid wood from fallen branches, while all the time encouraging the flame with his hands and his own breath. They then watched him suspend two crates of soft drinks plus some tins and sealed bags of food in a natural refrigerator created by a circle of rocks in the stream. There followed the crucial explanation of how to go about taking a dump and an introduction to the sacrosanct spade. By the time Basil was dry, there was just enough time for Bernard's tent to be raised before time for sleeping bags was declared.

Private Markham was back in Burma and had bivouacked with his buddies once more.

But as he'd expected, his sleep was limited. His lads were so hyper, they talked and joked until 3am when the last of them nodded off. However, he knew the following night would be different.

At 7am the drowsy face of Danny poked through Bernard's tent flap;

'When's breakfast, Bernie?'

'That's kind of you, Danny. Get one of the others to help you make it.'

'You're kiddin', Bernie,'

'Nope. We take turns at making the meals. If you give me fifteen minutes, I'll show you how.'

They breakfasted on porridge oats and milk, followed by fried eggs, bacon and bread. The sun was up on a clear day, a boon to Bernard. He would have hated leading the lads in rain and wind. Once the camp site was tidy, they kitted themselves out and began their journey. The approach to Ben Arthur from their base was steep, so the climb was slow. They had to stop regularly for Tommy, the third of the white lads. Tommy had asthma and needed his puffer, more so now in the light of the extreme exertion. Bernard was surprised at the athleticism of Jimmy, who was built like a mountain goat. He forged ahead of the pack. Bernard decided to let him lead, as long as he still had sight of him. Unfortunately, when they were well up, a mist descended. Bernard and Jimmy communicated by shouting to each other. As if by magic the mist cleared and there was Jimmy, seated on a rock at the base of The Cobbler's famous last. He hollered:

'Come on, slowcoaches, gerra move on!'

Bernard let the others pass, then retraced his steps to help the trailing Tommy.

Eventually the whole party gathered on Jimmy's rock for a rest, just yards from the eye of the needle. Suddenly, to the amazement of the lads, a woman, who must have been 60 years old or thereabouts, climbed up out of the mist, passed them with a nod, then proceeded to thread the eye and stand on the summit. She didn't hang about. Having come back through the eye, she stopped and spoke to Bernard:

'Well, that's my fifth since Friday. Must get on.'

The boys had noted how fit she was. Her legs were weatherbeaten and sleek, and looked as strong as would support a heavy table. She was awesome. It took a minute for one of them to speak. It was Danny:

'Warriz she, a ghost or somethin'?'

Bernard explained:

'She's a Munro climber. She's one of an elite called Munro climbers. They try to climb every mountain in the country over three thousand feet.'

Their reaction amused Bernard, because he knew they would feel, if the old lady had done it and any one of them chickened out, that lad would lose face.

Not surprisingly, Jimmy was the first through the needle and on to the top, where he raised his arms in triumph. One by one, the others followed to varying degrees of confidence, gasping as they struggled up the narrow ledge on the other side. Bernard kept calling out, telling them not to look down.

He was surprised to find Danny the last to move:

'I can't do it, Bernie. I can't stand heights.'

Bernard had to resist a laugh. Here was the leader of the pack, normally full of bravura, confessing he was really a scaredy-cat.

'We can do it together, Danny. You take my hand. I'll go first. When we get through the needle, whatever you do don't look down. Shut your eyes if you have to.'

Danny was now confronted with a terrible dilemma. Should he appear like a coward in front of his mates, or take the hand of a man whom he had called a queer on many occasions?

Jimmy made his mind up for him:

'Gerra shift on, Danny.'

When they were all stood on the summit, they were euphoric. They sang their favourite hits from the pop charts, while Bernard took photographs of the magnificent scenery, and of group members when they were unawares.

They were keen to know what the next adventure was. Bernard sat them down with his map:

'We go across that shoulder to the top of Ben Ime over there. It's almost five hundred feet higher than The Cobbler, but it's only a long gentle climb from here, not nearly as tough as what we've done already.'

The trek from one summit to the other took them an hour and a half. Once there, Joel, the third of the coloured trio, who was a strapping lad and had shared the carrying of cold meat sandwiches and drinks with Bernard, revealed the contents of his haversack. Bernard did likewise. All were tired and hungry by now, so consumed the goodies in no time at all. Bernard took more photographs, including one of the group, of a formal nature this time. Keen to include Bernard, a second was taken by Conrad.

While they rested, Bernard consulted his map again:

The next bit's tricky, lads. We descend the other side, but the first five hundred feet is pure scree. If you can keep on your feet, you'll be lucky. Otherwise, slide on your backsides.'

Danny was fired up for it:

'Gorra be just like sledgin' in the snow at Christmas, fellas.'

Bernard cautioned:

'Not quite, Danny.'

As they skidded and slid their way on legs and bottoms, there was a great deal of yelling and whooping, and often 'ouching'. By the end of the trial by scree, there was not a backside that wasn't bruised and aching. But somehow it didn't hurt.

The remaining descent of the nursery slopes was done by them all at a breeze, only stopping once by a mountain stream to take on water. They made the main road just south of The Rest and Be Thankful by mid-afternoon and walked its three miles to the point below their campsite. After a hearty meal, they had time to themselves. Some went exploring, some stayed in their tent and played board games they'd brought with them. When dusk descended, they all agreed on an early night.

At 3am they were wakened by shouting. They sat upright looking at each other, then arguing about it, then realising none of them was to blame. It could only have come from one source, the least likely of all. Bernard.

He was sitting bolt upright in his tent, trying to figure out why. Perhaps it was the whole outdoor experience with the lads, which although enjoyable had brought back Burma with a vengeance. Whatever the reason, he'd been visited once more by Captain Akio Kobayashi and his henchmen. His tent flap was drawn and the figures of two dark faces were staring at him. The voice was Jimmy's:

'Are ya all right, Bernie?

Bernard decided to level with them. Otherwise, his charges would think they were in the care of a madman:

'I'm okay, old friends. When I fought the Japs in Burma, I had a bit of a hard time.'

Danny broke in:

'Whar 'appened, Bernie?'

'Not now, lads. Maybe another time. Go on, back to your beds.'

It took the six of them half an hour to settle down to sleep again. Bernard could hear them talking the whole time and he was the sole subject. But his revelation had rocketed him up in their estimation. He had become 'a bloody hero' and Danny Monaghan would never call him 'a shirtlifter' again.

The following day, the Monday, had to be a shorter one. After breakfast they strolled down the valley to Arrochar. Apart from looking around, they discovered they could hire rowing boats and explore Loch Long. Two boats were enough, three lads in the first, Bernard with the other three. He made sure that the crews were a mixture of coloured and white, and chose Joel for skipper of the first, due to his strength.

Danny simply couldn't resist a wager, and was keen to assert himself again after his embarrassment at the threading of the needle:

'Let's 'ave a race, ta other side. Losers pay for cokes at finish.'

Joel responded for the other boat:

'Okay, man, yo're on. But we just three, we gets a start.'

Bernard refereed, remembering how he and his buddies had crossed the Chindwin and Irrawaddy Rivers.

'That won't work, lads, not with three rowers. Only two should row at any time. Members of either team can change places half way across. I won't row at all.

Bernard carried a whistle. At the peep both boats took off simultaneously. He laughed at the efforts of some who had thought it would be easy:

'Take long strokes, boys, and make sure you get plenty of the water.'

It wasn't quite the Cambridge and Oxford boat race, but it was very competitive, and resulted in a win for Danny's crew, by four lengths. Danny was on top of the world once more, and jumped into the shallow water:

'Ya beauty, we are the champs!'

When they had returned the boats, they lunched by the side of the Loch, then walked north on the main road back to the campsite. There they found the lorry first, parked on the road, and minutes later, Charlie, having a kip in the small tent. They let him rest until he was refreshed, then they busied themselves breaking up camp.

They loaded the lorry and were off, and for as long as they could see them, looked back at the mountains they had climbed the day before. As the return journey progressed, individual lads would nod off for short periods, but mostly they shared their weekend's experiences, ribbing each other rotten for things that had gone wrong. Sometimes they burst into song, and when they were too loud, Charlie would threaten to stop the lorry and throw them all out. But at one point he half-turned to Bernard:

'I don't know what thou's done, Skipper, but them load o' scallies are the better for it.'

If he expected a response to his compliment, he was disappointed. Bernard was sound asleep.

CHAPTER 14

A double blow

A NEW DECADE had long set in at Brewster's. As he helped behind the coffee-bar, watching his lads and lasses giving their all on the dance floor, he had to pinch himself to believe he had now spent eight eventful years at the Club.

It had never been easy. On more than one occasion he had stood in the local courtroom as a character witness for members, and he still employed the smashing of crockery to release their anger. Danny and Jimmy may have moved on to adult life, but their younger versions were just as much of a handful.

Abruptly, he was wakened from his reverie:

'He's amazin, isin 'ee Bernie?'

Bernard wasn't given a chance to respond.

'Oh yeah, I'm in love with 'im.'

The two girls holding up the coffee-bar were listening to the jukebox and drooling over the singer and his record *Are You Lonesome Tonight?* Not only was Elvis dominating the charts on both sides of the Atlantic, he was dominating Brewster's at Sunday dances. One of the girls swooned and had to be revived with water. She came round just as *It's Now or Never* started up, and Bernard prayed she wouldn't do the same again. Sometimes he wished he could subject them all to a half hour of his old classical records. That would teach them something about real music.

'Eh up, Skipper!'

Charlie was shouting across the floor from the top of the stairs. Bernard came over to him.

'What are you doing here, Charlie? This isn't your ball game.'

'Bloody right it ain't, lad. Anyways, I could 'ear the phone ringin' from 'cross the flamin' road. Fat chance o' you 'earin it wi' this racket goin' on.'

'Do you know who it is, Charlie?'

'It's your big mate from London, the one ye call Stork.'

Bernard went downstairs, closed the door of his office, and picked up the receiver.

'Hello, Stork. To what do I owe this pleasant surprise? Don't tell me you and Sylvia are having another one.'

'If only that was the reason, Bernard. I'm afraid I've got bad news for you. Cynthia's been taken into hospital. She has pancreatic cancer and it's not good.'

Bernard left Liverpool so early in the morning it was dark as pitch. By mid-day he was in London and by his sister's bed-side. He was shocked to see Cynthia so drawn and haggard. There had always been a large age-gap between them, but he felt that at 53 years she should have many years ahead of her. The figure before him was crippled with pain and looked like a woman of 70.

'This is not like you, Sis, giving everybody a fright and having them run around after you.'

It amused her and lifted her spirit:

'Yes, you're right, Bernard. I guess I'm not much use for anything at the moment, a proper bag of old bones.'

The conversation went on, as hospital conversations like this often do, avoiding the inevitable truth at all costs:

How are you getting on at work? I hope those lads of yours are not causing you too much grief.'

'They're no bother, really. It's just this business of growing up that's the problem. They just need a little time and understanding from people.'

'Stork says you're very good at your job, probably one of the best practitioners in the country.'

'Well, he would say that, the big softie.'

Towards the end of visiting time, Bernard felt he ought to touch on the pressing issue:

'I should really be looking after you.'

'Don't be silly, Bernard. Oh dear, men, they have no idea.'

Away with you.'

'Bernard, this kind of illness can be messy and unpleasant for families. Let the professionals do their job.'

He visited her the following day as well before he had to return to work. But only a week had passed before he received another call from Stork.

'It's bad, Bernard. She's been taken into a hospice and they say she's got two days at the most.'

This time he found his sister up to the eyeballs in morphine, and unable to communicate with him. Occasionally she tried hand signals, but they meant nothing to him. He was allowed to stay as long as he liked. At one point he turned to one of the nursing nuns.

'This is very sudden, Sister. I was talking to her in the hospital only last week.'

'Don't be afraid, Mr Markham. Your sister is comfortable now, no longer in pain.'

He sat for hours, only leaving her bedside for an occasional cuppa. At 20 minutes to midnight, a smile lit up her face and she exhaled one last breath. The nun leaned over the bed, folded Cynthia's arms across her chest, and placed a rolled up towel under her chin. Then, looking at Bernard, she turned the palm of her hand up and slowly lifted it skyward. Without saying anything, she had intimated to him that Cynthia was now on her way to God.

Bernard stayed with Stork and Sylvia while he made arrangements between Cynthia's passing and her funeral. It was helpful to have the company of old friends at this time, and their young children cheered him up no end. Nevertheless, it was not lost on him that, never having married and had a family of his own, he now had no relatives at all. It was a strange feeling.

Stork took some time off, so that he and his old buddie could visit some of their old haunts.

'Have you kept up your association with the AA, Bernard?'

'Not really, I've been too busy to think about alcohol in recent years.'

'You should keep it up, Bernard. You never know when you might need them. Then there's some of your lads of course. I'll bet they have drink problems.'

They went on to talk a lot about Sergeant McKinlay, bursting into laughter when reminiscing about the great man's ability to lose his temper one moment then crack a hilarious joke the next. But apart from that, they didn't discuss Burma.

'Do you remember Frankie and Paul, Bernard?'

'Oh yes, the brothers grim.'

Stork chuckled:

'Frankie's a plumber these days, and very good by all accounts. Whenever I see him, he loves to talk about how you sorted out Judge Carter.'

'What about Paul?'

'That's not so good. He went down for armed robbery, got five years for it. I've been to visit him once, but it wasn't pleasant. He was quite aggressive.'

'Oh well, some you win, some you lose.' By now Bernard was a hardened pro.

The day of the funeral arrived. It was bitter, and the leaves around the crematorium, which had fallen weeks before, had stiffened like cardboard, and when scattered by strong blasts of wind, were making a scraping sound.

Bernard was silent throughout the service, thinking his own thoughts, while Stork and Sylvia joined heartily in the singing of the chosen hymns. It was a modest company, made up of

Cynthia's neighbours, a few friends she had held on to from her childhood, and some people from the office where she worked. There was time at the reception for Bernard to get to know some of them. And one very austere gentleman made a point of singling him out:

'Mr Markham, I'm James Cartwright, your sister's solicitor. Miss Markham specifically instructed me to hand you this letter personally.'

He gave Bernard a brown envelope along with his firm's business card. Before leaving, he doffed his hat and said:

'Please accept our sincere condolences at your great loss, Mr Markham.'

Bernard nodded and smiled. He decided to read the letter later. And Stork talked Bernard into spending one more night in Ealing with the family.

Sylvia pulled out all the stops, cooking a sumptuous meal. Afterwards, with the kids bedded down, they had a few glasses of wine, watched live classical music on television, then retired upstairs to bed. Bernard took the spare room.

In the morning, Stork had to get up early for his work, so was surprised to find Bernard seated at the kitchen table. He looked ashen-faced. At first, the big man thought his friend was hungover:

'Not feeling so good, old friend?'

No answer.

'Is there anything wrong, Bernard?'

'I haven't slept a wink.'

'What, not at all?'

'You'd better have a read at this.'

Bernard passed him the letter which James Cartwright had handed to him at the reception and which he had read at bedtime:

My Dear Bernard,

I feel so ashamed. I could never work up the courage to tell you face to face. I'm so sorry.

The fact is I was never your full sister. When I was a toddler, Mum gave birth to a boy. It was a difficult labour, the poor little mite only lived for a few days, and Mum and Dad were advised not to have any more children. The boy's name was Bernard.

Some years later, Dad's work took us to Wales. As I got older, I became aware of Mum and Dad's longing for a son. Then a local priest came to the house and told them of a mining family in Rhawddrhiw in the Rhondda Valley. They had lost their mother in childbirth, and the father wasn't able to support the baby together with all of his other children as well. These were the days before legal adoption came into being in England and Wales. Arrangements were made for the handover of the child by the Church and between the father and our parents. Mum and Dad named the boy Bernard after the son they had lost.

I'm so sorry. Mum and Dad could never agree on when you should be told. I don't think Mum would ever have told you, so before he died Dad made me promise to tell you when you were 18 at the latest. But by then you were a soldier in active service and later you had that awful time in Burma. I should have told you after Mum died, and I would have got round to it had it not been for your alcohol problems and your breakdown. Please don't think I'm blaming you for that. Lots of soldiers took to drink and had breakdowns after the War. It's no wonder they did, poor lads.

I know you'll be angry and upset. But you're a strong and successful man now, Bernard. You'll find a way of dealing with this. I'm only sorry I could never find the courage to tell you straight.

Please believe me when I tell you that Mum and Dad loved you just as much as they would have had you been born their son. Nothing can change that. Nor can anything change the fact that I have always loved you too. forever your sister, Cynthia. Ps. You need to go and see my solicitor, Mr Cartwright, now. He has important documents for you, including your birth certificate.

Having read it, Stork looked up:

'Oh my God! What must you be feeling?'

'That's just it. I don't feel anything. I've thought about it the whole night, but I still don't feel anything.'

Stork decided the less he said for now the better:

'It's the shock, Bernard. You've had two shocks, a double shock. You need time to take this in.'

At that point Sylvia arrived in her dressing gown with her younger child in tow. So the buddies carried on as if nothing had happened. They had their breakfast, washed and shaved, and got their kit together, Stork for his work, Bernard for the trip back to Liverpool. They went out of the door together. Bernard turned to Stork:

'I don't want anything to do with this.'

'Bernard, don't do anything rash. You might regret it later.'

'Leave me be, Stork. I'm big enough to make my own decisions.'

'Let me at least come to Liverpool in a few weeks' time to see how you are.'

'Of course you can.'

The two old soldiers took their separate ways. One hour later Bernard was with James Cartwright:

'I do appreciate what a great shock this must be for you, Mr Markham.'

'It doesn't matter, I don't want anything to do with it.'

'Please, Mr Markham, think carefully. In this envelope there's your birth certificate, plus statements from your natural father and the Rhawddrihw clergyman at the time. They concern your identity.'

'I already have an identity, thank you, one that I've lived in for nearly forty years.'

Almost disdainfully, he lifted his case, turned on his heel, and left the solicitor's office for a bus to Charing Cross.

CHAPTER 15

Purgatory and a punch-bag

ON THE TRAIN back to Liverpool Bernard Markham sat in a brown study. He was reflecting that one of his girl members at Brewster's had confided in him only the year before that her parents had told her they'd adopted her as a baby. She had just turned 16. It hadn't been difficult for him to imagine that situation so long ago – her natural mother having to cope with the stigma of an illegitimate birth and having no choice other than to give her baby away. Bernard had said all the right things to the teenager. But now the boot was on the other foot.

Had anyone who knew Bernard been asked about his character, they would have described him, whether they liked him or not, as a strong man. But that would only have been partially true. At his core he was a sensitive man. He had been raised in the wealthy burgh of Hampstead by a well-off, middle-class family. They had sent him to a public school, which he hated. He was bullied by more confident, older boys, and a master who had taken a shine to him would occasionally take him on his knee. He hated sports for which he was persistently taunted. His only refuge was in his music.

And this background had left him without a shred of confidence in the company of girls. When he was dating Kathleen, he felt like a man for the first time. When she deserted him in the middle of their engagement, he lost hope, and even nurtured a hatred for the very idea of sex.

In the weeks following his return to work, the staff and membership of Brewster's were confronted with a much changed leader.

'Thou has no need to shout at me like as that, Skipper.'

For the umpteenth time Bernard had snapped at Charlie for nothing at all, and the old man had taken enough of it.

Susan had reached the same point:

'Any werk I do for ya these days is never good enough. You find fault with everythin'.'

She burst into tears and ran out of the Club into her aunt's across the road.

The youngsters were having secret conversations:

'Warriz it with Bernie? He says nothin' and just stares all the time.'

The management committee were confronted with a very low key manager at their next sitting. It appeared to them he had lost his enthusiasm. Councillor Lindsay began to hope they might soon be seeing the back of him. At the end of the meeting, he seized an opportunity:

'D'ya know somethin'? I reckon our clever clogs 'as been drinkin' earlier. I was downwind o' him and gorra noseful.'

Lindsay got no support on that one, but he wasn't mistaken. Bernard had been experiencing an empty feeling inside when he went to bed at night. It had made sleep difficult, so he went to his GP and told him about recent events. The doctor could only offer him sleeping pills which didn't do much good. Bernard's next move, made in desperation, was to re-acquaint himself with an old friend, the bottle.

And he hit it hard. He was in the pub at lunch-time, tippled in what time he had off in the afternoon, and after 10pm when the Club closed he went home and drank until midnight or 1am. He turned night into day. One morning he arrived at work in a terrible state. Charlie took just one look at him.

'Skipper, thou's not well. For all our sakes, go 'ome.'

'I'll be fine, Charlie.'

'So 'elp me, Skipper, if ye don't go 'ome, I'm off and I'm takin' Susan wi' me.'

It had the desired effect. Bernard turned and walked home. But to what?

He was heartbroken. He was heartbroken for the mother who had died giving him birth, the mother he had never been able to know. He was heartbroken for himself, having to cope with the fact that his parents of twenty to thirty years had not been his parents after all, that he wasn't who he had always believed he was. And he was heartbroken that he had nobody with whom to share his anguish. There were moments when he considered doing away with himself.

The doctor gave him a line signing him off for two weeks which only encouraged him to drink more. One night he stepped out of the pub and into the road without looking. He was hit by a taxi, the driver being unsighted by mist and rain. Thankfully, it was only a glancing blow. After a night in hospital, he was allowed home.

The next days were spent in a combination of classical music, alcohol and aimless walkabouts. After one such walk he returned to find his door unlocked. He automatically assumed he had forgotten to lock it when he'd gone out. But when he was inside, he discovered a familiar figure sitting on the couch. It was Stork.

'Hello Bernard. Your neighbour kindly let me in. How have you been?'

'Okay.'

There was none of the usual warmth that Stork had come to expect on the occasions he had met up with his old buddie. And the ensuing conversation pursued a one-sided pattern with Bernard the receiver and monosyllabic at best. What was worse for Stork was the look of Bernard. It was all too familiar to the big man. He had seen it on the faces of hundreds of his fellow prisoners when they laboured together on the Thailand to Burma Railway. It was a look of hopelessness, a signal they had given up and that death would be the only way out. Stork became unnerved by the chill in the atmosphere. He decided to get straight to the point:

'Bernard, did you read the documents at Cartwright's, the solicitors?'

'I told him where he could stick them.'

'Why on earth would you do that?'

'Because I'm happy with who I am, Stork.'

'Oh really? Well I must say, you look happy and I don't think.'

'Please don't lecture me, Stork. There's no point.'

'Bernard, you've got to confront this thing. If you don't, you can't go on.'

There was no response to that, but Stork was determined to keep at it. He and Bernard had been through a great deal together and he wasn't about to give up on his friend now:

'Bernard, I went to Brewster's first, expecting to find you there. Charlie told me all about the last weeks. They're all concerned about you.'

'There's nothing you can do, Stork. There's nothing anyone can do.'

'You should really pick up those documents. You would probably discover you have other family.'

'My family, the only real family I ever had, are all dead now.'

Stork felt he'd said enough for now. The two veteran Chindits spent the next 24 hours together. They watched television, went for walks, had a meal and a few drinks. Quite deliberately, they kept the conversation light. They talked about the amusing times in Burma which kept the platoon sane. They talked about the music club that Bernard had started for the young lads in London. Finally, Stork drew his friend into the subject of women:

'Is there still no special lady in your life, Bernard?'

'There is one I like. Trouble is she's a real Lady and married to a Knight. I've thought about saying something to her, but she's a different class from me.'

Stork decided to back off on that one. His old buddie had enough trouble already.

Late on the following morning, Bernard accompanied Stork to Liverpool Lime Street. They could hardly hear each other above the din created by the echoes of trains and commuters bouncing back off the station's roof and walls. Stork had to shout:

'Bernard, before I go, promise me something.'

'Anything. Just name it.'

'You're a dear friend. I wouldn't want you to do something silly.'

'Now you're the one who's being silly.'

Bernard's last remark did nothing to comfort Stork. As the train slowly creaked into life, he had a dreadful feeling in his water that it would be a long time before they would see each other again. This time, Bernard was on a journey on which Stork couldn't help. He had to make that journey on his own.

But Stork had accomplished more than he thought. Bernard spent a full day in deep thought about some of the things his buddie had said. And Charlie was surprised to see Bernard enter the Club three days before his sick leave was due to end:

'Eh up, Skipper. Thou must be feelin' better.'

'I just came in to make a phone call, Charlie, that's all.'

After asking Susan to let him have the office to himself for ten minutes, he took out of his wallet the card he'd been handed at his sister's funeral. He dialled the number:

'Hello, is that Cartwright's, the solicitors?'

'Yes, how can I help you?'

'Could you put me through to Mr James Cartwright please?'

'Certainly, hold one moment.'

'Good morning, Mr Markham. How nice it is to hear from you again.'

'About those documents, Mr Cartwright, I'd better come through for them. And by the way, I do apologise for the last time.'

'No need to apologise, Mr Markham, quite understandable in the circumstances. I could of course post them to you special delivery, but they're very personal, so if you don't mind......'

'Not at all, I'll be there the day after tomorrow.'

So Bernard made the pivotal journey to London. He collected the documents, but deliberately waited until he was back in the peace and quiet of his Liverpool home before reading them.

The following day he was back at work with only a week left to prepare for the Club's next big day. Bernard had been campaigning for a while to get the Club's name changed to Brewster's Youth Centre. He felt that the name Boys' Club was now old-fashioned and that the change was needed because girls were no longer attending just to accompany boyfriends but more often to take part in programmes of their own. With Lady Cecilia on his side, the largely chauvinistic management committee had reluctantly relented, and a date had been set. A goodly number of city councillors and other dignitaries were expected.

Bernard hated such occasions. They were always top heavy on ceremony. To his independent mind, the cabal of labour councillors who would inevitably be present would say all the right things, however incoherently, while pandering to the public for votes as they did. And as was their regular habit, they would wine and dine themselves at the public's expense into an even higher level of incoherence.

But on the night Bernard was careless. He took a pint of beer at the pub for Dutch courage. One pint became two, and so on. Charlie stopped him before he went upstairs to get ready for the guests. He passed him some of his favourite strong mints:

'Tak these, Skipper. If I can smell it off thee, them top brass will an' all.'

At least Bernard was pleased that the youngsters on his members' committee had all turned up. That gave him encouragement and a sense of normality.

After the company were given time to mingle, listen to music and help themselves to the buffet, it was time for speeches. Only Lady Cecilia and Councillor Lindsay spoke. She was brief and very much to the point, seeing the change as one which was following a national trend, and much needed in the drive towards male and female equality. She ended by praising the excellent work that Bernard had done for the past almost nine years. Then, before giving way to Lindsay, she congratulated him on his recent elevation to the vice-chairmanship of Liverpool City Council.

Lindsay spoke for far too long, mostly about politics and the coming elections. People started to shuffle their feet and move around in their chairs. There was a lot of coughing and going off to the toilets. The young people began to wish they'd gone to the pictures. And the finish, about the Club at last, got right up Bernard's nose:

'I'd just like ta say, on behalf o' mesel' an' the Council, we fully support the werk done by organisations like Brewster's. They keep trouble off the streets by givin' young'uns somethin' useful to be gettin' on wi'. Our OAPS can sleep soundly in thir beds now. Finally, it gives me great pleasure ta declare Brewster's Boys' Club the new Brewster's Youth Centre.'

There was a round of applause, out of relief more than anything. Bernard had a raging headache by this time, and Lindsay didn't help by approaching him:

'Well lad, was that good enough for ya?'

'Not really.'

Clearly, Lindsay was looking for praise, but the Club Leader was in no mood to oblige. Why it was that Bernard chose this moment of all moments was something he himself was never able to fathom. But choose that moment he did. All the grief, confusion, anger and heartbreak of the previous six weeks was vented at the closing speaker, as Councillor Lindsay became Bernard's punch-bag.

'What makes ya say that, Mr Clever Clogs?'

'You bloody hypocrite, Lindsay. You don't give a damn for young people, probably because they don't have a vote. And if they did, they certainly wouldn't vote for you and your pals. When it comes to youth work, all you lot want to do is keep the adult population feeling safe and happy.'

'That's rubbish. The Labour Party in Liverpool has always looked out for young'uns.'

'That's because they've never had a choice. You lot could stick a stuffed parrot on a perch at election time. As long as a red badge was pinned on its breast, and it repeated the same old manifesto time and time again, the opposition would have no chance.'

The argument had become the main feature of the night, as the company formed a natural, old-time ring around the two heavyweights.

'And what would ya know about that, Markham? A toff like you? Whadya know about the struggles o' werkin class folk – folk like mesel' who werked down the pit when I were a kid?'

'And you got out of it as soon as you could, I imagine. Was it the chance to be a union rep? Now there's another two-faced lot.'

'That's a terrible thing ta say, just what ya get from a bloody tory.'

'As it happens, I'm not a tory voter, nor would I ever vote for the Labour Party. They're just tories in disguise.'

'One thing's for sure, matey. You've never known 'bout sufferin'.'

'Is that a fact? Well, let's see. During the War, me and some of my buddies were prisoners of the Japanese, and I don't need to tell you how that went. Is that suffering enough for you, Councillor Lindsay?'

At that point Charlie intervened, if only to save his boss's skin:

'Eh up lads. If thou's gonna keep this goin', can I suggest ye carry on in boxin' ring downstairs in gym?'

Lady Cecilia was glad of Charlie breaking in:

'Yes gentlemen, I think you should call quits.'

Bernard responded, still high as a kite:

'I haven't even started.'

Lindsay was fine with that:

'Then just you go for it, Markham.'

'You miners! To hear you talk, you'd think you'd written the book on suffering. Nobody else in the whole wide world has suffered unless they've been down a pit.'

'That's cos we didn't see much o' the world. We were in darkness half o' the time wi' backs bent and bloody sore, and spittin' coal dust out o' our guts.'

Lindsay could see that had quietened Bernard, so he pressed home:

'What da ya have to say about that, Mr Markham?'

'Fair enough, but you can stop calling me Mr Markham.'

'Why? Should I call ya Bernie, like the kids do?'

'That neither.'

Bernard puffed his chest out and raised his chin:

'I do know something about mining, Councillor Lindsay. I was born in the Rhondda Valley. I'm the son of a colliery labourer by the name of David Williams.'

'What in God's name are ya gabblin' about, lad?'

'My name is Thomas Williams.'

And he stormed out of Brewster's, leaving the company to pick whatever bones they could out of what they had just witnessed.

CHAPTER 16

A pilgrim and his progress

TWO MORNINGS AFTER Bernard's astonishing revelation, he was visited in the coffee-bar by his Chairwoman:

'Who's been a naughty boy, then?'

'I know. I can't stand that man. But there's no excuse for the way I attacked him, he didn't deserve it. And I shouldn't have talked about miners in that manner. I'm writing a letter of apology to him right now.'

Cecilia nodded:

'Yes, that would be the sensible thing to do, Bernard. Or is it Tom?'

'Oh right. You'd better sit down, Ma'am. I'll make us a cuppa.'

Over the next twenty minutes he told her the whole story.

'Goodness, how awful. You poor man.'

'It's strange, it doesn't feel so bad now that it's off my chest.'

'What will you do?'

'It's quite simple, Cecilia. I have to go.'

'Oh no, must you?'

The Lady was doubly moved. She hadn't wanted to hear that, for she would miss him. But also, it was the first time he had addressed her by her first name, despite countless requests of him over eight years to do just that.

'I can't stay, Cecilia. Everyone at Brewster's and around the City won't know who I am now. And anyway, perhaps it's time to move on.'

'It's a pity. Crichton-Smythe is retiring in eighteen months. If it hadn't been for your outburst, you would have been his natural successor. Your competitors are all old army men. I mean they're really old.'

'I was thinking of applying for a job in Scotland. It looks interesting and would mean promotion.'

'What will you do for references? Will you ask Lindsay?'

'No. Even if he accepts my apology, I'd rather not.'

'Well, you don't have to ask, you'll get an excellent one from me. And I assume you would want it as Thomas Williams.'

'Yes, thank you Cecilia. That would be great.'

'But you'll need a second referee, and it would have to be Crichton-Smythe. How are you going to manage that in the light of what's happened?'

'I haven't worked that out yet.'

'Let me speak to him. Like me, he's a member of the Standing Commission on Museums and Galleries. It meets next Wednesday and I'll most likely bump into him.'

'I can't expect you to do that, Cecilia.'

'Oh don't be naïve. And anyway, he's always going on about the leg he lost in the War. That business in Burma and India gives him something in common with you. Also, as an officer he's known plenty of soldiers who had difficulty with their pasts. He'll understand.'

Once again, the Club Leader had cause to be grateful to her. She had done so much for him.

'I don't know what to say, Cecilia. But I do have a confession to make.'

'Go on then.'

'I've always had a bit of a thing for you. I'm sorry.'

Lady Cecilia Blakeley-Hunsworth blushed to the roots of her hair, but not for the reason he thought:

'Oh dear, confessions all round I'm afraid. I had a thing for you too.'

'Blimey! Why didn't you say?'

'Oh come on Bernard, it would never have worked. If we'd had an affair, we could never have kept it a secret, everybody would have known about it. And my husband John is a very ruthless man. He would have destroyed you.'

'I suppose so. It's a lovely thought though, Your Ladyship.'

Cecilia laughed, then got back on track:

'Now, we'd better get organised. Lindsay's friends will be plotting against you as we speak. What are your movements over the next ten days.'

'Well actually, after I send the job application in, I'm thinking of using up the remainder of my annual leave.'

'Going anywhere nice?'

'I'm going to Wales, to Rhawddrhiw, my beginning according to the birth certificate. I might find an older brother or sister. My father might even still be living.'

'Oh that would be wonderful, wouldn't it?'

On that note they parted, with Cecilia promising, if he did get the Scottish job, the Youth Centre would give him a good send-off.

He didn't know it then but he was never to see her again.

The following week, only one day before setting out for Wales, Bernard got a telephone call from Crichton-Smythe which was typically short and to the point:

'Got the whisper from Lady Blakeley-Hunsworth, old chap, about the Thomas Williams business. And just received request from the Jocks for a reference. Will do it at the double. Best of luck.'

It occurred to Bernard that the politicians had in all likelihood been on to Crichton –Smythe already about his inappropriate behaviour, and his boss was under pressure to give him an excellent reference, in other words to get rid of him.

The trip to Wales was the first real opportunity for Bernard to live in the skin of Tom Williams. And recently, having been caught up in the latest national craze, he'd paid the deposit on a brand new Mini. Wales wasn't far from Liverpool and the car would make a pleasant change from the train journeys he'd made over many years. Between Chester and Crewe he turned right into Wales. He marvelled at how green the country was. Everything seemed to be green and a deep green at that. He enjoyed his journey southward through the hills until he reached the Rhondda Valley and finally the village of Rhawddrhiw. The village centre was modest. Beyond a bridge which spanned a narrow river was a main street with a few shops, a post office and a pub with the sign *The White Daffodil* over the front door. He entered the pub and was welcomed by the landlord:

'Pleased to meet you, Sir. We don't see many new faces these days. I'm Sam.'

'Pleased to meet you, Sam. I'm Tom, Tom Williams. I'm here to try and find old relations of mine.'

'Well now, that old gentleman in the corner might be the man to help you.'

'Has he lived here long?'

'Oh yes, Dai Evans is ninety odd, and knows everything about Rhawddrhiw. We call him the Chronicler. But speak loud to him, he's a bit deaf.'

After introductions, Dai thought hard:

Williams you say? That's a hard one. There have been many by that name over the years.'

'My father was David Williams of seventeen Caer Street.'

'Well now, is that not just like the thing? I stay in Caer Street, number forty-two. When I'm finished my lunch, I'll take you over there.'

Williams returned to the bar and ordered a pint. Sam talked as he poured:

'Old Dai will keep you right as long as you keep the volume of your voice up. He's very good, and very fit for his age. He has a walking stick and goes the length of the riverbank and back every other day, sometimes towards the hills, at others to the

Rhondda. He has a pint with cawl and bread at lunch-time and some days, if the weather's not too cold, we see him again in the evening when he has another pint.'

'Did you say cawl, Sam?'

'Oh yes, that's a speciality of ours. It's a traditional Welsh dish. Sounds splendid, but it's just a soupy stew, popular with OAPs because it's hot and cheap. Can I get you some?'

Williams turned up his nose:

'I don't think so, thanks all the same.'

'Can I get you something else then?'

'I'll come back later, Sam. The old boy seems ready now, and I'm keen to get over there.'

Tom Williams and Dai Evans crossed the bridge and made their way to the miners' rows on the other side of the river:

'What's the name of the river, Dai?'

'That's a good question, that is. And I've never really known the answer. You'd be hard pressed to find it on any map. When we were kids, we called it the Lechy. We paddled in it, threw stones and cuddled fish. It's only a mountain stream really, and runs into the Rhondda not far south of here.'

'Here we are, Dai, Caer Street.'

'Now Tom, I must tell you this could be a lucky bag. The pit closed a while back and many folks left the village. Some of the houses are empty.'

Sure enough, number 17 was empty. Williams peered through the two front windows, but not a stick of furniture could be seen. He tried the door, but it was locked fast. His disappointment was palpable.

The old man had picked up on it:

'Tom, you were born here, weren't you?'

'Was it so obvious?'

'Fact is I knew David Williams very well. We worked down the pit together. It was terrible what happened to him. His missus, Eleanor I think her name was, was such a lovely girl. She died giving birth to her fourth child. There was something not right about it. I think that doctor botched it up.'

'I suppose my father's not around any longer either.'

'I'm sorry, Tom. He died just after the War. I didn't want to tell you in the pub, I'd just met you. And anyway, it was no-one else's business.'

'What about the rest of the family?'

'They were all your sisters. Two of them got married, and one of them went off with her husband to Australia. The single girl stayed on here but sadly died when she was still comparatively young. That just leaves the other married girl. She lives in the next village, Carregdu. Her name is Pritchard, Mavis Pritchard I think.'

'Would I be able to look her up?'

'How long are you intending to stay, boy?'

'Sam has rooms above the pub. I've asked him for two nights anyway, maybe more.'

'Well then, you can drive me to Carregdu on one of the days and I'll help you. Meanwhile, what you doing right now?'

'Nothing really.'

'Come with me to the end of the road. It's only a short climb from there to the old pit.'

As the pair of them made the gentle climb, Bernard quizzed the old man:

'When exactly did the pit close down, Dai?'

'Coming on for two years now, I'd say. They were going for less mines and bigger mines. They had changed from the old room and pillar method to longwall mining with all the new-fangled machinery.'

'That must have been a sad time.'

'For some, yes it was, but many were able to adjust quite happily. There were those who took their families to mining towns in England, but many left the industry, especially the younger ones.'

'Why was that, Dai?'

'They went into building industries mostly. It pays better wages and the work's not so hard on them. It's understandable really. A number of them still live here, mind. Busses come in the morning and take them to towns like Pontypridd.'

'Is that why half of the homes are occupied and half not?'

'Exactly, you catch on well, boy.'

They had reached the pithead. A light breeze was blowing and there was an eerie, ghostly feel to the place. Tom had to force himself to imagine it in its heyday, bustling with miners working on the surface, or going down the lift shaft, or coming up dog dirty and tired but relieved another one was over. All around him was a plethora of abandoned machinery, already well rusted, and along the side of the mine ran a massive slag heap. Crowning the whole scene was the pithead wheel which made a sound like a baby in pain as it rocked to and fro an inch at a time in the breeze.

'You must have lived through a lot up here, Dai.'

'I'll say! Sometimes a man would be crushed in a collapse. I think the worst trouble was in 1901, the year the Old Queen passed away. Eleven men died after an explosion caused by escaping gas. Every time I talk about it, I hear that alarm again, and see myself rushing to the pithead to join the rescue crew. The women were running after us in a fearful state. They had to hitch up their skirts to keep up.'

'How did it go?'

'We worked without a rest for two days, and we only succeeded in saving three of the injured men. It broke our hearts. And there wasn't a household in Rhawddrhiw that wasn't affected by it.'

'That must have been awful.'

'It was Gareth Jones that really got to me. He was only fourteen years old. We brought him up and laid him out. His body was all mangled, but his face. Oh God, his face! It was so peaceful, as if he'd simply fallen asleep. I still see that face in my sleep.'

'How did his parents take it?'

'His father was elsewhere that day. I got the job of telling his mother. Worst job I ever had to do. I go to the old bone orchard regular to lay flowers, at the grave of my wife Gwyneth, you understand. But I always keep one flower back so that I can walk over a bit and place it at Gareth's family stone.'

'I'm sorry, Dai. I didn't mean to bring this all back to you.'

'Not at all, boy. In an odd sort of way it helps me, and I don't get many chances nowadays to talk about it.'

'Did you and Gwyneth have any children?'

'No, sadly. Not that we didn't try. Poor girl had two miscarriages and the doctor told us we should stop. However, that's quite enough talk about grief. Let me tell you what's happening in the village today. There's still a male voice choir, you know.'

'Do you sing, Dai?'

'Me? Heck no. I must be the only Welshman who can't get a note out in key.'

Williams burst out laughing:

'Yes, I know how you feel. I was the only public school boy who hated rugby.'

'Ah, the good old rugby. Our lads play on the village green during the winters. In the summer season, like as now, the posts are down so they can play cricket. As it happens, there's a match against Carregdu tomorrow. Sunday matches are great to watch. Would you like to go, Tom?'

'It would be a pleasure, Dai.'

Williams had an evening meal followed by a couple of pints at *The White Daffodil*. Then he stretched out his legs in front of its log fire and read about South Wales for a bit. Soon he was regularly nodding off, so decided to turn in for the night.

In the morning after breakfast, he walked the length of the riverbank towards its source in the hills, taking photographs as he went. For a time he could hear the deep sonorous tones of the male voice choir reverberating throughout the valley. And he got a shock when a roe deer shot across the path in front of him like an arrow from a bow. Come the afternoon he had joined old Dai who was sat on a bench on the village green, waiting for the needle match between Rhawddrhiw and their neighbours:

'Tom, when we go to Carregdu tomorrow to find your sister, have you thought how you're going to approach her?'

'I'm not sure. I certainly wouldn't want to just walk in on her.'

'Leave it to me. I'll speak to some of the boys in the Carregdu team at the tea-time interval. They know me well, their fathers and grandfathers before them worked down the mine with me. One of them will know Mavis Pritchard, I'm sure.'

'Here we go, Dai. The openers are coming out to bat.'

'Oh good, and it looks like we've got first use of the pitch.'

Watching the cricket relaxed Williams. There were thirty spectators at most, scattered thinly around the boundary with only an occasional cheer or pair of hands clapping. In the great expanse, every smack of willow on leather was followed by a rifle like recoil, and often his attention was stolen by the wide variety of trees fringing the ground and the hills beyond.

He lost track of the score. He was enjoying an inner peace of the sort that Bernard Markham had rarely known in the past twenty years.

Dai had to bring him back to reality:

'Tom, my eyes are no good. Will you have a look at the scoreboard for me?'

Williams looked across the ground to the far side. A schoolboy was on duty at the scoreboard, hanging black slates with white numbers on to hooks, changing them only at the end of each over.

'A hundred and forty-six for seven, Dai.'

'It's an antiquated system, is that. We should have a modern rolling board with a covered enclosure for the scorer, but we never have any money.'

'Five overs to go, Dai.'

'It won't be enough. Carregdu will get the runs easy, they have better batsmen.'

The Rhawddrhiw innings closed at 159 all out. Dai and Tom walked over to the pavilion where refreshments had been prepared by the home players' wives. They had sandwiches and tea, and Dai spent some time chatting to the away team. After a short delay to the restart due to a sudden shower of rain, the spectators returned to their seats:

'You seem to know the visitors well, Dai.'

'Yes, I was talking mostly with Elwyn Price, their burly fast bowler, and telling him about you and your reason for being here. Mavis Pritchard lives around the corner from him. He says, if it's all right with you, he'll go round to her house tonight, prepare the ground so to speak.'

'That's very kind of him, and fine with me.'

'Very well then. We meet him at Carregdu's village square at ten tomorrow morning.'

Dai's prediction proved right. The away team knocked off the runs for only four wickets with ten overs to spare. The teams and spectators alike gathered at *The White Daffodil* afterwards for a few pints where the main talking point was test match cricket and the current tour of England by the wonderful West Indians.

Tom Williams picked up Dai at the old man's house at 9.30 the following morning, Monday. It was a short drive, only seven miles, to Carregdu. They were met by Elwyn Price as Dai had arranged.

'Morning, Dai. How do you do, Mr Williams?'

'Very well, Elwyn. This is really too kind of you.'

'It's no bother. I'm on a late shift today, as it happens.'

'Do you want to climb in? Then we'll……'

'No thank you. Eh, I'm afraid the news is not good, Mr Williams. I did speak to Mavis. She says to tell you she knows who you are, but she's very sorry, she doesn't want to turn the clock back. I'm afraid she can't see you.'

On the way back to Rhawddrhiw, not a word was exchanged. Dai was too long in the tooth to speak at a time like that, for the younger man was clearly hurting. Williams parked in his usual place at the back of *The White Daffodil* and went for a riverbank walk on his own. Dai went to the post office to collect his pension, and from there he picked up a few provisions from the shops. The new friends met up again at the pub in the evening:

'How are you feeling, Tom?'

'I'm not too bad, surprisingly. I should have expected it. In my job I've seen a lot of sadness in the lives of the sort of young people I deal with. I suppose I got carried away. In real life, there are few happy endings to something like this.'

'You're very brave, boy. I can think of men it would break, and that's a fact.'

'Ah well, at least I know where I stand.'

'Are you sorry you came here now?'

'Not at all, Dai. I'm having a great time. I think I'll stay a night or two yet.'

'Well then, that's great that it is, boy. What have you got in store for me?'

Dai and Tom spent the next day visiting Treorchy and Pontypridd, and generally taking in the sights of Glamorgan. But the time passed too quickly for them both. On the Wednesday morning, Dai walked to the pub after his breakfast and met with Tom who was standing by a packed case waiting for him:

'I guess this is good-bye, Dai.'

'I guess so, boy. But let me tell you, I haven't had so much fun in years.'

'Glad to be of service, Dai. I suppose you'll find other fish to fry, though.'

'Oh yes, Dai the Chronicler plans to live to a hundred, and get a telegram from the Young Queen.'

Bernard laughed:

'So, it will be a long time before they put you in the bone orchard, eh?'

'Dashed right it will. And anyway, I'm in no hurry to spend eternity beside my Gwyneth. She would only nag me and I wouldn't be able to escape to the pub.'

Williams was quite emotional:

'I'm going to miss you, you old beggar.'

'And I you, boy. Now mind, don't allow yourself to become bitter. Bitterness destroys a man. It's not worth a light. Always think of today and tomorrow.'

'I'll do as you say, Dai. Don't you worry about me.'

Williams started his Mini and swung it towards the bridge. As he did, he heard Dai shout out:

'Make sure you get that job in Scotland!'

CHAPTER 17

Colliershire Union of Youth Clubs

'BERNARD.........BERNARD.........BERNARD.......'

It was driving Tom Williams mad. Since his return from Wales, no matter how hard he tried, he couldn't convince his young members of his correct name. Finally, he decided to give up and just accept it.

As things panned out, it didn't matter anyway. He was invited to Scotland for an interview. And his reputation, buoyed up by Lady Cecilia's and Crichton-Smythe's references, were enough to secure him the post. He was handed the envelope by Charlie, who had stooped to pick it up from the letter-box:

'Thou's got job, Skipper. It's a thick'un.'

He was to organise inter-club activities and other initiatives for some thirty or forty youth organisations affiliated to a new merger between Colliershire's youth clubs and boys' clubs.

'I were right, eh Skipper?'

'Yes, Charlie. But I'm going to miss you. A good team in Lancashire were the Yorkshireman and the Welshman.'

'Ay, and that be enough for old Charlie as well. I'm callin' it a day. I'm three score and ten this year.'

'You're seventy? How did the City Council not pick up on that?'

'Them never asked me age. When I 'it sixty-five, I just kept goin'. I don't reckon an owld man shovellin' coal would catch the eye o' top brass.'

Susan was due to go off on a long holiday the following day, so she and Tom took their leave of each other:

'Best o' luck, Bernie. Oh, listen ta me, never called ya Bernie before.'

'And good luck to you, Susan. You've been a fine secretary. I hope the next chap appreciates you as much.'

'And I 'ope yer new secy makes ya yer mornin' cup o' cha.'

Williams did not want any fuss over his departure. Above all, he hated the idea of ceremony. And thankfully, he was not approached by Councillor Lindsay and his friends with any such suggestion. He decided to have a party in the coffee-bar with his young members, one or two old members like Danny, Jimmy and Rohan, and Bob Craig, the Treasurer, who had been a stalwart throughout. He went through the motions of asking Charlie, only to get the expected response – a mouthful about 'the devil's music and young nutters'. And the fact that Lady Cecilia was in Italy on holiday, and had only been able to leave him a letter, convinced him he'd made the right decision. He still had feelings for her, but had to accept that a liaison between them would never have worked, could never have worked, just as she had said herself. Nonetheless, he would always treasure her memory. She was the only woman after his fiancé Kathleen that he had wanted. And he would hold on to her letter:

Dear Tom,
I'm so glad you got the job. Many congratulations. Sorry I can't be there to say good-bye properly. I wish you all the luck in the world.
Our loss is Scotland's gain.
Cecilia B H

Williams had a great time. And so did the kids, although, that was largely due to the new sound which was sweeping the country and had been born and bred in Liverpool. The Beatles were on their third number one hit single, *She Loves You*. Sensationally, it had soared to number one by noon on the first day of release.

Bernard's ears were assailed by the record time and time again, likewise by its predecessors, *Please Please Me* and *Twist and Shout*. But Bernard liked it, he had an ear for originality, and the atmospheric, ringing sound was certainly different.

At 9pm the members stopped the music to make a presentation to Brewster's departing Leader. They had clubbed together for a new record-player and pamphlets of musical scores for piano, a mixture of modern and classical. Williams was almost overwhelmed so he kept his thankyous short. But inside he felt good. His presents had come from the right people.

Before starting his new job, he had a spare week to clear his Liverpool home, travel to Colliershire and set up the council home he'd been allocated in the new town of Crack Willow. His office was to be six miles away in the county's administrative capital, Kirkleonard.

So there was time for Tom Williams, onetime Bernard Markham, to take stock of his life. He had reached a major crossroads. Much of his previous life had been hard, indeed traumatic. He had fought and suffered in a War created by an insane world. And at the age of 40, it had been revealed to him he was not the son of the people he had always known as his parents, the folk who had raised him. There was little left of that life, apart from his good friend Stork, whom he was unlikely to see so often now. The burning question now was:

How in future would he juggle the two identities, Bernard and Tom?

Stork had always told his buddie that he possessed a great intellect, and this time, now approaching middle-age, he was to put that intellect to its best ever use.

As far as the Scots were concerned, his name would be Tom Williams at all times, and he would tell them nothing, or next to nothing, of his past life. But since his return from Burma, and despite his drinking and his breakdown, he had grown a backbone of steel. And it was pure Bernard Markham. Not that the steel was entirely of his own making, for Bernard had been helped by a whole load of people. In his mind he listed them – his adoptive parents and sister, and his greatest ever friend and anchor, Stork. But there were also the buddies he'd left behind in Burma who died too young. How could he forget them and their support? And how could he forget the people who had saved his life? – Katashi, Maya, Indi and Chai. He thought of the doctors and nurses who had tended to his rehabilitation. He thought of Cecilia, his ally in the early part of his career. And lastly, he thought of Dai the Chronicler, the wonderful old Welshman who had restored his faith in mankind and helped him to look to the future once more.

Cleverly, he saw a way ahead. He would get his way with the powers that be by dressing smartly and speaking in his plum English accent, while always introducing himself as Tom Williams. If the powers were labour councillors, he would inform them he was born in the Rhondda Valley to a mining family. He would have the best of both worlds and nobody but nobody would ignore him. Loved or hated, he would not be ignored.

There remained only one thing for Williams to do before he left. He sat down and wrote a long letter to Stork and Sylvia, bringing them up to speed and letting them know, once he had settled into the new job, he would be in touch. That done, he pushed off north in his Mini, leaving the City which had made him into the complete professional to the Beatles, Gerry and the Pacemakers, and all the other groups who added up to the Liverpool sound. He was off to the land of the Scots, a people who knew as much as anyone about the subject of pain and suffering. Scotland would do just fine for Tom Williams AND Bernard Markham.

His early days were spent in admin at his Kirkleonard office. There was much to do, and he leaned heavily on the experience of office work, gained in 1944 when he was grounded by the British Army in Poona. Within six weeks he had convinced a very old fashioned board of management that they needed to fund the post of a part-time secretary, if he was to roll around Colliershire and make meaningful contact with all their affiliated clubs. Once a Mrs Crawford arrived and got her feet under the desk, he was free to do what he felt was the important part of his job, meeting young people and establishing working relationships with them.

In the midst of all his toing and froing, it occurred to Williams that his nightmares from Burma and his malarial attacks had markedly reduced in recent years. If he hadn't worked it out before, he was now fully aware that work was the only antidote that made a difference. He still enjoyed a few drinks from time to time, but what the hell, he thought, he was human.

On one of his early visits he entered a youth club in the port of Rossryan. He was immediately impressed by two young lads of 15. Without being asked by their voluntary leaders, they seemed to take a natural leadership role with their younger club mates. One was sporty and clearly an extrovert. The other was shy and reticent, but nonetheless supportive of others. Williams approached the latter and offered his hand.

'How do you do, Sir? My name's Williams, Tom Williams. I'm from the Union of Youth Clubs.'

The boy didn't quite know what to make of this strangely dressed and spoken man. He had never been addressed as 'Sir' before, that was for sure. It was a term he normally used himself to either answer, or approach. his school teachers.

'I'm Malcolm Ingles.'

It was all the boy could think of saying. He was overawed, for the odd gentleman was obviously very important. He retreated to safer ground.

On the other hand, not to be outdone, the other lad stopped his football, approached Williams, and stretched out his hand:

'Hi there, I'm David Samson. Are you a new leader?'

After the introductions, Williams quizzed David for some time about the club, how he had got involved, how long he'd been attending, what sort of activities took place during a normal week, and if he knew Malcolm well:

'Yeah, Malcy and I have been pals for yonks.'

As they walked home together after closing time, the two young friends chatted about the mystery man and his visit to the club:

'Strange old guy, eh?'

'Yeah, asked a lot o' questions. Ah thought he wis nosey.'

'Ah thought he wis quite friendly.'

'Well, ye ken what they say, friendly as in ower friendly, like intae men, no women.'

'Ye mean queer? He didnae strike me as queer.'

'D'ye think he's important? Ah mean, the posh voice, the tie, the hat an' all?'

'Yeah, Ah think he's been an officer in the army or somethin' like that.'

Tom Williams had gathered enough about his new job to see that it was mainly admin, and frustratingly so. Even his rounds of Colliershire's youth clubs were not going to meet his need to develop strong bonds with young people. He would only be able to chat with them briefly in the passing. He had to come up with a solution, one which would take his youth work to another and challenging level.

In 1960 the Countess of Albemarle had headed up a new Youth Work Development Committee to look into ways of countering the current anti-authoritarian behaviour of young people, thought to have come about due to the loss of fathers and other male role models in the two World Wars. The outcome of their deliberations was professional training for students in youth and community service, based in the colleges of Leicester, Glasgow and Edinburgh. Just as Williams was settling into his new post, the first of those students were graduating and picking up posts for themselves. And they were guided by a model of practice known as social group work.

As an experienced practitioner, it wasn't necessary for Williams to have the qualification. Not only that, but he had practised social group work in his service to young people long before it had become known by that name. He was a man who had never read a textbook, but a man ahead of his time and possessed of an intellect that would keep him ahead of the game. On his next visit to Rossryan, he laid the first few bricks of his next construction.

'Malcolm, David, can I have a word?'

One nudged the other:

'Ah tellt ye he wis queer. We'll never see the end o' him noo.'

'Shut up. Let's hear what the man has tae say.'

Williams found a quiet corner:

'I'd like to set up a youth committee which would have a say in the planning of the Union's activity programme, and I'd like to invite you both to be its first members.'

This was a concept way beyond what the lads had experienced before. Malcolm was apprehensive:

'Ah dinnae ken. It depends what ma Dad says, then there's ma school exams.'

'Of course, I fully understand.'

On the other hand, David was up for it, so Williams continued:

'I was thinking of a Sunday afternoon, just once a month, at my house in Crack Willow. You could get there by bus. I'd make your lunch.'

The idea of going to the man's home didn't sit well with Malcolm at all:

'Ah dinnae ken.'

'Well, why don't you both have a think about it until next time we meet? Meanwhile, I'll ask lads from other clubs around Colliershire.'

Decades on from that time it would become strictly unethical for any professionals working with children to invite them into their homes. But in Williams' best times, the fifties and sixties, attitudes were still liberal.

It took Williams six weeks to drum up enough interest from the young people in his idea. Once he had six of them keen, including David Samson and Malcolm Ingles, he agreed a date with them for the first get-together at his home.

In varying degrees they were wary of him, but they were fascinated by him as well. Despite the way he projected, he came across as a sincere man. He was also funny at times, and not at all distant or aloof. As his new young friends arrived in ones and twos at his house that first Sunday, he welcomed them warmly, and his newly acquired Dalmatian dog, Tessa, made a fuss of them:

'Hello there, in you come, I'll get the kettle on. There's lemonade if you prefer.'

Once they were settled, and realising they didn't know each other very well, Williams opened with an ice-breaker:

'Let's play an interesting game of introductions. I divide you up into pairs. Each pair spends ten minutes getting to know each other, who they are, where they come from, which club they go to, and what they do in their club. Then, each pair in turn stands in front of the whole group, one of the pair introduces his partner, then it's the partner's turn to introduce him.'

No one pair was from the same club. They found the informality put them at their ease, and when on occasion the process went wrong, they giggled and laughed.

Then an impatient David Samson broached the reason for the visit:

'Mr Williams, we were going to talk about the Union of Youth Clubs.'

'Not just yet, David, There's plenty time for business later. I'd like to hear what you all thought about the test match series between the West Indies and England.'

The meeting began to get heated. Some lads were really into cricket, like George who fancied himself as a fast bowler, and Willie who batted at number three for the school. Other lads would have preferred football as the subject. Williams didn't care. They were all warmed up and beginning to enjoy their day out.

At an appropriate juncture Williams brought the meeting to order. Then they discussed the existing Union of Youth Clubs' programme. They intimated what they liked, what they didn't, and agreed what changes could be reasonably made. David Samson and George volunteered to help at some of the Union's inter-club competitions.

Williams called a halt for lunch at one o'clock. Beforehand, he had prepared sandwiches, crisps and lemonade.

They carried on debating after that until Williams consulted his watch:

'It's three o'clock, friends. You'd best be on your way for your busses back home. They don't run so often on Sundays.'

As his lads filed down the path and called out 'Cheerio, Mr Williams,' he called back:

'Tom, call me Tom, friends.'

The monthly meetings continued and proved to be a resounding success, but Williams knew he would need something more substantial than that if he was to help his young lads to develop, and a place other than his own home. He consulted the handbook of youth service facilities which had been posted to him by the county organiser when taking up his post. He came to S:

Strathconan Residential Centre, property of Colliershire County Council, large room for games or conferences, fully-equipped kitchen, dining-room, male and female toilets, two dormitories, two single rooms for group leaders. Has the capacity for a maximum of 24 persons. Bookings can be made for weekends or weeks Monday to Friday. School or youth groups particularly welcome and initial contact should be made with the Warden at the following address or telephone number................

At the next meeting of his house group, he floated the idea of a residential weekend. He christened it Senior Member Training and told them it would be good for their leadership and communication skills, not just in their clubs but in their future lives. At first, this all sounded a bit like school to them, but when Williams added there would be time for outside activities like football and orienteering, they went for it whole-heartedly. A total of twenty teenagers, aged 15 to 19, put their names down for the first weekend. Williams felt he was getting somewhere. It was the autumn of 1964, more than one year after his arrival in Scotland.

On the Friday night of that first residential weekend, sensing his charges needed to take in the atmosphere and let off some steam, he let them loose. The younger ones drifted around the village of Strathconan before returning for table-tennis, or board games like chess and monopoly. Those old enough were allowed to go to the local pub with strict instructions to be back by a certain time.

After lights out Williams could hear the excitement filtering through from the dormitories. They were too hyper to sleep. When the murmuring finally stopped, Williams looked at his bedside clock. It was nearly 3am. He smiled and thought:

They'll pay for this in the morning

It was now 7.30am:

'Jesus, what's that?' yelled George in shock.

He wiped cold water off his drowsy face and looked up, thinking the water tank must have sprung a leak.

'Ya boy!' exclaimed Malcolm at the same experience.

And so it went on down the line of bunk beds, as Williams proceeded to flick water from a bowl on to their faces to waken them up:

'On your marks, lads! Breakfast is at eight o'clock.'

On a serious note, Williams was agonising about what he should do about the two young girls in the group. He had fitted them into the domestic arrangements by giving them the second leader's room to share, but what sort of subject was he going to come up with at the first debating session after breakfast?

Williams was a conjuror. He didn't believe in preparing typed-up programmes before such events. He liked to wing it. So he went into the kitchen when Mrs Reilly, the Warden, was busy on breakfasts and asked her if she would join the morning session. She was only too pleased to be invited, and could see his reason for asking.

His next problem was to come up with a subject for discussion.

David wagered:

'Ah'll bet it's cricket or football.'

Malcolm countered:

'Na, he's too canny for that. It'll be somethin' we're no expectin'.'

Malcolm was more right than he could possibly have known:

'This morning, ladies and gentlemen, we're going to discuss the vexing question in our country at the moment concerning the law on abortion.'

A massive and endless groan emanated from some lads, a stunned silence from the others. The two girls, Brenda and Vicky who were both 17, brightened up visibly. Mrs Reilly gave a nod of approval.

As a youth worker it had always been Williams' greatest regret that he had never provided adequately for the needs of his girl members. Central to that weakness was a lifelong angst at his own sexuality. At social events when growing up, he was awkward in the company of women, and later in life he turned against the very thought of sex. But as he grew older, he learned to include women in his life and work, and that particular morning was a case in point.

He wrote out questions on slips of paper which included:

Should an unmarried mother have the right to terminate her pregnancy?

When does life begin – when the baby is born or when still in the womb?

Nor did his surprises finish with that:

'Now listen up, friends. You get quite enough of me. I'm going to divide you up into two smaller groups, and I want Brenda to chair one group, and David to chair the other. I'll give you ten minutes to consider the questions and prepare. You can talk among yourselves as much as you like.'

He was making it up as he went along, and most of them struggled, being often inarticulate when they tried, and subdued when they didn't. But it mattered little. He was opening their minds to issues which they were unlikely to address in their school curriculum. Mrs Reilly had been a guide leader in her younger days. At first she was shocked by his unconventional approach, but soon she adapted and played a supporting role to the two young leaders.

In the afternoon the boys played football in the grounds, while Mrs Reilly took the girls into town.

The early evening after dinner was spent in another debate, this time about Harold Wilson's Labour Government and their first months in power. Williams opted for new chairmen and divided each group equally into tories and socialists. The debate got very heated:

George was all in favour of Mr Wilson:

'Now that the tories are out, I hope they never come back. They don't care about working class people like us.'

Willie, the cricketer, countered in the best posh voice he could muster while gripping his imaginary lapels:

'Speak for yourself, my dear chap. I'm afraid the facts tell us............'

At 8pm they broke off and the rest of the day was their own free time.

There were occasional moments in Williams' career when he rued his decision to turn his back on a 9 to 5, Monday to Friday job. At 5am that Sunday morning, one such moment occurred.

He was wakened by David:

'Tom, can you come through? It's Malcolm.'

Malcolm's head was buried in his pillow, and he'd been groaning for two hours, keeping some lads awake. He had a raging toothache. Williams gave him painkillers but to no avail. At breakfast time he was still in agony.

The nearest emergency dentist on a Sunday was twenty miles away. Williams wasted no time. He handed out instructions to Mrs Reilly and the more able boys so that they could keep things on track for the time being, and he took off with Malcolm.

The tooth was duly extracted and they returned to base. One hour later it became obvious to all that Malcolm was spitting out an inordinate amount of blood. Williams drove him back to the dentist like the clappers, and didn't spare the rod:

'Not much of a job that you've done on my lad.'

The dentist took it that Williams was the boy's father. Williams had fully intended he would. The job was completed properly.

That Sunday was the day of Malcolm. But more than that, it was the day that kicked off one of Williams' closest and longest lasting friendships.

On one of the Union officer's visits to Rossryan Youth Club, he and Malcolm fell into casual conversation. Previously, Malcolm had retreated from the man he judged to be queer. But now, the double dash to emergency had changed his opinion. On those journeys Malcolm had been unable to speak due to the pain, the freezing of his lip and the excess blood. In his mind, however, new thoughts about his eccentric leader were taking hold. Now he viewed him almost as a father figure:

Williams began:

'How are you doing, old chap? How are the choppers?'

Malcolm smiled:

The conversation continued and found a greater depth:

'I hear your Dad's not too well.'

'He never is. He was a prisoner of war and has been strange all the time I've known him.'

Williams instinctively knew where this was going:

'How do you get on with him?'

'He hits me. He's always hit me, like he always hit my Mum, before they separated.'

This time it was the leader who retreated. He knew when enough was enough, at least for the moment.

If Williams had his equals as a social group worker, as a one to one counsellor he was peerless. Untrained he may have been, but what he had gone through in Burma and consequently in several hospitals due to his physical and mental conditions, and countering that, the kindness shown to him by a few special people which had brought him back to the land of the living, had bred into him a level of compassion for his fellow man which nobody else seemed to possess. And that compassion was directed at the most vulnerable young people under his auspices. Often as not they came to him. The eccentric older man and the younger rough round the edges urchin were attracted to each other like positive and negative magnetic poles.

While he felt Malcolm's need was the greater, he was no less devoted to David. This lad was a competitor who liked to win, always keen to take part in new initiatives, ideal leadership material:

On another club visit Williams posed him a question:

'What would you like to be when you leave school, David?'

'Ma Dad thinks Ah should join the Civil Service.'

'I didn't ask you what your Dad wanted you to be.'

'Well, Ah'd like to play for Dunclifton Athletic at football, but Ah don't think Ah'm good enough to be a pro.'

'That's as maybe. But a lad like you should do something that you love. I can't see you as a civil servant, David, I really can't.'

David spent the rest of that club night doing some hard thinking. The conversation had left its mark.

The Senior Member Training weekends at Strathconan were always innovative. On one occasion Williams opted for the theme of confidence building. The idea was for individuals to speak in front of the whole group. The less confident could choose an alter ego from a list of famous people, like Bob Dylan, the musician, or Bobby Moore, the footballer. The task of the audience was to identify the alter ego by asking the speaker questions only answerable by yes or no. The more confident would draw a subject out of Williams' deer-stalker hat and, given only a minute to prepare, had to speak on the subject for a minimum of three minutes.

The activities on such weekends were a form of alternative education for the youngsters. And the learning was fun.

Over his years in Colliershire Williams never fitted in with the schemes of his younger, more ambitious colleagues. Whilst they had great respect for him, they thought him out of step with the modern thinking. In return, Williams thought them at times petty, egotistic, calculating, and worst of all, straying from what to him was always of paramount importance, the individual needy youngster. It wasn't unknown for him to storm out of meetings of his fellow managers, announcing he had better things to do, then go for a walk somewhere with Tessa his dog to cool down.

He was a purist. When young, he had committed himself to young people, especially the most vulnerable. Over the years, the Service would change its name as it began to cater for other age groups beyond youth, like adult returners to education and out of school care groups. Williams remained dedicated to youth work.

What his colleagues never fully appreciated were the additional benefits he brought to the Service, benefits above and beyond the call of duty. One such was his long term association with Toc H, a Christian organisation founded in Belgium in the midst of World War One, which five years later founded a youth centre in London. As a former soldier, and a passionate youth worker, Williams fell in love with Toc H, and used its many arms to bolster his youth projects by bringing youngsters from abroad over to the UK to make a contribution to the work and establish relationships with his local young volunteers.

He also used his long term ties with the YM/YWCA to enhance his youth work, and the support he had received from the

AA, no longer needed for himself, was now transferred through him to benefit that section of his young people whose lives had been damaged by alcohol.

When David Samson reached 19, he was a senior volunteer and leader with the Union of Youth Clubs, but jobwise he was looking to move on from the civil service office he had joined after leaving school. He approached the man who had become his mentor:

'You were right about the Civil Service, Tom. It's not for me.'

'But what will you do, David?'

'Well actually, I was thinking of applying for a place on the youth and community course at Edinburgh.'

Williams was delighted. And in the years that followed, he was further delighted when his young protégé qualified and went on to have a successful career.

The time he invested in Malcolm also bore fruit. With the people skills he had picked up, many of them from Williams, he took up social work, the perfect cure for his own troubled childhood.

By the time the shaman left his post at Colliershire UYC, he was 50. He had perfected his method of dealing with the dual persona of Bernard Markham and Tom Williams, but there was still something missing in his life. He looked on in envy at the family lives of his colleagues. Above all, he longed for a son. At this point in time, David Samson and Malcolm Ingles had come closest to filling that void.

And now he was moving on to an area organiser's job and converting an old chip shop in Crack Willow into an office where he would head up a team of professional youth and community workers. But if any of his colleagues entertained the notion he was about to anchor his feet behind a desk and let younger men do all the youth work, they were in for a rude awakening.

Williams would find new opportunities for face to face work with a new breed of young people.

CHAPTER 18

Old friends and not so old friends

IT WAS 2015. John Gray had been retired for eight years. And recently, David Samson and Malcolm Ingles had also retired.

All three had kept an eye on their old mentor by making regular visits to his home. At 92 years of age, Williams had become frail. Whenever John Gray spoke to him on the phone, he was distant, and tended to cut the conversation dead after only a minute, not at all the accommodating person his friends had come to know so well.

Sensing something wasn't quite right, Gray made a visit. He was let in by Gerry, Tom's adopted son.

Gerry shook his head, which said it all. Nevertheless, Williams perked up at the sight of his friend:

'Hello John, good to see you. How are you, boy?'

'More importantly, Tom, how are you?'

'I'm afraid it's just the sands of time, boy. I guess it's *my* time.'

Normally, Gray would have come up with a clever answer to that, but leaning on his past experience of caring for close relatives in their last days, he could see the tell-tale signs of deterioration in Williams' face and body, so decided to change the subject:

'My son Kevin has reached the quarter final of this year's Scottish Amateur Snooker Competition.'

'Oh good, I'm really pleased for him. You must tell him.'

Williams had long been concerned about Kevin on Gray's behalf. Ten years before the boy had experimented with drugs and done himself some damage. The two men exchanged their news for a while, until Williams raised something he'd been holding on to for years:

'John, I need to tell you something, and I want you to have a photograph.'

'Of course, Tom. What is it?'

'Do you remember me telling you about the chap who came here with his father's ashes. We scattered them in my garden.'

'Yes, I remember thinking at the time how unusual that was, but at the same time what a wonderful gesture it must have been, a tribute to you really.'

'Yes, it was. His name is Robert Taylor and I knew him when he was little. His father was Leonard Taylor, an old buddie of mine in the Chindits. We called him Stork, on account of the fact he was so tall, and so thin as well. In Burma we were always starving.'

'You meant a lot to each other, didn't you?'

'He was the best friend I ever had. We went through so much in the War, and afterwards, through all my bad times, he stood by me.'

'You mentioned a photograph. Tom?'

'Yes John, it's in that top drawer, just to your right, next to my glasses.'

Shortly, Gray was studying three smiling figures. They were standing side by side in a garden, against a backdrop of city skyscrapers.

'That's not Tokyo is it, Tom?'

'You bet it is, boy.'

Gray worked out that the figure on the left was probably Stork. He stood head and shoulders above the other two. The figure on the right was clearly Williams.

'Who is the Japanese gentleman in the centre?'

'Why don't you have a guess, John? Think of what I told you about Burma.'

'Oh no, it can't be.'

'Look at the back, boy.'

Gray turned it round and read:

Stork, Katashi and I, Tokyo, August 1988.

'That's amazing. It's Katashi, the guard who saved your life. How on earth did you find him?'

'Stork was a very clever man. And he had made so many useful contacts through his job with the MOD. When he retired from government work in the seventies, he did an unwavering search through Japanese Army records. Mind you, it took him nearly a year.'

Gray had always been good at maths, and had a good memory:

'You crafty old codger! When you retired in July 1988, you said you were going on holiday to visit Poperinghe in Belgium where Toc H started.'

'Well, you know I didn't like to talk to our colleagues about my time in Burma.'

'I can't take that photograph from you, Tom.'

'You must, Tom. Apart from Stork, you're the only one I told about my imprisonment by the Japs. Gerry doesn't know, and I'd like to keep it from him and his boys. Please John, while Gerry's upstairs, put it in your pocket.'

To Gray, that was as good an indication as any that Williams didn't have long. As it turned out, it was his last visit to Williams' home. A few weeks later, he received a call from David Samson to say that the old man was in hospital:

David explained the situation:

'There were nurses coming in several times a day to tend to him. They tried to get him to agree to hospital but he resisted every time. Then I spoke to him, telling him for his own sake and those who cared about him, he should agree to go in. Well, he went ballistic at me, as you can imagine, you know what he's like. However, this morning, he relented.'

On John Gray's first visit to the hospital, Williams was in an assessment ward on the ground floor. He was sitting up and looked not bad at all. Two young nurses were adjusting his bed. Williams couldn't resist a comment. He pointed at John:

'Ladies, I have to tell you that you're in the presence of a nationally recognised poet.'

'Whoo-ooh!' one of them exclaimed.

Glad to see there was still some spirit in the old boy, John Gray smiled and said:

'Tom, you shouldn't say that to young nurses, you'll get me carried away.'

The two former colleagues chatted for some time, the session being split into two halves by the patient and his bed being moved to a private room.

Williams finally brought the conversation to a close:

'You'd best get on, boy. Remember your jacket now. I'll see you next time.'

Three days later David Samson informed John Gray that their old mentor was on a regular dose of morphine and slipping fast. Gerry was given a bed beside his father to be with him through the night. And during the daytime hours there were many visitors – Gerry's sons, Gerry's friends, Malcolm and David, John and many others. There was Derek, one of the unemployed teenagers of the eighties who had become the *Kwid Kids,* the young community service group. There was Donald and Bobby of the *Kon-Tiki Kids,* the four man crew who had sailed the raft down the River Latham for charity. They were all men of 50 plus now.

Williams had no shortage of people wanting to visit him. He had done so much for them, they wanted to show their appreciation. And that satisfied a need in David Samson who intimated to Gray:

'That's good. I didn't want him to die on his own.'

Gray made two more visits to his friend's bedside. On the first, the change in Williams was immediately clear. Despite the morphine making speech impossible, he would repeatedly sit up with a struggle and make frenetic hand signals all the time, as if he was trying to say something important.

When the doctors finally withdrew his food, and increased his morphine to the point that he was almost totally out of it, Williams went in to a deep recurring dream in which he was a soldier on a long journey. He passed countless teak trees and undergrowth dominated by bamboo. There were deep ravines and rivulets to negotiate, and the journey was made to the endless calls of exotic birds and monkeys. Occasionally, there was time to bivouac, and friends he hadn't seen for more than seventy years appeared and spoke to him:

'Well Kiddo, Ah tak ma hat aff tae ye. Wha wid 'o thocht it? Ninety-twa years auld? And me thinkin' ye widnae last a month. Weel done, laddie, weel done.'

Sergeant McKinlay turned, then barked at Stinka for not changing his socks.

'Oh come on, Bernard. It's ten minutes since I made my last move, and look at the sky. It's getting dark, and lights out will be called soon.'

Bernard paid him no heed, so Smudger took a huff, upended the chess board, and went off to his bivouac groundsheet.

'I'm so glad, Bernard. I always spoke up for you when the Sarge or anyone else suggested it. I knew you were no fairy. And I was right, you never were.'

Thomo smiled at him and went off to gather firewood.

In one of his few remaining moments of consciousness, when he couldn't distinguish between fantasy and reality, Williams was certain that Stork was standing by his bedside:

'Don't be afraid, old friend. It's just one more step. What a time we've had, the things we've been through! We were survivors, you and I. But rest now, Mr Williams, I'll see you on the other side, and then we'll do some serious catching up.'

On John Gray's final visit, Williams was in a coma, his breathing laboured. Gray sat on a chair by the bed in solemn contemplation for what seemed an eternity, until a young nurse came in to do her half hourly check on her patient:

'Are you a friend of Tom's? He's a fascinating old gentleman, isn't he?'

For some inexplicable reason, Gray began to tell her that Williams had been an exceptional man:

'He was a Chindit in Burma during the War. He fought against the Japanese…….'

By the puzzled expression on her face, the history lesson was lost on the young nurse. And Gray didn't get into it anyway. The emotion of the previous weeks had at last come to the surface. His voice faltered and a tear blurred one eye.

She offered the standard panacea for such a regular occurrence on the ward:

'Would you like a cup of tea?'

Gray raised his right hand in a gesture of decline, for by now he couldn't speak at all. Discreetly, she tucked in the bedcover and left.

The release of emotion had brought Gray to the decision that it was time to say good-bye.

Years before, he had come to the conclusion he would not be the man he was had it not been for the guidance he had received from the old shaman. He got out of his chair and leaned on the side of the bed:

'Thanks, Tom. Thanks for everything you've done for me.'

Then he thought about Williams' horrific tales of capture and torture by the Japanese, and how he had done him the honour of entrusting him with them. He looked down at Williams' forehead and focussed on the spot he imagined to be the one on to which the cold water would remorselessly have fallen from the dripping tap. Instinctively without thinking, he bent down and kissed it.

Williams was still in the coma when last he was visited by David Samson. Despite knowing he wouldn't get a response, David kept talking to his old tutor non-stop and finished with his own gratitude:

'You've been a good man, Tom, and you've done a huge amount of good for a great many people, especially me.'

Samson took a hold of Williams' hand. And to his surprise, he felt his own hand being squeezed.

Malcom Ingles had been going in every day. On what turned out to be the last one, he was beside young Martin, Gerry's son. Martin adored his grandfather. Before he left, he stroked Williams' head and wept.

Malcolm stayed for another hour, keeping watch on his close friend's breathing. The breaths became louder and longer drawn out. They had reduced to less than 10 per minute, when suddenly, almost unnoticed by Malcolm, the room had gone quiet. With a sigh and a smile, the immense, beloved shaman was gone.

Chapter 19

The Last Post

In the run-up to Tom Williams' funeral, a tribute was posted in local newspapers. But such was the celebrated youth worker's reputation, the news spread like wildfire around the UK, particularly to branches of Toc H and the YM/YWCA.

In Brewster's Youth and Community Centre in Liverpool, Councillor Danny Monaghan, Club Chairman and now 76 years of age, asked the secretary to type up a tribute to their first professional worker, the then Bernard Markham. When it was done, he opened the coveted glass cabinet and placed the wording underneath the formal photograph taken of Bernard and his lads when they stood on the summit of *The Cobbler* in 1956.

Gerry knew very little about his father's involvement in the Burma campaign of 1943, but he was aware that Tom had been a marine commando before that. Accordingly, he was determined there should be a presence at the funeral by veterans of Tom's old regiment. He got in touch with The British Legion, who were only too pleased to arrange it, and three old soldiers turned up for the occasion.

The church in Crack Willow began to fill up. David Samson was a bit disappointed and turned to John Gray:

'I thought there would have been a lot more people.'

'Well David, half of the people who knew Tom well will have passed away long since.'

As they waited for the minister to begin, the congregation swapped their memories of the deceased, and there were the usual observations of who was unexpectedly there, and who wasn't there but should have been.

One old man came in late and sat on his own at the back. He had a shock of pure white hair and was unconventionally dressed for a funeral – green sports jacket, open-neck shirt and brown twill trousers.

Just as the service was about to commence, one of the veteran commandos moved to the side and in front of the congregation. Holding the regimental standard upright with his left hand, he stood to attention. Clearly, he was going to maintain his position throughout the service, and with his bushy moustache he cut an impressive figure.

Gerry and the family had decided to keep the singing traditional. It included *The Lord's My Shepherd* and *All Things Bright and Beautiful* in memory of Tom's love for animals.

And all had the opportunity to contemplate their own memories of Tom, when a piece of Puccini, one of his favourite composers, was played.

The minister read from a passage in the bible, and as prearranged, invited David Samson to do the tribute.

David tried to do the impossible, encapsulate Tom's long and complex life into a few short minutes. He started with Tom's birth in the Rhondda Valley of which the shaman had been so proud, moving on to his army service in the War, in particular his time as a Chindit in the 1943 Burmese campaign. David then outlined Tom's youth work career, from his early days in London and Liverpool, to his later triumphs in his adopted Scotland, not forgetting to include his long associations with Toc H, the YM/YWCA, the AA and the Society of Friends, known better as the Quakers. The Friends had encouraged Tom to become a prison visitor, and many young men who had committed terrible crimes became used to the eccentric old gent. He wanted them to know that there was at least one person who wouldn't pass judgement on them, who would simply talk to them and be a friend. Even after retirement, he had continued to serve young people and the community, until ill health stopped him in his late eighties.

David then highlighted how important it was to Tom that he had gained a family in his later life. To have a son, a niece, a daughter-in-law and three grandsons had fulfilled a need in him like no other.

Finally, David touched on Tom's specific contribution to Crack Willow. As a new town it had lacked community activity in its early days. Tom had convinced his young colleagues and volunteers that the best remedy was to knock on doors and get local people interested in starting up new groups. He was right, it worked. One of his finest innovations was the *Big Summer Show*.

The main theme of David's speech was that Tom Williams, as a youth worker, had been unique. The more vulnerable young people were, the more Tom would support them. And they knew him to be a man they could trust, more so than any other professional.

John Gray was invited to read poetry. His first choice was the opening verse from *Fern Hill* by Dylan Thomas. The great Welsh poet had written it only two days after the atomic bombs were dropped on Japan, and Gray felt it was relevant to Williams' experiences in Burma. Gray finished with the opening lines from *The Soldier* by Rupert Brooke:

The poem had always been important to Tom Williams. It reminded him of his buddies who had fallen in Burma:

If I should die, think only this of me;
That there's some corner of a foreign field
That is forever England. There shall be
In that rich earth a finer dust concealed.

And John Gray had come to the conclusion neither he, David, Malcolm, or any other of Williams' modern friends had ever quite replaced the buddies in Tom's heart.

When the service concluded, the congregation walked slowly up the hill from the church to the cemetery. Malcolm made time to chat with the old, white-haired latecomer. He had travelled up from Edinburgh to represent his branch of the Society of Friends. He was a Quaker.

At the graveside committal, the family took up five of the eight cords. In honour of their support to Tom in his final years, Gerry asked David, Malcolm and John to take the remaining three. One of the veteran soldiers put a bugle to his mouth but struggled with the first notes. Had Sergeant McKinlay been present, he might well have said:

'Stert again, boy. Noo, afore ye do, spit!'

As the strident, steady notes of *The Last Post* rang out across Crack Willow's hillside cemetery, Thomas Williams, onetime Bernard Markham, onetime Kiddo of *Operation Longcloth*, was lowered to his final resting place.

And 8,000 miles away to the East, with Burma's monsoon season at its height and most withering strength, a mighty Irrawaddy River surged towards the many branches of its delta, and out into the Andaman Sea.

Printed in Great Britain
by Amazon